The Case Against Bureaucratic Discretion

Steven G. Koven

The Case Against Bureaucratic Discretion

palgrave
macmillan

Steven G. Koven
University of Louisville
Louisville, KY, USA

ISBN 978-3-030-05778-7 ISBN 978-3-030-05779-4 (eBook)
https://doi.org/10.1007/978-3-030-05779-4

Library of Congress Control Number: 2018965746

This Palgrave Macmillan imprint is published by the registered company Springer Nature Switzerland AG
The registered company address is: Gewerbestrasse 11, 6330 Cham, Switzerland

Preface

This book is partially alarmist and partially hopeful. The alarmist element arises out of concern that government bureaucracies are becoming forces in their own right rather than neutral tools of democratically elected officials. In recent years, questionable behavior of agents of the state (bureaucrats) has focused attention on government abuse. Deaths at the hands of local police, Central Intelligence Agency prisoner interrogations (Abu Ghraib), and Federal Bureau of Investigation interjection into politics (Clinton and Trump inquiries) are just a few examples that raise questions about whether the so-called neutral bureaucracy is operating as intended. This relates to the ancient question of "who will guard the guards."

For democracies to function as planned, it is necessary for elected representatives to be able to control the actions of career bureaucrats. This question of democratic accountability should be of interest to students of public administrators, political theory, and political science as well as a public concerned about government infringement on personal liberty. The obvious fear of "runaway" bureaucracy is that government organizations will use their claims of expertise, access to inside information, and the need for secrecy to become rogue organizations, unaccountable to the people or their representatives.

The partially hopeful element of the book highlights the actions of whistleblowers who uncover organizational abuses. Actions of government representatives such as police officer Frank Serpico, Veterans Administration doctor Sam Foote, and Army Sergeant Joseph Darby suggest that employees within large organizations can expose wrongdoing. Corrective action is possible, even in massive and relatively closed organizations. Whistleblowers bear a cost for their disclosures, yet their internal moral compass compels them to act. The reality of these whistleblowers provides some reason for hope.

Many of the actions of government raise questions, yet one should not tar all agencies with the broad brush of dangerous overreach. However, awareness of this potentiality is a necessary step in order to guard against its actualization. For many citizens, government organizations work. For others they are the face of an oppressive state. Finding the balance between a government that effectively performs its duties and a government that respects the constitutional rights of individuals is not an easy task. This book hopes to further the discussion while highlighting the need for democratic accountability. On a personal note, I would like to thank Palgrave Macmillan and their editors for giving me the opportunity to explore in some detail the still relevant quandary of who will guard the guards.

Louisville, Kentucky Steven G. Koven

Contents

PART I

Theory

CHAPTER 1

Theoretical Grounding of Bureaucratic Ethics

1 Introduction

The term "bureaucracy" possesses negative connotations usually surrounded by images of incompetence, laziness, sloth, and inefficiency. The concept of responsiveness or the potential for nonresponsiveness deserves equal, if not more, attention. In theory, bureaucracies are neutral organizations, tools to be used for good or ill. In reality, they have the capacity to become independent policymakers that operate beyond the cognition of average citizens. Classical theorists recognize both the need for bureaucracy and the dangers they pose. In the modern era, when the tentacles of the state can reach almost any corner of the world, this danger is perhaps more unrelenting than ever. An ever enlarging government bureaucracy slowly but surely may erode individual liberties and the ethos of democracy, if not checked by outside or internal forces. This chapter describes the growth of the administrative state and the ethos of bureaucracy that can support the state. It provides examples of autonomous actions by government organizations and their potential to act in manners contrary to established law.

S. G. Koven, *The Case Against Bureaucratic Discretion*,
https://doi.org/10.1007/978-3-030-05779-4_1

2 Growth of Administrative State in the US

2.1 Pre–New Deal Growth

Administration of one type or another is necessary for governing large numbers of people. One person cannot do it all; some delegation is essential. This is both an ancient and modern axiom. For example, the Bible (Exodus 18: 1–27) informs readers that upon leaving Egypt, Moses' father-in-law Jethro advised him that he would "surely wear away" if he continued to take it upon himself to sit in judgment of everyone who came to him to instruct them about the statutes and laws of God. Jethro recommended that Moses identify able men who "fear God, men of truth, hating covetousness." These men would "be rulers of thousands, and rulers of hundreds, rulers of fifties, and rulers of tens." Moses would have jurisdiction over "every great matter" but others would judge "every small matter." This burden-sharing arrangement would enable Moses to "endure" and enable the people to "go to their place in peace."

Crafters of the US Constitution took heed of the administrative prescriptions found in the Bible. They recognized the need for both delegation and oversight, ever fearful of the dangers posed by concentrated power. These apprehensions correspond with a framework that prioritizes both limited government and the protection of individual liberty. The US Bill of Rights as well as other amendments to the Constitution explicitly outlines such protection. The first ten amendments (Bill of Rights) prohibit the government from intrusion into personal prerogatives, such as religious worship, right to assembly, or freedom of speech. The Bill of Rights enumerates procedures the government must follow to protect against unreasonable search and seizure or cruel and unusual punishment. Among other protections, amendments outline procedure for redress of breaches in constitutional rights. These protections help ensure freedom from an intrusive, oppressive, and expansive public sector.

The US founders intended the size and scope of the public sector to be modest. The first agencies of the federal government were the Departments of War, State, Navy, Treasury, and Office of the Attorney General. At the end of the Federalist period (1800), about 3000 appointed civilian officials labored in the federal government. The original State Department consisted of nine employees in addition to the Secretary of State. The War Department did not reach 80 civilian employees until 1801. Over time, the number of agencies and personnel increased steadily. An expansion of governmental responsibilities led to the creation of the Department of the Interior in 1849, the Department of Justice in 1870, and the Post Office Department in 1872. By 1881, the number of federal personnel grew to about 95,000; by 1925, federal workers increased to nearly half a million (Wilson 1975, p. 77).

Clientele pressure represents one factor that contributed to the growth of the federal bureaucracy. The Department of Agriculture and the Department of Commerce and Labor arose to protect the interests of farmers, industrial workers, and business. In 1862, (a time when approximately three-fourths of Americans lived off the land) the government created the US Department of Agriculture (USDA). Originally, the department principally confined its activities to research and education with the goal of developing and disseminating new farming techniques. Over time, however, the USDA expanded its services into activities such as economic forecasting, nutritional programs, food stamps, consumer services, rural development, natural resources, and environmental protection (Stillman 1987, p. 42). In 1888, labor organizations such as the Knights of Labor helped secure creation of a Department of Labor. In 1903, the Department of Labor was renamed the Department of Commerce and Labor. During the nineteenth century, client-oriented pressures also led to the creation of bureaucracies at the state level (Wilson 1975, pp. 88, 90).

Regulatory agencies added to the growth of bureaucracy. The inability of states to regulate powerful private entities such as the railroads facilitated the creation of the Interstate Commerce Commission in 1887. Political pressures fostered the establishment of other regulatory bodies such as the Federal Reserve Board in 1913, the Federal Trade Commission in 1914, and the Federal Power Commission in 1920. Creation of each of these regulatory bodies occurred in a charged political environment. Proponents of regulating massive organizations (such as railroads, banks, utilities, and corporations) were able to muster sufficient political strength to pass legislation that reined in the power of these entities (Woll 1963, p. 42).

The growth of regulatory agencies represents a source of anxiety for some citizens. Critics of these organizations view regulatory agencies as a "fourth" or hidden branch of government because they play an unpublicized role in shaping policy (Stillman 1987, p. 42). The ability of the public to influence the behavior of nonelected officials in these regulatory bodies remains a constant source of concern. In the era of Donald Trump and Tea Party populism, fears of a "deep state" have gained traction. This fear is consistent not only with bureaucratic growth but also with the great discretionary power of career bureaucrats. The ability of these bureaucrats to exert their authority over average citizens is profound. Their power is often obscure to the average citizen. Many citizens therefore view bureaucrats as unaccountable threats to their liberty since career officials are not directly subject to the electoral will of the people. This seepage of accountability represents a corruption of the principle of government by consent of the people.

2.2 *New Deal and Post–New Deal Growth*

The Great Depression shattered confidence in the ability of the private sector to maintain economic growth. The New Deal of President Franklin D. Roosevelt embraced a more expansive role for government to provide assistance to those in need. The New Deal employed large numbers of people for public works and other endeavors. Two prominent programs of the New Deal period include the Civilian Conservation Corps and the Works Projects Administration. These programs helped to fill the economic void produced by the massive Depression beginning with the stock market crash of 1929. With the New Deal, a large permanent bureaucracy emerged. In 1932, the federal bureaucracy comprised 572,000 employees; by 1939, 920,000 employees; and by 1950, 2.6 million (p. 49). Philosophically, the Great Depression shifted attitudes away from the view that poverty is the result of individual characteristics such as indolence, drug abuse, or alcoholism. With the Great Depression, people who were previously hardworking and prosperous found themselves unemployed and in desperate economic straits. It became much easier for them to accept the notion of an expansive government. This government could correct for market failure that was evident. The government became the employer of last resort as Keynesian policies of government spending became accepted.

With the declaration of war against Japan on December 8, 1941, and the subsequent declaration against Germany on December 11, 1941, unemployment was no longer an issue. Federal government spending expanded by 132 percent between 1941 and 1942; spending increased by 111 percent from 1942 to 1943. By 1945, expenditures for defense accounted for 37 percent of the nation's gross domestic product. In 1940, 14.6 percent of the nation's labor force was unemployed. Unemployment declined to 1.9 percent by 1945. By 1950, defense spending as a percent of gross national product declined to 5 percent. Defense spending as a percent of total federal spending declined from 90 percent in 1945 to 32 percent in 1950 (Tassava 2008).

National security remained a concern even after World War II. The National Security Act of 1947 established the Central Intelligence Agency (CIA) to collect, coordinate, and disseminate foreign intelligence. In 1946, Congress created the Atomic Energy Commission to foster and control the peacetime development of atomic science and technology. Congress set up the National Science Foundation in 1950 to promote basic and applied research and the National Aeronautics and Space Administration in 1958 in response to the USSR's launching of the Sputnik satellite in 1957 (p. 51).

The next great wave of government activism occurred during the 1960s with Lyndon Johnson's Great Society programs. Johnson's Great Society introduced programs such as food stamps, worker training, Medicare, and Medicaid. Numerous regulations were enacted relevant to environmental pollution, worker safety, and consumer protection (Cohen 2000, p. 54). The Johnson administration created agencies such as the Department of Housing and Urban Development, Department of Transportation, and Appalachian Regional Commission. In addition, the Great Society expanded grant programs to state and local governments in support of hospitals, schools, and highways (Stillman 1987, p. 50).

More recently, the Homeland Security Act of 2002 established the Department of Homeland Security (DHS). The new department consolidated 22 agencies related to homeland security into a single Cabinet-level agency. Organizations such as US Customs, Immigration and Naturalization Services; Immigration and Customs Enforcement; Transportation and Security Administration; Federal Emergency Management Agency; US Coast Guard; and the US Secret Service were consolidated into the new DHS. The creation of the DHS represents the largest US government reorganization in 50 years. In fiscal year 2017, DHS received a net discretionary budget of $40.6 billion and comprised more than 240,000 employees (United States Department of Homeland Security 2017).

Solely exploring numbers of federal agencies and the size of the federal workforce, however, underestimates the true influence of government. While the official count of US federal employees (not including uniformed military personnel and postal workers) has not changed considerably in recent years a more careful investigation reveals that the US public sector has "stealthily" expanded using the proxies of state and local government, for-profit businesses, and nonprofit organizations (Dilulio 2014). Raw personnel data, however, grossly underestimates the true size and scope of the federal government. Government organizations such as the Department of Defense conceal their true size by hiring outside contractors. The government obscures numerous national security–related expenditures. In addition, the US government does not openly reveal "black budget" programs that cover expenses related to military research and covert operations. Examples of black budget expenditures include spending for the F-117 stealth attack aircraft and the B-2 stealth bomber. For a long time the government denied the existence of these aircraft.

The public sector also accounts for a large proportion of the revenues to state, local, and nonprofit organizations. Between 1960 and 2017, the number of state- and local-government employees tripled to more than 18 million. Federal money contributes greatly to the growth of lower-level governments. Between the early 1960s and early 2010s, the inflation-adjusted value of federal grants for the states increased more than tenfold (Will 2017).

In an example of federal influence, contributions from the national government help fund many local police departments. In addition, agencies such as the Defense Department supplemented their workforce with an almost equal number of for-profit contract employees. In 2006, there were nearly as many private contractors as US military soldiers in Iraq—100,000 contract employees versus 140,000 troops. Finally, a large proportion of the revenues to nonprofit organizations flow in one way or another from the public sector. If payments to state and local government, payments to for-profit businesses, and funding of nonprofit organizations are summed, government spending in 2017 was 3.5 times bigger than in 1960 (Will 2017).

2.3 *Explanations for Growth of Government*

Various theories exist as explanations for government growth. Wagner's Law posits that increases in the size and scope of government correspond to changes in society, particular to changes in urbanization and industrialization. According to this view, as society transitions from an agricultural to an industrial economic base, the demands on law enforcement, fire protection, transportation, education, and sanitation systems increase. Urbanization, with its potential for conflict, creates a need for government to take on more responsibility in supplying vital services. Other explanations for government growth focus on revenue created by economic growth, policymakers underestimating the true cost of programs, and politicians wishing to curry favor with constituents (Nice and Fisher 2016, p. 49).

Crises, surges of demand for government activity, clientele pressure, and budget maximization are commonly cited explanation for government growth. The Great Depression and World War II directly led to vast increases in the size and scope of the public sector. Franklin Roosevelt's New Deal created an array of agencies to address the economic catastrophe of the 1930s. In 1933, one in four Americans were out of work, thousands of banks closed, and industrial income fell by more than 50 percent (Stillman 1987, p. 47). By 1945, these problems became moot. Clientele groups also put pressure on government to intervene in the marketplace.

An alternative perspective looks at internal motivations of public officials as an explanation for increased spending. Public choice theorists contend that bureaucracies increase because of the self-interest of bureaucrats. The budget maximization model of public choice theory contends that rational bureaucrats will always seek to increase their budgets in an effort to increase their own power (Niskanen 1971). Under this perspective, bureaucrats assume their salaries, prestige, power, and benefits will increase as their organization grows (Beetham 1996, p. 25).

Some scholars categorize explanations for government growth into "citizen-over-state" theories and "state-over-citizen" theories (Garrett and Rhine 2006). The citizen-over-state theories begin with the premise that government responds to the demands and will of the people. In contrast, the state-over-citizen theories posit that the size of government is independent of citizen demand; government grows because of inefficiencies in public sector activities and/or self-interested actions of bureaucrats.

Subcomponents of the citizen-over-government theory include (1) government as a provider of goods and reducer of externalities, (2) government as a redistributor of income or wealth, and (3) government as responding to interest group pressure. The government as provider of goods and reducer of externality explanation contends that personnel grow because voters decide to fund numerous services. Government expands when voters elect legislators who favor a more extensive public sector. In addition to added services, government critics argue that lower productivity tends to increase the size of the public sector. The near-monopoly nature of many publicly provided goods and services encourages higher wages for public sector workers; unionization can lead to excess staffing.

A second factor in citizen-over-state theories of government expansion assumes that government serves as a redistributor of income and wealth. Growth in government can occur because over time new voters elect candidates that commit to an increase in resources that are committed to redistribution. Candidates promise transfer payments to groups of lower-income citizens in order to gain their support. Studies indicate as the middle class feels threatened, or as growth of income slows, demand increases for redistributive public policies (Kristov et al. 1992).

A final factor in citizen-over-state theories relates to interest group pressure. Well-organized interest groups can apply political pressure more effectively than can individual citizens. Through concentrated lobbying, interest group pressure can exert great influence. Legislators are more likely to adhere to the demands of organized groups than the demands of unorganized taxpayers. The mass of taxpayers assume the costs of higher government spending. Empirical evidence supports a positive relationship between the numbers of political action committees (surrogate for interest groups) and federal government spending. As described with regard to groups such as farmers and labor unions, interest group pressure can lead to the creation of new bureaus and agencies. Government size increases in response to the organized pressure. Through lobbying, interest groups obtain desired policies.

Inherent in these citizen-over-state theories of government expansion is the idea that government is "demand driven" or that government grows because citizen calls for government services increase. In contrast, state-over-citizen theories of government growth posit that size of government is independent of citizen demand. Government grows because of inherent inefficiencies in public sector activities and self-interested incentives of bureaucrats.

State-over-citizen theories present a picture of self-interested bureaucratic actors expanding public spending for their personal benefit. Prominent among the state-over-citizen theories are (1) bureaucracy theory, (2) fiscal illusion, and (3) monopoly government. Bureaucracy theory (one aspect of public choice theory) suggests that bureaucrats generate budgets that are in excess of what citizen demand warrants (Niskanen 1971). A bureaucrat can acquire a budget in excess of the efficient level because of the difficulty in monitoring public sector efficiency. Bureaucracy theorists such as Niskanen (1971) argue that unlike the private sector with its focus on profit the public sector does not possess an easy-to-operationalize measure for success. A bureaucrat's objective is to maximize the quantity of services supplied. Under this model, excessive production of services may produce a "dead weight" loss. Niskanen proposes that government bureaucrats are able to increase spending because of their monopoly positions. Due to their monopoly position, a loss of accountability occurs; excessive production of services may produce a "dead weight" loss in the public sector. Bureaucracy theory does not deny the citizen demand models of government but it suggests that bureaucrats can generate budgets that are in excess of what citizen demand warrants.

Niskanen's insights borrow from Parkinson's Law that notes the number of employees employed in a bureaucracy rises irrespective of the amount of required work. According to Parkinson's Law, officials make work for each other. The monopoly nature of bureaucracies adds to a loss of accountability. Funding agencies do not possess good information to judge performance on monopolies (Garrett and Rhine 2006). When excessive production occurs, taxpayers do not receive equal value for their contributions.

The fiscal illusion theory proposes that the bureaucracy grows because voters are deceived about its true size. The theory assumes that citizens measure the size of government by the quantity of taxes they pay. In order to create a fiscal illusion, governments increasingly use taxes that are non-intrusive to citizens. Federal withholding of income taxes and withholding of local property taxes through monthly mortgage payments reduce the perceived intrusiveness and perceived burden of taxes. When governments automatically withhold taxes from earnings, taxes are less likely to stimulate resistance.

The monopoly government theory proposes that government not only provides basic goods (such as police and fire protection) but also "bundles" narrowly defined issues with popular basic services. The "bundling" of goods and services helps legislators achieve their goals of increasing the probability of reelection, personal monetary gain, and the pursuit of personal ideals. Monopoly government theory borrows from the private sector where a monopolist can increase profit by bundling products into a single package. Consumers purchase an entire package of products and must accept the less desired goods along with the more desired goods. Prominent economists extended the monopolist view of government in a "leviathan" government model (Brennan and Buchanan 1980). In the "leviathan" government model, the sole objective of government is to maximize revenue. Citizens lose all control and the model views political competition as an ineffective constraint on government growth. The leviathan view is the mirror opposite of citizen-over-state theories. In the leviathan model, only constitutional constraints on the government's authority to tax and issue debt can limit bureaucratic growth.

3 General Ethos of Bureaucracies

3.1 *Prescribed Legal Behavior of Bureaucrats*

Legislation of duly elected representatives gives legitimacy to government bureaus (Frug 1984, p. 1300). Legislative bodies (e.g. US Congress, state legislatures, and city councils) can create agencies to manage crises and redress social problems. Growth of regulatory bodies led critics to charge they were not accountable to the people. These critics assert regulatory agencies have powers that exceed those of the three recognized branches (the legislative, executive, and judiciary). The independence of regulatory bodies is justified by the need to maintain separation of powers as well as checks and balances. Regulatory bodies can protect against the risk of arbitrary use of political power by politicians (Maggetti 2010, p. 1).

The power of regulatory and executive branch agencies is limited. The US Congress and other legislative authorities can conduct hearings and investigations of alleged misdeeds within the executive branch. On occasion misbehavior results in high-profile probes such as Benghazi hearings of 2015, Internal Revenue Service hearings of 2013, Iran-Contra hearings of 1987, and New York City police corruption investigation/Knapp Commission of 1970. These forums expose the shady underbelly of bureaucratic activity.

Forums limit abuse by enhancing public awareness and imposing penalties. Accountability occurs when overseers reveal questionable behavior. Bureaucrats (especially "street-level" bureaucrats) can abuse their power of discretion and violate constitutional rights. Bureaucrats can engage in acts of malfeasance that decrease the efficiency and effectiveness of the organization. When overseeing organizations expose misbehavior, they promote proper conduct. Legislative oversight is necessary; however, investigation of real or perceived abuse can become highly politicized as demagogic political figures seize the opportunity to advance their careers.

For the most part, bureaucrats and agencies seek to operate within the parameters of their legal authority. Agencies operate under legislative directives such as the Administrative Procedure Act (APA) of 1946. This act governs the manner in which administrative agencies of the federal government propose and establish regulations. At the time of passage, advocates of the APA viewed it as a "bill of rights" for average citizen. The APA attempts to ensure due process and protect residents from secretive acts of the government. The APA requires government agencies to keep the public informed of their procedures and rules, provides for public participation in the rulemaking process, establishes uniform standards for an agency's rulemaking and adjudication, and defines the scope of agency judicial review authority. The APA represents a compromise between those favoring a more expansive public sector and those fearful of the dangers of the top-down rule and central planning.

Politicians and citizens are ever worried about the dangers posed by an expansive state. Franklin D. Roosevelt commented that the practice of creating administrative agencies with the authority to perform both legislative and judicial work threatens to develop a "fourth branch" of government. The APA represents an attempt to control the power of an expanding state while protecting principles of constitutional government. The APA is not a definitive settlement of tensions that arise between advocates of a powerful state and protectors of constitutional rights. It approaches a first step on the road toward assuring constitutional protections (Postell 2017, p. 243).

At the heart of the question of legality is the need for bureaucrats to carry out their responsibilities within the parameters of rule-based behavior. Bureaucrats should not allow personal conceptions or private interests to guide behavior. Discretion exists in that bureaucrats often receive broad mandates such as protecting safety or educating children and then interpret how to accomplish the task. The degree of discretion to exercise has been a constant source of consternation within the legal and public administration communities. In theory, the legislature acts as the principal and the bureaucracy the agent carrying out the wishes of the people. In reality, there is a constant fear that government bureaucracies will cease to become the servants of legislatures and cease to be servants of the people. The recurring fear is that public bureaucrats become masters rather than servants. Bureaucrats violate principles of democracy if their perceived responsibility to accomplish broad mandates entices them to take matters into their own hands irresponsibly.

3.2 *Sense of Responsibility of "Ideal" Bureaucrat*

Varieties of perspectives compete with each other to define the "responsible" bureaucrat. Two frames of reference present contrasting images of capable bureaucratic behavior (Frug 1984). According to the first model (formalistic model), the responsible bureaucrat acts as part of a well-functioning machine and endeavors to achieve the goals of others. The bureaucrat may not agree with the desired goals/ends, but takes no part in influencing policy. Bureaucrats act with neutrality; they do not exercise discretion. As part of the well-functioning machine, the ideal bureaucrat fulfills a specified function and integrates with functions of others in the organization. This model views bureaucracies as well designed. One assumes operational problems fix themselves with small adjustments. There is no reason to believe that the operation of the organization will pose a threat that outside forces (such as the courts or elections) should control.

Instrumental relationship to ends, technical design, and efficiency are central elements in the first (formalistic) model. In theory, bureaucrats respond to constituents' commands. The ideal bureaucrat does not rely upon private factors but upon the impersonal requirements of the organization. Bureaucrats are independent of the personal will of others and subservient only to general, impersonal laws (p. 1300). The responsible bureaucrat carries out responsibilities that allow the machine to achieve desired ends.

In contrast to the first model, the second model (expertise model) of bureaucracy views the responsible bureaucrat as a member of a social system. The social system molds individuals into a functioning group. Writers of bureaucratic theory often refer to this view of bureaucracy as "organic," to contrast it with the "mechanical" nature of the formalist model (Perrow 1979). The organic model pictures a bureaucracy as a natural community organized to pursue a common purpose. Loyalty, rather than discipline, is essential; the effective organization depends more on the psychology of its members than on judiciously following rules. The organization must internalize as part of its collective consciousness the common purpose that unites its members. Theorists focus on how organizations can foster cooperative pursuit of a common goal. The responsible administrator therefore is committed to pursuing the common goal and molding the organization in such pursuit.

Frug (1984, p. 1321) describes the expertise perspective as one where "shareholders, employees, and the general public are equally disqualified from reviewing executive decision making because they all lack the ability to second-guess the complex judgments that enter into such decision making. No one outside his own particular specialty can adequately judge another person's work. No one else has the right instincts that can give concrete meaning to the organization's purpose.... Only those inside the bureaucracy have the appropriate intuitions about how it works and how best to effectuate its purpose." Internal considerations control the organization. If the organization is not functioning properly, the solution is to find the "right people" to make it work. The expertise model's description of the relationship between the bureaucracy and its constituents parallels the internal organization of the bureaucracy. The model does not view constituents as directors of organizational policy. The constituents' deference to discretion is broad and general because they recognize that only someone on the job can make the actual day-to-day decisions that set institutional policy.

Frug (1984, p. 1321) views the expertise model as the mirror image of the formalist model. The formalist model posits a machinelike, objective organization controlled by the arbitrary, subjective desires of the bureaucracy's constituents. The expertise model, by contrast, depicts a flexible organizational purpose energized by a creative executive. Limits of professionalism, expertise, and competence that constrain organizational flexibility within appropriate bounds influence the organization. The responsible administrator under the first model serves constituent desires within the confines of a well-run machine. Under the second model, the responsible administrator uses his or her expertise within a like-minded group to pursue a common purpose. The second model not only concedes but also celebrates the role of subjectivity and discretion in bureaucratic operations.

3.3 *Utility of Responsible Discretion*

Discretion is not a total one-way street. Dobel (1999, p. 1) notes that every elected, appointed, and career official must exercise discretion in carrying out the duties and responsibilities of office. He asserts that societies depend upon the conscientious judgment and skill of these officials to provide the foundation for public order. Public officials have to consider their personal morality and strike a balance among institutional and personal dimensions of public judgments. Dobel presents three models to understand conflicts between discretion and democratic responsiveness. The legal-institutional model emphasizes the public official's subordination to legal and institutional authority. The personal-responsibility model asserts that public officials must incorporate personal responsibility into their judgment. The effectiveness or implementation model highlights discretion and politics involved in decisions of public officials. This model posits a need to use power, to be flexible, and to act effectively. Dobel recognizes that responsible judgment of public officials requires moral resources. Governments cannot dictate all judgments of officials in advance; integrity therefore is essential. Dobel surmises, "public integrity should be conceived of not as rigid and determined, but as dynamic and accountable. Defensible public discretion is exercised by real human beings and sustained by personal integrity" (p. 22).

Rourke (1984, p. 42) contends that giving administrative agencies discretion reflects basic forces in American political life such as the belief in the value of individual justice. This belief in individual justice runs deep in the political tradition of the United States. There is a conviction that rather than relying on legal codes, common law practices that consider unique features of each case better serve justice. When administrators exercise discretion, they can tailor decision to circumstances. Rules may need to bend to particular situations in order to provide justice. Discretion is necessary since policymaking in the modern state is experimental. Legislators anticipate that agencies may eventually have to deal with issues legislatures do not foresee. There is an expectation that administrative discretion can devise policy by trial and error and day-to-day decision making. Legislatures may also turn over authority to bureaucrats in an effort to shift the onus of making unpopular decisions onto others. Rourke observes that reform groups have long favored delegation of discretionary power to administrators because they believe administrators are more likely to be professional and nonpolitical in their decisions. He concludes that in the United States there has been persistent criticism of administrative discretion because it seems to flout commitment to democracy. However, he states, "there are valid grounds for believing that administrative discretion, if not as American as apple pie, is certainly compatible with our political culture and very convenient for many of the groups interested in or affected by the exercise of such discretion" (p. 44).

Responsibility links to discretion. Pennock (1960) characterizes responsibility as the exercise of judgment and discretion in light of careful analysis and conscientious weighing of values. Cooper (1990, p. 58) emphasizes that expectations imposed from outside should be balanced with ethical reasoning. Burke (1986) argues for responsibility that derives not just from formal laws but also from a broad understanding of bureaucrats' place within an encompassing set of institutions and processes. Denhardt (1988) focuses on individual moral reasoning as a basis for responsible action. She claims the no outside structure should give a priori justification for any course of action. Discretion is necessary for application of moral reasoning. Plant (2018, p. 538) concludes that by the late 1990s the prevailing view was that responsible administration requires a balance between compliance and individual reasoning. He states that by the late 1990s, "Discretion on the part of public administrators was accepted as inevitable, given the nature of complex modern policy formation and execution."

Discretion in terms of whistleblowing or "guerrilla" activity is the focus of O'Leary's (2006) text. O'Leary focuses attention on actions of career bureaucrats who work against the interests of superiors in order to achieve specific outcomes. O'Leary cites the actions of Chiune Sugihara and Mark Felt as examples of public servants that used their power to achieve outcomes that were not the preference of immediate supervisors. As a Japanese diplomat living in Lithuania during World War II, Sugihara disobeyed orders by issuing thousands of visas to Jewish refugees. In issuing the visas, he saved many people from certain death. Upon returning to Japan, Sugihara lost his job in the foreign ministry and spent much of the rest of his life feeling humiliated. Felt, the number two official in the Federal Bureau of Investigation (FBI), provided valuable information about Nixon administration abuse to the media and was instrumental in bringing down a sitting president (p. 2). Felt did not follow FBI policy of staying detached from partisan politics. His actions, however, had a profound effect on the course of American history.

In retrospect, we view people such as Sugihara and Felt as heroes in that they uncovered wrongdoing or saved the lives of innocent people. Certainly, they did not have to do what they did; they exercised discretion. Many perceive the value of their actions today as responsible and beneficial to society or beneficial to humanity. In exercising discretion, however, their actions ran counter to the values of classical bureaucracy. The heart of bureaucratic thought exists in the writings of classical theorists. Additional perspectives such as human relations, contingency theories, new public management theory, and organizational culture schools of thought supplement the classical view (Shafritz and Ott 1987; Rainey 2003). Classical administrative theory, however, remains an essential starting point for understanding the roots of modern organizations and the manner in which they function.

4 Classical Theory of Administrators in Bureaucracies

4.1 Woodrow Wilson

Scholars term Woodrow Wilson as the father of public administration. His contribution to the field relies upon a sharp line of distinction between politics and administration. Wilson defines politics as the enactment of law and formulation of public policy. In contrast, he defines public administration as the execution of the law (Wilson 1887, p. 212). Wilson views principles of good administration as the same for all types of government. According to Wilson, French and German scholars at the turn of the twentieth century most fully refine the "science" of administration. He contends that democracies such as the United States could learn from autocratic regimes in Prussia and France about efficient government (Ostrom 1973, p. 27).

Wilson posits that modernity is associated with a system of "good" administration. The basic principle of such a system includes the following:

- A government controlled by that single center of power.
- Unified power is more responsible than divided.
- Legal documents (such as a constitution) determine the composition of the center of power.
- Politics sets the tasks for administration but the field of administration lies outside the proper sphere of politics.
- All modern governments will be similar in structure so far as administrative functions are concerned.
- A hierarchical ordering of a professionally trained public service provides the conditions necessary for "good" administration.
- Perfection in the hierarchical organization maximizes efficiency. Least cost expended in money and effort is the measure of efficiency.
- Perfection of "good" administration is a necessary condition for modernity and for the advancement of human welfare (pp. 28–29).

Wilson's seminal 1887 article, "The Study of Administration," represents a groundbreaking advance in the development of public administration as a field of study. At the time of the first American textbook in administration (1893), Wilson had been giving lectures in administration for six years. Wilson's role as a pioneer is apparent in the fact that at the time he taught administration at Princeton and Johns Hopkins University only two other schools in the United States offered courses in administration (Turner 1956, p. 251).

Perhaps, Wilson's best-known contribution to public administration is his emphasis on professionalism and adaptation of a "businesslike" approach to government. In establishing the view that administration lies outside the proper sphere of politics Wilson lays the intellectual justification for removing public entities from the "hurry and strife" of politics. Wilson advocated civil service reform as a means of making public service unpartisan and businesslike. He recognizes the danger of borrowing systems used in nondemocratic regimes. Wilson nevertheless asks why the

United States should not be able to borrow from others even if they are autocratic regimes.

Wilson argues that if he sees a monarchist managing a public bureau well he could learn his business methods without adopting his political preferences. The bureaucracies in monarchies can serve their king while US agencies can serve the people. In theory, US scholars can "scrutinize the anatomy of foreign governments without fear of getting any of their diseases into our veins" (Wilson 1887, p. 220). His prescriptions for a technically schooled civil service, separation of administration from politics, and a focus on efficiency advance US administrative science.

4.2 *Max Weber*

Weber concurs with Woodrow Wilson in that perfection in bureaucratic administration depends on exclusion of politics from administration. According to Weber, bureaucracy relies upon application of rules in a rigorous and machinelike manner. Weber views the bureaucracy as an instrument that can work for anyone who controls it; bureaucracies serve any political master. The individual bureaucrat is a cog in the large machine. Weber opines that once perfected, it is impossible to replace or dispense with the bureaucratic organization. If the organization falters, chaos can result. Weber believes it is difficult to find replacements among the masses for the functional administrative specialists. Dominance of the bureaucracy depends upon its capacity to monopolize information behind a wall of secrecy, to preclude rivalry among officials, and to monopolize professional expertise (Ostrom 1973, pp. 32–33).

Weber identifies very specific features of the "ideal" or fully developed bureaucracy. The following main features characterize Weber's conception of the ideal bureaucracy:

- Each office has a well-defined sphere of competence with duties clearly enumerated.
- Offices exist within a hierarchy; each lower office is under the supervision and responsibility of a higher one.
- Authority is restricted to official duties; there is a complete segregation of official activity from private life.
- Officials hold office by appointment (rather than by election), and because of contractual relationships between themselves and the organization.

- Officials are selected because of objective qualifications acquired by training, established by examinations, diplomas, or both.
- Career tenure is expected; protections exist against arbitrary dismissal; promotion is by seniority, achievement, or both.
- Activities of the bureaucracy rely upon general, consistent, abstract rules; rules require the categorization of individual cases based on objective criteria.
- Official conduct duties in a spirit of impersonality without hatred but also without affection.
- The bureaucracy frequently has a nonbureaucratic head. The head sets the rules; bureaucrats follow the lead of the head (Etzioni-Halevy 1983, p. 28).

Weber is clear regarding his view of the need to subordinate the views of appointed officials to those of political leaders. Weber states,

> The honor of the civil servant is vested in his ability to execute conscientiously the order of the superior authorities, exactly as if the order agreed with his own conviction. This holds even if the order appears wrong to him and if, despite the civil servants remonstrances, the authority insists on the order. Without this moral discipline and self-denial, in the highest sense, the whole apparatus would fall to pieces. (Gerth and Mills 1958, p. 95)

Weber exalted the benefits of bureaucracy; he notes that bureaucracy is, from a technical point of view, capable of attaining the highest degree of rationality and effectiveness. Hierarchy facilitates control and discipline; employment on the basis of qualifications allows for competent work. Rules save effort by standardization; impersonal detachment promotes objectivity and prevents irrational action. Impersonal detachment nullifies favoritism and discrimination. Weber's prescriptions constitute an "ideal type" of organization or a prescribed organization in its purest form. Weber asserts that the closer the organization comes to the ideal the more effective it is likely to be.

Weber also notes that bureaucratic tendencies inevitably come into conflict with democracy. Democracy, according to Weber, accepts the concept of equal rights of the governed. Democracy therefore is committed to preventing the development of a closed status group of officials and minimizing the authority of such officials. Democracy promotes expanding the influence of the people. Weber recognizes that once a bureaucracy is established, it is among the social structures that are the hardest to destroy. He states, "Bureaucracy has been and is a power instrument of the first order-for the one who controls the bureaucratic apparatus" (p. 228). Scholars of bureaucracy observe that in the course of official duties bureaucrats acquire a great deal of information that is not always at the disposal of their political superiors. As a result, nonelected bureaucrats may come to dominate the democratically elected leaders. This poses a threat to modern democracy.

Etzioni-Halevy (1983, p. 34) affirms the view that bureaucracy can threaten democracy. The ability of bureaucracies to control information makes redress of grievances difficult. Political checks on bureaucracy are problematic because of their resistance to control. Weber's construct of the ideal organization exalts virtues such as efficiency, consistency, continuity, and predictability. His assertion of bureaucratic necessity for modern society helps insulate the Weberian organization from criticism. Bureaucracy is efficient because of its precision, speed, consistency, continuity, record keeping, unity, coordination, and minimization of interpersonal friction.

Weber's writings, however, raise various "red flags." Fry and Raadschelders (2008, p. 40) note that Weber recognizes the possibility that a caste of administrators can emerge (a new aristocracy) whose power is grounded in specialized skills. Political leadership is necessary to protect the rule of law from autonomous bureaucratic action. Weber argues that bureaucrats may develop interests of their own and start to shape policy. He holds that bureaucratic officials should not engage in politics, but should only undertake impartial administration. A sense of duty placed above personal opinion should be part of the administrator's ethics. Weber maintains that a bureaucracy must be able to be inspected and controlled to prevent it from becoming a law unto itself. Democracy requires the prevention of a closed status group of officials from taking power (p. 43).

Weber not only describes the necessary factors for the modern organization but also discusses the dangers posed by efficient organizations that may begin to believe they are indispensable. In an inversion of democratic principles, the subordinates (bureaucrats) of the true rulers (the people) become the masters. The bureaucracy and bureaucrats then consolidate their hold on power. Bureaucracies enhance the power of bureaucrats through lifetime employment, control of information, an aura of expertise, and self-aggrandizement.

4.3 *Frederick Winslow Taylor*

Frederick Winslow Taylor is a pioneer of managerial analysis (Rainey 2003, p. 25). He is the major figure in the scientific management school of thought that involves systematic analysis of tasks performed by workers. Taylor is commonly associated with private sector management but his scientific management attracted the enthusiastic support of those in government who believed that his techniques were universally applicable. The use of scientific management in the public sector is consistent with the view of Woodrow Wilson that the public sector should be more "business-like" and Max Weber's beliefs that organizations should be more efficient. With acceptance of Wilson's notion to separate politics from administration, it became permissible to search in the private sector for general administrative techniques that could enhance efficiency in the operation of American government (Fry and Raadschelders 2008, p. 56).

Taylor's ideas continue to have relevance in both business management and public administration. Scholars link Taylor's scientific management to time and motion studies. Today, production engineering and ergonomics use similar practices (Lutrin and Settle 1985, p. 31). The names of the procedures change but the basic methodology remains similar. Taylor identified the basic social problem of his time as that of inefficiency.

Taylor identifies management as the primary cause for inefficiency although workers also share in the blame. According to Taylor, management is deficient in terms of both lack of knowledge as to what constitutes a proper day's work and its indifference to proper practices. Workers contribute to inefficiency through organized restriction of output (known as "soldiering"). Taylor blames poor management for soldiering. He argues that authoritarian management and a piecework incentive system foster worker resistance. Inefficiency also occurs because workers are not likely to know how best to perform assigned tasks. Taylor distinguishes between "first-class" and "second-class" workers. The first-class worker is willing and able to perform tasks efficiently; the second-class worker is able to perform tasks but will not do so. It is management's responsibility to develop first-class workers, put them in suitable positions, provide them with good working conditions, and give them detailed instructions on the best method of performing their tasks (Fry and Raadschelders 2008, p. 62).

In Taylor's mind, a "science of management" could replace rough rules of thumb. He sought to make workers as predictable and efficient as the machines they tended. Management has the responsibility to develop method; once management identifies the proper method workers are responsible for implementing it. Scientific management consists of standardization of methods, adoption of the best tools, and cooperation between management and workers. Essential principles of scientific management include (1) the development of a science of management, (2) the selection and training of workers, (3) bringing science and workers together, and (4) an equal division of work and responsibility between managers and workers (p. 63).

Three important aspects of Taylor's scientific management relate to time and motion study, wage incentive systems, and organizational structure. Time and motion study breaks down activities and specifies optimal routes for performance. It seeks the "one best way" of performing tasks. Taylor's wage system calls for exact time standards for performing tasks. Organizationally, Taylor advocates the establishment of a cadre of technical experts in positions of power. The organization should assign experts to the planning department and personnel should exercise authority because of their knowledge, not their position in the hierarchy (p. 67).

Taylor's aura of science enhances perceptions of organizations as legitimate and well run. This in turn enhances autonomy and can shield public organizations from outside criticism. The emphasis on internal expertise, productivity, and efficiency of scientific management may weaken desire for external oversight.

4.4 Henri Fayol

Henri Fayol along with Frederick Taylor is widely acknowledged as a founder of modern management methods. His writings became popular in the United States with the English translation of his 1916 book *General and Industrial Management*. "Fayolism" bears similarities to "Taylorism" and scientific management. Like Taylor, Fayol focused on managerial practices to minimize misunderstandings and increase efficiency in organizations. He referred to Taylor in his writings and considered Taylor a visionary. According to Fayol, the organizational chart that depicts lines of authority and how they relate to one another is the principal tool of management. He stresses the concept of unity of command, one of his 14 principles of management. The principle of unity of command views each employee as taking orders exclusively from one superior. He notes that everyone in every type of organization should know his or her place on the organizational chart (Lutrin and Settle 1985, p. 32).

From his practical experience as an engineer with a mining company Fayol described 14 basic management principles, which he felt could be used in all management situations. These principles include the following:

1. Division of Work—the object of division is to produce more and better work with the same effort.
2. Authority and Responsibility—authority is the right to give orders and power to exact obedience; responsibility refers to obligation to perform duties. These go together.
3. Discipline—the state of discipline for any group of people depends essentially on the worthiness of its leaders.
4. Unity of Command—for any action, an employee should receive orders from one superior only.
5. Unity of Direction—one head and one plan for a group of activities having the same objective.
6. Subordination of Individual Interest to General Interest—the interest of one employee or group of employees should not prevail over that of the concern.
7. Remuneration of Personnel—payment should be fair and as far as possible afford satisfaction for the employee and employer.
8. Centralization—centralization or decentralization is a matter of finding the optimal degree. The optimal degree is dependent on circumstances.
9. Scalar Chain—chain of superiors ranging from the ultimate authority to the lowest ranks.
10. Order—a place for everything and everything in its place.
11. Equity—produced from a combination of kindness and justice.
12. Stability of Tenure of Personnel—generally, the personnel turnover of prosperous concerns is more stable than that of unsuccessful concerns.
13. Initiative—superior managers exercise initiative.
14. Esprit de Corps—harmony and cooperation among personnel is a great strength (Fayol [1916] 1987).

Fayol's ideas have become a fundamental part of modern management. As an authority of good management, Fayol's insights help advance professionalism, legitimacy, autonomy, competency, command, and influence of government agencies. He recognizes that as government agencies strengthen, they may become less accountable to elected officials.

4.5 *Luther Gulick*

Luther Gulick's status in the field of public administration is such that scholars refer to him as the "Dean of Public Administration" (Fry and Raadschelders 2008, p. 85). His academic scholarship spans a period of 70 years. His first publication appears in 1920 in a book-length version of his doctoral dissertation written at Columbia University; a 1990 article appears in the journal *Public Administration Review*. Gulick served in many public service and academic roles. From 1921, when he was 29, until 1962, Luther Gulick presided as president of the Institute of Public Administration, the nation's oldest organization formed to promote scientific management in government. He went on to serve as the chairperson of the Institute of Public Administration until 1982. Under his leadership, the Institute undertook numerous administrative studies.

Between 1936 and 1937, Gulick served as a member of the President's Committee on Administrative Management (also known as the Brownlow Committee). He coedited the *Papers on the Science of Administration*, published by the Institute of Public Administration in 1937. President Franklin Roosevelt appointed Gulick along with others to make recommendations for the reorganization of the executive branch of the federal government. With the onset of World War II, Gulick served in a wide array of capacities in Washington, DC. In the 1950s and 1960s, he served as New York City's first administrator.

Luther Gulick's insights in *Papers on the Science of Administration* adopt a classical approach to administration that rests on a belief in the virtues of hierarchy and centralization of authority in the chief executive. Gulick supports a belief in efficiency as the central value of administration and a conviction (like Taylor and Fayol) that there must exist certain principles for good administration applicable to all organizations. These doctrines formed the basis for the administrative reform movement (Spicer 1998, p. 299). Gulick's conception of an ideal government is one where a chief executive, supported by special staff, draws up plans; the legislature accepts or rejects the plans; the executive implements adopted plans; and the public exercises control through participation in political parties and pressure groups (Fry and Raadschelders 2008, p. 92). In theory, this would produce efficiency as well as meaningful democratic control.

Gulick advocates integrating and placing the administrative branch of government under the leadership of strong and competent executives. He contends that principles derived from an aversion to executive power defined the original focus of American government. Gulick asserts that there is a need to revise these principles in order to create an administrative branch capable of planning and implementing democratic policies. Gulick advises reforms guided by the following principles:

- all agencies consolidate into a few departments
- related work administered as a single unit
- work placed under a single official selected on the basis of proven ability
- power commensurate with responsibility
- reducing the number of elected officials
- providing staff to department heads for performance evaluation
- vesting responsibility for each function in a specific official
- eliminating boards or commissions for administrative work; they should be limited to quasi-legislative and quasi-judicial functions
- giving chief executives the power to appoint and discharge department heads
- administrative work headed up by a single chief executive who should be directly elected and responsible to voters or their representatives
- chief executive should have staff to search for better methods of operation (Fry and Raadschelders 2008, p. 98; Gulick 1925, p. 400).

Scholarship that defines the work of the chief executive is perhaps Gulick's greatest contribution. Gulick formulated the acronym POSDCORB to describe the work of a chief executive. According to Gulick, the chief executive should focus on the following:

- Planning—working out in broad outline the things that need to be done.
- Organizing—establishing the formal structure of authority through which work subdivisions are arranged.
- Staffing—bringing in and training staff.
- Directing—making decisions and embodying them in orders.
- Coordinating—interrelating the various parts of the work.
- Reporting—keeping those to whom the executive is responsible informed.
- Budgeting—fiscal planning, accounting, and control (Gulick [1937] 1969, p. 13).

Gulick goes further than other classical theorists venture in citing the potential dangers scientific expertise poses to democracy. He notes that experts may assume they can better assess what the people need than the people themselves. This poses a threat to democracy. Experts may also assert authority in areas in which they lack competence. This poses a threat to efficiency. As a warning, Gulick observes that a government program that relies upon a professional group of experts will eventually come under the direction and leadership of that profession. He believes the answer to the danger of technocracy is a sense of professionalism that imposes responsible self-discipline and recognizes that experts cannot be the final authority. For democracies such as the United States, the common person must be the ultimate judge of what is in their interest (Fry and Raadschelders 2008, p. 96).

Gulick rejects the strict separation of administration from politics, yet adopts scientific methods. He views the application of scientific methods as a means to substitute competence for ignorance and to replace the jack-of-all-trades with the expert. Gulick attempts to discover immutable laws of administration. Meier (2010, p. S284) notes that although much of academic public administration dismisses the contributions of Gulick, the absence of attention to his work is problematic. His observations especially related to the dangers of technocracy remain prescient and highly relevant.

4.6 *Contributions of Classical Scholars to Understanding Discretion*

Modern society rests on principles advocated by classical theorists such as Woodrow Wilson, Max Weber, Frederick Taylor, Henri Fayol, and Luther Gulick. Each of the classical scholars contributes to an understanding of how bureaucracies and bureaucrats act. Classical theory outlines the prescriptions for the development of the professionalized administrative state. Theories describe attributes required to promote outcomes such as effectiveness, efficiency, consistency, and equal treatment. Woodrow Wilson as the "father" of public administration allows public sector management to advance into the domain of business practices. Wilson removes the province of government employment from the clutches of machine-style sinecures and introduces concepts such as good management to the operation of government activities. In addition, Wilson's advocacy for training civil servants and introducing merit-based promotion advances efficiency in the public sector.

Weber notes that bureaucracy is the dominant form for modern societies. He views legal authority as superior to the older paradigms of charismatic and traditional authority on a number of dimensions. Charismatic authority (based on personal qualities of the leader) fails because there are no defined spheres of competence to protect against arbitrary exercise of power and no system of rule to ensure equal treatment or due process. Traditional authority grounds itself on respect for the past. According to Weber, such authority is susceptible to the indulgence of personal whims. Subjects are dependent on the favor of the ruler and personal relationships influence judgments of the traditional authoritarian. Weber's ideal bureaucracy reduces arbitrary discretion; it operates under a strict set of rules and implements those rules without hatred or passion. In theory, bureaucracy promotes equal treatment through detachment and neutral professional expertise.

Frederick Winslow Taylor is associated with both private and public sector management. His obsession with oversight works to reduce on-the-job discretion and on-the-job "soldiering" (organized underperformance). The concept of "one best way" in and of itself is a statement about uniformity and consistency. Fayol furthered the thrust of Taylor in developing principles that encourage efficient management. With a strong emphasis on the organizational chart and manager's power to exact obedience, Fayol fits clearly in the formal-rational approach to administration. Gulick's extensive contributions include a more extensive role of administrators in policy. His rejection of the strict politics-administration dichotomy recognizes that administration involves interpreting policy directives. Discretion often occurs as those at the bottom of the organizational chart interpret directives differently or even create their own rules.

In general, classical theorists try to systematize, legitimize, and routinize behavior of public officials. This behavior is justified in the names of consistency, efficiency, and equity. At the same time as classical theorists attempt to standardize behavior, organizations differ widely in terms of level of discretion. As persuasively described by Lipsky (2010), much discretion can occur at the "street level" where broad policy prescriptions are interpreted and implemented. Employees can subvert policy in a multitude of ways. Subversion can occur with the blessing of administrative and political leaders or can occur without the awareness of upper-level administrators. In the extreme, organizations can become autonomous unaccountable entities with allegiance only to internal sets of norms and values. Discussion of abuses of discretion appears below.

5 Potential Abuses of Bureaucrats: Danger of Discretion

5.1 Passive and Hidden Resistance

Scholars have long identified the potential of entrenched bureaucracies to thwart the policy thrusts of elected officials and thereby obstruct the political will of the people. Max Weber argued that an inherent danger exists in the tendency of bureaucrats to exceed their administrative function and assume a political role (Beetham 1996, p. 61). Bureaucrats may feel that their control over official knowledge combined with a belief in the superiority of their administrative values provides license to alter or disregard political directives. Local leaders attempt to subvert higher-level directives through noncompliance. Bardach (1977, p. 66) notes that failure to properly implement policy follows four scenarios: (1) the diversion of resources; (2) the deflection of policy goals; (3) the resistance to explicit, and usually institutionalized, efforts to control behavior; and (4) the dissipation of personal and political energies in game-playing.

High-profile examples of bureaucratic abuse abound. Passive resistance falsely presents an image of compliance while ignoring directives. Tokenism is a popular form of passive resistance where actors appear to be publicly contributing to a program while privately providing only a small (token) contribution. Forms of tokenism include procrastination in making contributions or contributions of inferior quality. For example, in the past, federal officials have made only token efforts to enforce federal fair campaign legislation. The Berkeley, California, Police Department made only token efforts to enforce the laws against marijuana use. In many areas, the chronically mentally ill receive only token services (p. 98). Today, many localities resist strict implementation of federal drug or immigration violations.

O'Leary (2006) describes how bureaucrats can alter policy by appearing to be team players but engaging in "guerrilla" actions such as leaking information to the press. In 24 stories of "guerrilla government," O'Leary details how career administrators circumvented the policy desires of superiors in the organization. Actions range from obtaining secret records, leaking emails, influencing votes of legislators, feeding questions to congressional representatives, and other activities. These "guerrilla" actions counter the stereotype of bureaucrats as neutral implementers of policy. The neutral implementer and separation of politics from administration perspectives have been in ill repute for quite some time. O'Leary notes that for better or worse, interests and values of bureaucrats drive actions. She surmises "guerrilla" activities ebb and flow, however, but never completely disappear (p. 91).

"Guerrilla" activities can be as simple as putting a work order at the bottom of the desk drawer and forgetting about it, to slipping information to a legislative staff person, to outright insubordination. O'Leary states that in the absence of hiring a full-time detective, higher-level managers "have limited knowledge about, and control over, the career public servants in their organizations. Professional bureaucrats dominate information creation, analysis, and transmission, giving them a capacity to structure or suppress alternatives, and premises" (p. 91).

Bureaucratic opposition to policy may be intense and individual bureaucrats may justify insubordinate actions through sanctimonious conviction. In one example, officials at the Department of Interior and the Nevada Department of Wildlife (NDOW) maintained that saving wetlands became more important than the task of pleasing superiors, upholding departmental policy, or appeasing potentially hostile groups. Career officials felt their action was simply the right thing to do. A desire to do something good for nature superseded their legal obligations to implement official policy. In the Department of Interior and the NDOW career bureaucrats worked behind the scenes to develop support for an environmental bill and later were ghostwriters of parts of the final bill (p. 26).

Often policymaking of lower-level bureaucrats goes undetected, especially if there is lax oversight. Discretion or judgment about implementing or failing to implement policy exists. Discretion can be high among street-level bureaucrats such as teachers, police officers, and parole officers. For example, teachers in School A may emphasize curriculum or ideological viewpoints that their local School Board or the national Department of Education does not endorse. Police in City B may decide to ignore specific high-crime districts or allow open drug dealing to occur in particular neighborhoods. Parole officers in Prison C may issue earlier parole to people with similar ethnic backgrounds as themselves. FBI agent D may decide not to pursue a case against a high-profile politician. Police officer E may personally dislike the person he/she arrested for narcotics possession and advocate for a stiff penalty. At the same time, Police officer F may ignore a narcotics possession of individual G who is an influential member of the community.

Davis (1969, pp. 9–14), in a classic exposition of discretionary judgment, provides numerous examples of how decisions made by career bureaucrats influence outcomes. The following five examples describe the ability of career bureaucrats to shape outcomes in a relatively unobtrusive manner.

- Through a plea bargain a prosecutor agrees with one defendant to reduce a felony charge but refuses to do so for another defendant.
- The manager of a public housing project evicts the mother of four children on the ground of undesirability without giving a more specific reason.
- Police round up minority youth and keep them jailed through high bail and delayed proceedings.
- A traffic officer warns a violator instead of writing a ticket, because the violator is a lawyer and the police of the jurisdiction favor lawyers.
- An assistant attorney general institutes a prosecution against a corporation. His successor dismisses the prosecution, without stating facts, without stating reasons, without relating the case to policies, and without public statement.

A significant number of scholars maintain that the politics-administration dichotomy attributed to Woodrow Wilson (1887) is no longer tenable (Appleby 1949; Long 1949; Rohr 1989; Waldo 1948). However, if non-elected bureaucrats make their own rules it undermines principles of democracy. Rohr (1989, p. 49) suggests that even passive resistance to legitimate policy presents problems for democratic societies. Active resistance represents a more direct threat.

5.2 *Active Resistance*

Very open resistance to policy thrusts of elected officials or political appointees within bureaucracies is a reality. One does not have to look very far to see examples where career bureaucrats or locally elected officials acted to circumvent directives of superiors. The most notorious examples illustrate that active resistance can completely derail or delay implementation of policy formulated by elected representatives or organizational superiors.

Perhaps the most obvious example of active resistance to public policy relates to school integration. Public school integration did not automatically occur following the 1954 *Brown v. Board of Education* Supreme Court decision. Rigid ideologically positions can deter implementation of policy, especially when highly charged issues such as integration, abortion, or environmental protection are involved. Resistance is often justified in the minds of the actors in order to attain a "greater good" such as saving the environment or preserving a cherished way of life. Striving for the greater good can also motivate "guerrilla" action of bureaucrats or noncompliance by local leaders. Politicians may be motivated to take high-profile stands against unwanted legislation. However, these actions erode foundations of democracy by replacing legitimate legislation with policy preferences of unelected bureaucrats or preferences of provincial politicians.

Resistance hinders democracy. The history of school integration is illustrative. The landmark case of *Brown v. Board of Education* clearly established that the doctrine of "separate but equal" in public schools was not constitutional. However, political figures such as Arkansas Governor Orval Faubus refused to accept the decision and, in 1957, called out National Guard troops to resist the federal policies. As is now well known, President Dwight D. Eisenhower intervened by federalizing the Arkansas National Guard and sending elite airborne soldiers to Little Rock to enforce the court order.

Other events mirror that of Little Rock. In 1956, Virginia Senator Harry Byrd encouraged "massive resistance" to school desegregation. Rather than integrate, in 1959, leaders in Prince Edward County, Virginia, closed its entire public school system. Private schools educated the county's white children. Tuition grants from the state of Virginia and tax credits from the county supported the private schools. It was not until 1964, when the US Supreme Court outlawed Virginia's tuition grants to private education, that Prince Edward County reopened its schools, on an integrated basis. Integration of the University of Mississippi in 1962 triggered a riot ending in two dead, hundreds wounded, and many others arrested. The University of Alabama admitted its first African-American students in 1963 after President John F. Kennedy federalized National Guard troops and deployed them to the university.

In contrast to state resistance to national policy, bureaucrats within the ranks of administrations also can hinder or alter policy. In another example of ideologically based resistance to established law, high-ranking officials within the Reagan administration worked to funnel weapons to enemies of the Nicaragua government. The so-called Iran-Contra affair evolved from efforts to achieve the "greater good" of stopping or hindering the spread of Communism. In the Iran-Contra case, the US National Security

Council (NSC) successfully provided aid to groups (contras) opposing the government of Nicaragua. This act was in direct opposition to congressional legislation (Boland Amendment of 1984) that banned direct or indirect US military aid to such groups.

Congressional hearings of 1987 revealed that National Security Advisor John Poindexter had personally authorized the diversion of money to the Contra rebels in violation of the Boland Amendment. The CIA's William J. Casey also played a part in the plan. As a military aide to the NSC, Lt. Col. Oliver North had been the main negotiator to obtain funds and weapons. During the hearings, North repeatedly explained that he was under orders from his superiors. The Iran-Contra affair raised serious questions about the ability of foreign policy officials to circumvent policy and the effectiveness of congressional oversight of foreign affairs. The Iran-Contra affair revisits the ancient question from Roman poet Juvenal of "Who will watch the watchmen?" (Mathews 2017). This question still resonates today.

Open or covert defiance of legal directives has consequences. They undermine the legitimacy of political leader and violate principles of democratic rule. Bureaucratic actions can shift the locus of power from elected officials to more opaque, less transparent actors. In the extreme, these actors and their organizations can establish and implement policy that is in accord with their personal or ideological interests, rather than the interests of the majority.

6 Plan of the Book

The intent of the book is to illuminate the tensions between the principles of democracy and bureaucracy. Bureaucratic discretion remains a double-edged sword. Those who benefit from discretion praise the "flexibility" of officials. Those harmed by discretion are not favorably disposed. Discretion has acute implications for democracy. The implications of discretion on democracy are the focus of this book.

This chapter outlined the theoretical underpinnings of bureaucracies and potential danger of discretion. Chapter 2 describes the general ethos of democracy, democratic theorists, and alternative perspectives of democracy. This discussion provides perspective for the later conversation of the need to provide controls on bureaucratic actors. The chapter posits that citizen input, voting, and oversight from other branches of government can guard against bureaucratic abuse. Chapter 3 describes possible checks on the bureaucracy. In addition, the chapter explores the varieties of organizational cultures that influence conduct.

Chapters 4, 5, and 6 apply the concept of discretion to local law enforcement, national law enforcement, foreign policy, and veterans' affairs. Chapter 4 describes controversies surrounding local police action. Chapter 5 discusses the history of discretion in the FBI including actions of former FBI officials J. Edgar Hoover, Mark Felt, and James Comey. Whistleblowing at the Phoenix Veterans Administration hospital highlights the potential for internal control within bureaucracies. Chapter 6 reviews the history of discretion in the foreign policy bureaucracies such as the CIA and National Security Agency. Finally, the concluding chapter summarizes the basic argument of the book that if unchecked bureaucracies pose a threat. The chapter offers recommendations to increase oversight and democratic accountability.

References

Appleby, P. (1949). *Policy and administration.* Tuscaloosa: University of Alabama Press.

Bardach, E. (1977). *The implementation game: What happens after a bill becomes a law.* Cambridge, MA: MIT Press.

Beetham, D. (1996). *Bureaucracy* (2nd ed.). Minneapolis: University of Minnesota Press.

Brennan, G., & Buchanan, J. (1980). *The power to tax: Analytical foundations of a fiscal constitution.* Cambridge: Cambridge University Press.

Burke, J. (1986). *Bureaucratic responsibility.* Baltimore: Johns Hopkins University Press.

Cohen, J. (2000). *Politics and economic policy in the United States* (2nd ed.). Boston: Houghton-Mifflin Company.

Cooper, T. L. (1990). *The responsible administrator* (3rd ed.). San Francisco: Jossey-Bass.

Davis, K. C. (1969). *Discretionary justice: A preliminary inquiry.* Baton Rouge: LSU Press.

Denhardt, K. G. (1988). *The ethics of public service: Resolving moral dilemmas in public organizations.* Westport: Greenwood Press.

Dilulio, J. (2014). *Bring back the bureaucrats. West.* Conshohocken: Templeton Press.

Dobel, J. P. (1999). *Public integrity.* Baltimore: Johns Hopkins University Press.

Etzioni-Halevy, E. (1983). *Bureaucracy and democracy: A political dilemma.* London: Routledge & Kegan Paul.

Fayol, H. (1916 [1987]). General principles of management. In J. M. Shafritz & J. S. Ott (Eds.), *Classics of organization theory* (2nd ed., pp. 51–66). Chicago: The Dorsey Press.

Frug, G. E. (1984). The ideology of bureaucracy in American law. *Harvard Law Review, 97*(6), 1276–1388.

Fry, B., & Raadschelders, J. (2008). *Mastering public administration: From Max Weber to Dwight Waldo* (2nd ed.). Washington, DC: CQ Press.

Garrett, T. A., & Rhine, R. M. (2006, January/February). On the size and growth of government. *Federal Reserve Bank of St. Louis Review, 88*(1), 13–30. Retrieved January 31, 2017, from https://files.stlouisfed.org/files/htdocs/publications/review/06/01/GarrettRhine.pdf

Gerth, H. H., & Mills, C. W. (1958). *From Max Weber: Essays in sociology*. New York: Oxford University Press.

Gulick, L. (1925). Principles of administration. *National Municipal Review, 14*(7), 400–403.

Gulick, L. (1937 [1969]). Notes on the theory of organization. In L. Gulick & L. Urwick (Eds.), *Papers on the science of administration* (pp. 3–45). New York: Augustus M. Kelly Publishers.

Kristov, L., Lindert, P., & McClelland, R. (1992). Pressure groups and redistribution. *Journal of Public Economics, 48*(2), 135–163.

Lipsky, M. (2010). *Street-level bureaucracy: Dilemmas of the individual in public services*. New York: Russell Sage Foundation.

Long, N. (1949). Power and administration. *Public Administration Review, 9*(3), 257–264.

Lutrin, C., & Settle, A. (1985). *American public administration: Concepts and cases* (3rd ed.). Englewood Cliffs: Prentice-Hall Inc.

Maggetti, M. (2010). *Legitimacy and accountability of independent regulatory agencies: A critical review*. Center for Comparative and International Studies, ETH Zurich and University of Zurich. Retrieved February 27, 2018, from https://www.ethz.ch/content/dam/ethz/special-interest/gess/cis/cis-dam/

Mathews, R. (2017). Iran-Contra affair. *Encyclopedia Britannica*. Retrieved January 11, 2017, from https://www.britannica.com/event/Iran-Contra-Affair

Meier, K. (2010). Governance, structure, and democracy: Luther Gulick and the future of public administration. *Public Administration Review, 70*, S284–S291.

Nice, C., & Fisher, P. (2016). *Public budgeting* (2nd ed.). San Diego: Birkdale Publishers.

Niskanen, W. (1971 [1994]). *Bureaucracy and public economics*. Cheltenham: Edward Elgar.

O'Leary, R. (2006). *The ethics of dissent: Managing guerrilla government*. Washington, DC: CQ Press.

Ostrom, V. (1973). *The intellectual crisis in American public administration*. Tuscaloosa: University of Alabama Press.

Pennock, J. R. (1960). The problems of responsibility. In C. J. Friedrich (Ed.), *Responsibility* (pp. 3–27). New York: Liberal Arts Press.

Perrow, C. (1979). *Complex organizations: A critical essay* (2nd ed.). Glenview: Scott Foresman.

Plant, J. F. (2018). Responsibility in public administration ethics. *The Public Interest, 20*(Supplement 1), S33–S45.

Postell, J. (2017). *Bureaucracy in America: The administrative state's challenge to constitutional government*. Columbia: University of Missouri Press.

Rainey, H. (2003). *Understanding and managing public organizations* (3rd ed.). San Francisco: Wiley.

Rohr, J. (1989). *Ethics for bureaucrats: An essay on law and values* (2nd ed.). New York: Marcel Dekker.

Rourke, F. E. (1984). *Bureaucracy, politics, and public policy* (3rd ed.). Boston: Little Brown & Company.

Shafritz, J., & Ott, S. (1987). *Classics of organization theory* (2nd ed.). Chicago: Dorsey Press.

Spicer, M. (1998). The science of administration, the founders, and theories of political association. *International Journal of Public Administration, 21*(2), 299–321.

Stillman, R. (1987). *The American bureaucracy*. Chicago: Nelson-Hall.

Tassava, C. (2008, February 10). The American economy during World War II. *EH.Net Encyclopedia*. Retrieved February 27, 2018, from http://eh.net/encyclopedia/the-american-economy-during-world-war-ii/

Turner, H. A. (1956). Woodrow Wilson as administrator. *Public Administration Review, 16*(4), 249–257.

United States Department of Homeland Security. (2017). Retrieved January 11, 2017, from https://en.wikipedia.org/wiki/United_States_Department_of_Homeland_Security

Waldo, D. (1948). *The administrative state: A study of the political theory of American public administration*. New York: Ronald Press.

Will, G. (2017, February 25). 'Big government' is ever growing, on the sly. *National Review*. Retrieved January 9, 2017, from http://www.nationalreview.com/article/445230/

Wilson, W. (1887). The study of administration. *Political Science Quarterly, 2*(2), 197–222.

Wilson, J. Q. (1975). The rise of the bureaucratic state. *The Public Interest, 41*, 77–103.

Woll, P. (1963). *American bureaucracy*. New York: W.W. Norton & Company.

CHAPTER 2

Theoretical Grounding of Democratic Accountability

1 Introduction

Many view the ethos of bureaucracy as antithetical to democracy since bureaucracies tend to produce closed systems that are not accountable to the people. The secrecy, obfuscation, opaqueness, control of information, and aura of acquired wisdom protect bureaucracies from popular scrutiny. This secrecy can endanger polities and diminish regime legitimacy. A complete exposition of democratic theory is beyond the scope of this book; however, an overview of major democratic and elite theorists provides perspective about the danger of bureaucracy.

The democratic method has numerous advantages. First democracies force decision makers to take into account the interests, rights, and opinions of people in society. Policymakers must at least consider the views of the populous. Second, democracy can help decision makers formulate policy. Since democracy brings many people into the process of decision making, it takes advantage of many sources of information and assessments. Democratic decision making tends to be aware of the means necessary to advance the interests of the people. Third, many assert that democracy has beneficial effects on the individual moral and deliberative qualities of citizens. When citizens participate in making decisions, they have to listen to others, they are called upon to justify themselves to others, and they are forced to think in terms of the common good and justice (Mill [1861] 1991, Chapter 3). This chapter posits that an understanding

S. G. Koven, *The Case Against Bureaucratic Discretion*,
https://doi.org/10.1007/978-3-030-05779-4_2

of the virtues of democracy is necessary to begin to assess bureaucracies. The chapter introduces a fuller debate over how to check the power of bureaucracies.

2 General Ethos of Democracy

2.1 Classical Greek Perspectives

2.1.1 Plato

Scholars view Plato as perhaps the best known, most widely studied, and most influential philosopher of all time. Plato is the founder of the Academy in Athens, the first institution of higher learning in the Western world. In his treatise *Republic*, Book VI, Plato argues that some people are more intelligent and more moral than others and by nature of those characteristic should rule. Plato contends that democracy is inferior to other forms of government because democracies pay inadequate attention to the expertise that polities need to govern properly. According to Plato, those who are expert at winning elections will eventually dominate democratic politics. These individuals may be less skilled at governing and may not possess the wisdom of other citizens. Governance therefore suffers. Plato believed that most people do not possess the kinds of talents that enable them to consider carefully the difficult issues of politics. Successful politicians rely upon manipulation and mass appeal to achieve office. They are skilled at arousing popular sentiment, yet may not necessarily be the ablest rulers.

In the treatise *Republic*, Plato criticizes direct and unchecked democracy because he fears excessive freedom can lead to anarchy. Plato contends equality or the belief that everyone has an equal capacity to rule brings to politics all kinds of power-seeking individuals, motivated by personal gain rather than public good. Democracy therefore opens itself to demagogues, potential dictators, and tyranny. Plato asserts that democracy is unstable; it lacks leaders with proper skill and morals. For Plato, democracy depends on competent leadership. Without able and virtuous leaders (who come and go by chance), democracy is inferior to other forms of government.

Plato is also pessimistic about human nature. He believes most people are fundamentally irrational, driven by their appetites and egoistic passions, and informed by false beliefs. If people choose to be just and law-abiding, it is only because they lack the power to act criminally and are afraid of punishment. According to Plato, democracy is inferior to aristocracy (rule of a philosopher king), "timocracy" (rule by those who value power attained by means of military conquest and the acquisition of honors, rather than intellectual means), and oligarchy (rule by the wealthy). Oligarchy degenerates into democracy when the lower class expands. Democracy degenerates into tyranny when a champion emerges to reestablish order in the midst of chaos. The tyrant is the worst form of leader and the most unjust. Tyranny comes closest to complete lawlessness as tyrants seek the basest pleasures in life.

Plato exalts rule by the philosopher king since he believes philosopher kings can distinguish between true and false beliefs. These rulers love knowledge and pursue the common good; only the philosopher king can heal the ills of society. Plato contends the philosopher kings are necessary to counteract the destabilizing effects of false beliefs. For Plato, philosopher kings do not primarily seek wealth or honor. The goal of the philosopher king is to spread happiness by bringing citizens into harmony with each other. Philosophers rule not only because they are best prepared, but also because if they do not rule, the polity may fall prey to economic decline, factionalism, or civil war. Philosopher kings approach ruling as a duty (Korab-Karpowicz n.d.).

In Book V of the *Republic*, Plato presents his conception of the "just city." Such a polity cannot come into being until philosophers rule as kings or kings become philosophers. Plato views this as the only possible route to reach complete happiness in both public and private life. Philosophers love truth. Necessary characteristics for rule include hatred of falsehood, moderation, courage, quick learning, good memory, and a pleasant nature. In contrast to this happy state of affairs under the philosopher king, Plato presents democracy as a form of government that arises when wealth disparities grow. Too much luxury makes the oligarchs soft and the poor revolt against them. This leads to people holding office without having the necessary knowledge. For Plato, only an aristocracy led by the wisest men (unwilling philosopher kings) is a just form of government.

2.1.2 Aristotle

In addition to Plato, scholars also consider Aristotle a founder of Western philosophy. Aristotle continues to influence thinkers throughout the political spectrum. His writings led to divergent interpretations because he is inclined to consider opposing arguments in a careful and nuanced manner. Though he is generally critical of democracy, Aristotle admits that the case for rule by the many has some merit (Miller 2017).

In the tract *Politics*, (Books IV–VI) Aristotle addresses the contentious question of how to organize regimes. This involves the eternal question of who should rule. By closely examining regimes that actually existed in ancient Greece, Aristotle draws conclusions about the merits and drawbacks of various forms of rule. In order to answer the question of who should rule, Aristotle collects empirical evidence. He sent his students throughout Greece to collect information and histories of the Greek city-state and used the information to reach conclusions.

Aristotle posits that human beings are by nature political animals, who naturally want to live together. He uses two criteria to place regimes into categories. The first criterion to distinguish among different kinds of regimes is the number of those ruling: (1) one person, (2) a few, or (3) the many. The second criterion questions whether those in power, however many they are, rule only in their own interest or in the interest of all citizens. Aristotle labels regimes that defend common interests "correct regimes" and those that only endeavor to benefit the rulers he calls "errant" regimes. In errant regimes, the city is not a partnership of free persons. It is deviant. Correct regimes are what Aristotle terms monarchy (rule by one man for the common good), aristocracy (rule by a few for the common good), and polity (rule by the many for the common good). Correct behavior therefore is synonymous with working for the common good. Aristotle labels flawed or deviant regimes as tyrannies (rule by one man in his own interest), oligarchy (rule by the few in their own interest), and democracy (rule by the many in their own interest). An ordered ranking of regimes puts monarchy on top, aristocracy the next best, followed by polity, democracy, oligarchy, and tyranny. The distinction between oligarchy and democracy relates to whether the wealthy or the poor rule. All cities have these two groups: the many poor and the few wealthy. Conflict between these two groups produces political instability and may even lead to civil wars.

Aristotle contends that the monarch or one who rules because of superiority in virtue exemplifies an exceptional regime. The monarchy (rule of the best) is the absolute preeminent form of government; the monarch is uniquely qualified. Tyranny is a perversion of monarchy where the tyrant rules solely for personal benefit and pleasure. Tyranny represents the worst kind of regime, according to Aristotle. In contrast, Aristotle believes the polity (many rule in the interest of the political community as a whole) is the best "practical" regime. According to Aristotle, the problem with perverted democracy is that in such a regime the many rule in their own interest, exploit the wealthy, and deny them political power. In a more enlightened form of rule, the government protects the interests of the wealthy as well as the interests of the masses. Such a regime considers the common good. This type of regime combines aspects of democracy with those of an oligarchy.

Aristotle calls attention to the economic classes of city-states. A large middle class presents the most stable condition. Aristotle states that a political community that has extremes of wealth and poverty is a city of slaves and masters. Envy consumes the slaves; contempt characterizes the masters. People in the middle class are relatively free from the insidious nature of envy. Members of this class are likely to regard one another as similar, and are willing to rule and be ruled. This is a great fortune for both governing and the governed. Tyranny arises from headstrong democracy and from oligarchy, but it is much less likely to form when there is a large middle class.

Aristotle contends that in extreme democracy people are deluded into thinking that everyone is equal. The masses then follow the lead of corrupt and selfish demagogues and plunder the property of the hardworking and the capable. In contrast, the "true" forms of government are those in which the one, or the few, or the many, govern with a view to the common interest. Governments that rule with a view to the private interest are perversions. Tyranny is a kind of monarchy that supports only the interest of the monarch. Oligarchy supports the interest of the wealthy, democracy, of the needy. None of these forms of government seeks the common good. Aristotle characterizes the polity as a kind of "mixed" constitution typified by rule of the "middle" group of citizens. This middle group represents a moderately wealthy class between the rich and poor. For Aristotle, democracies can be polarizing. In extreme democracies, the multitude disregards the law in their exercise of power. The masses supersede the law by decrees; demagogues rule by decree. In contrast to extreme democracy, the right kind of democracy is a polity where leaders promote the interests of the entire community. Success depends on good leadership.

Aristotle claims people of moderate wealth are readiest to obey reason. The wealthy tend to become arrogant on a grand scale, the poor malicious in petty ways. Acts of injustice by the wealthy are committed either through arrogance or through malice. Aristotle cautions there can be an enduring polity only when the middle class is able to rule either on its own or in conjunction with the rich and poor. The rich and poor compete for power. Each group tries to dominate. Such competition is a recipe for instability and conflict rather than endurance (Clayton n.d.).

Aristotle offers practical political advice regarding how regimes may be preserved. He contends democracies undergo revolution because of wanton behavior of popular leaders. Such leaders harass the property owners, causing them to unify against the masses. These leaders also stir up the poor against the rich, which in turn allows demagogues to maintain power. Oligarchies undergo revolution when they treat the multitude unjustly. Revolution in oligarchical regimes can also come about from competition within the oligarchy. To preserve regimes one should ensure fair application of the laws. For continuing legitimacy, education in the principles of moderate democracy and moderate oligarchy is necessary (Clayton n.d.).

For Aristotle the best kind of democracy consists of large numbers of people that are lacking in leisure, and are unable to hold frequent assemblies. Because the people lack the necessities, they must spend their time working. For Aristotle, this is more pleasant to them than engaging in politics since in the best kind of democracy political office does not provide personal gain. Authoritative offices flow to the wealthy, yet the people can retain control of auditing and adjudication. Authoritative positions should fall into the hands of the best persons. Others will monitor their activities. By adjudication, Aristotle explains that the rich will not be able to use their wealth to put themselves above the law.

With regard to those (such as bureaucrats) that have influence on governing, Aristotle advocates putting individuals in power who are most virtuous. The purpose of the city is to develop virtue in citizens. Those who have the most virtue are the most fit to rule; they will rule best, rule on behalf of all the citizens, and establish laws that lead others to virtue. Aristotle emphasizes the importance of developing excellence of character as the way to achieve what is finally most important, excellent conduct. People who possess character excellence do the right thing, at the right time, and in the right way. Those who are going to rule ought to have three things: (1) affection for the established regime, (2) a great capacity for the work involved in rule and (3) virtue as well as justice. Institutions and laws are important, but equally important is the moral character of citizens (Clayton n.d.).

2.2 *Early European Perspectives*

2.2.1 Thomas Hobbes

Hobbes' 1651 tome *Leviathan* established the social contract theory that served as a foundation for later political thinkers. Hobbes championed the absolute rule of monarchs; however, he also developed fundamentals of liberal thought. Liberal ideas include individual rights, individual freedom, the natural equality of people, and legitimacy residing in the consent of the people. Social contract theory entails an agreement that rational, free, and equal persons enter into. Hobbes uses the idea of a social contract to argue that people should submit to the authority of an absolute sovereign. Hobbes fundamentally rejects Aristotle's view that people are naturally suited to life in a community and do not fully realize their natures until they exercise the role of citizen. For Hobbes, human beings are by nature unsuited to political life; there is no self-restraint in competition. A ruthless and bloodthirsty few make the moderate feel forced to take violent preemptive action in order to avoid losing everything. Aggression and anarchy ensue.

Hobbes contends that democracy is inferior to a monarchy because democracy fosters destabilizing dissension among subjects. In democracies, Hobbes believes politicians succeed only by making loud and manipulative appeals to citizens. Furthermore, politicians do not have an incentive to consider the common good. For Hobbes, democracy has deleterious effects on subjects, on politicians, and on the quality of the outcomes (Christiano 2015).

The idea of the social contract is essential to understanding Hobbes' view of governing. Hobbes proposes in his most famous statement that in a state of nature human life is solitary, poor, nasty, brutish, and short. In the absence of political order and law, everyone has unlimited natural freedoms, including the freedom to plunder, rape, and murder. In such a state, there is an endless war of all against all. To avoid this outcome, free men contract with each other to establish a political community or civil society. In this social contract, people gain security in return for subjecting themselves to an absolute sovereign. The absolute sovereign can be a single person, a group of people, or an assembly of individuals. The sovereign's edicts may be arbitrary and tyrannical, yet Hobbes views absolute government as the only alternative to the anarchy of the state of nature. Humans consent to abdicate their rights in favor of the absolute authority.

Some scholars treat Hobbes as a precursor of modern liberalism even though he embraces absolute rule. His conduciveness to modern liberalism appears in his endorsement of the idea of autonomy. Hobbes supports two kinds of autonomy: intellectual autonomy and moral autonomy. Intellectual autonomy refers to knowledge, moral autonomy to reason. Hobbes is mainly concerned with the problem of how people willingly disengage from a state of nature (where there is a war of all against all) and move into civil society. He ultimately views democracy as unstable since desires of individuals differ (Apperley 1999, p. 167).

For Hobbes three kinds of government exist: government by the one (monarchy), by the few (aristocracy), and by the many (democracy). He views democracy the least stable form and likely to digress either into the anarchic state of nature or become a de facto aristocracy of orators, interrupted sometimes with the temporary monarchy of one orator. Hobbes highlights three concerns about democracy under the categories of competition, diffidence, and glory. He maintains that people compete for the chance to speak but not all have the opportunity to promote their own interest. Second, democracy contributes to the war of all against all, because the desire to receive praise appeals to individual vanity. Vanity along with competition is a principal cause of insecurity. Finally, in democracies, there is mistrust and belief that people will pursue private interests at the expense of the public interest (p. 169). Hobbes concludes that in a democracy the unworthy are promoted to the detriment of the state.

2.2.2 John Locke

Along with Thomas Hobbes and Jean-Jacques Rousseau, Locke establishes the standard view of social contract theory. Locke is often termed the father of modern democracy for theories that he developed in *Two Treatises of Civil Government* (1680–1690). His influence on English politics and the American constitution is significant. Concepts advanced by Locke include the equality of people, the consent of the majority, the division of power, and the right to rebellion. In contrast to Hobbes, Locke sees the state of nature not as a war of all against all but as a society of people living together according to their reason. Locke emphasizes equality of people as creatures of God. His writings greatly influenced Thomas Jefferson as he wrote the US Declaration of Independence in 1776.

Locke contends that people have basic rights including the right to property, which he defines as a person's life, liberty, and estate. The right to property is justified by ownership of the fruits of one's labor. Locke contends that political society comes into being when individuals come together and agree to give up their individual power to punish those who transgress the law of nature. People hand over the power to punish to a government. The people then become subject to the will of the majority. By agreeing to such a compact individuals submit themselves to the will of the majority. In return, individuals receive laws, judges to adjudicate laws, and an executive body to enforce laws. In the compact, each person gives over to a government the power for self-protection.

Locke's most significant contribution to democratic theory deals with his interpretation of sovereign power. Locke divides the sovereign power into two parts: legislative and executive. He assigns to the legislature responsibility for making laws. Since the public selects the legislative body, the legislature holds power as a trust or fiduciary responsibility. The power to remove or alter the legislature remains in the hands of the people. According to Locke, the transfer of the right to rule from the people to the sovereign is revocable. If the legislative or the executive body engages in nefarious acts, the people may decide to rebel and punish the wrongdoers.

Basic elements of Locke's theory of legitimate relate to the common good, the consent of the governed, and the rule of law (Marini 1969, p. 9). Locke maintains that pursuit of the "common good" distinguishes legitimate from tyrannical government. Legitimate government serves the common interest rather than the special interest of the governors; those who govern in their own interest are tyrants. Locke urges pursuit of the common good as the only acceptable motive of rulers. Locke is aware that those who rule will slip sometimes into aggrandizing themselves and does not claim that the people will always be able to tell whether a given political act is in the public interest. He only asserts that ultimately the majority of citizens will know whether their welfare has been regularly disregarded (p. 10).

Locke is aware of divergent interests in society, yet believes the political society should be concerned with the welfare of citizens as a whole rather than the welfare of individual citizens. Locke's purpose is not to maximize participation in government decision making but to address the problem of arbitrary government. He states that it is only when leaders prefer their own personal interests to the community good (in violation of the trust the community places in them) that society should be concerned with limiting the power of leaders. His basic argument is for the rule of law by a government resting ultimately upon the consent of the governed and governing in the interest of the society.

The idea of government of laws and not of men is a recurrent theme. This is a foundation of what we have come to call limited government, and according to Locke, it implies several characteristics. First, government of laws implies continuing acquiescence of the governed. The laws acquire legitimacy from consent rather than from some personal authority of the rule-maker. Second, governance ought to proceed by standing rules or declared laws rather than arbitrary dictates. Third, leaders should design laws for the good of the society and not for the private separate advantage of the rule-maker. A basic principle of Locke's theory is the consent of the governed that places the legitimacy of government upon the original sovereignty and continual consent of citizens. For Locke, people do not govern themselves but those who represent the community govern. The community has the power to remove leaders. In the elected form of government, removal can occur through voting. In any form of government, revolution can occur if consent is lacking and rule is abusive.

According to Marini (1969, p. 17) Locke's theory of democracy differs from classical democratic theory in that he does not assert that the "majority is right or that each citizen must consent in person or by mandated deputy to a governmental act before it is legitimate." In contrast, Locke argues that political legitimacy simply rests upon consent. His theory is much less a theory of self-rule than a theory of responsible elected rule. Locke describes freedom as the rule of law; he talks of responsible government and of government under law, but not government by the people. He sees responsible government as government for the good of the society, which rests upon the consent of the governed. For Locke, a person or a plural body rules, people do not rule themselves.

2.2.3 *Jean-Jacques Rousseau*

Jean-Jacques Rousseau is one of the most important theorists of democracy. He believes all political power must reside with the people; government officials receive their orders from the people and follow a "general will." In his most important work *The Social Contract* (published in 1762), Rousseau outlines the basis for a legitimate political order. Rousseau claims in order to prevent a brutish condition without law people must come together through a social contract to both preserve themselves and remain free. He believes this is possible because submission to the authority of the general will of the people protects individuals against subordination to the wills of others. Submission also ensures that people obey themselves because they are, collectively, the authors of the law. The government is responsible for implementing and enforcing the general will. It is composed of a smaller group of citizens. Rousseau believes in direct, rather than representative, democracy.

Key to understanding Rousseau's views of democracy are concepts such as the social contract, the general will, virtue, and the legislator (Bertram 2017). Rousseau's central doctrine in politics is that a state can be legitimate only if the general will guides its members. In *The Social Contract*, Rousseau addresses the question of how to reconcile the freedom of the individual with the authority of the state. Rousseau establishes an alternative to the Hobbesian perspective of a war of all against all. The Hobbesian perspective, according to Rousseau, leads to the establishment of state authority and law that reinforces inequality as well as exploitative social relations. In this situation, the interest of the rich subordinates the interests of the poor and weak.

In Rousseau's alternative, each person enjoys protection while remaining free. Rousseau argues that the general will is the source of law and applies to each citizen. Freedom and authority are not contradictory, since legitimate laws derive from the general will of all citizens. In obeying the law, the individual citizen is only obeying himself or herself as a member of the political community. Citizens favor laws that secure the common interest impartially and are not burdensome. For the impact of the laws to be the same for everyone, the situation of citizens should be substantially similar. In a state where citizens enjoy a wide diversity of lifestyles and occupations, or where there is a great deal of cultural diversity, or where there is a high degree of economic inequality, the impact of the general laws is unlikely to be the same for everyone.

Rousseau notes that in a well-ordered society, individuals submit to a law that safeguards their freedom by protecting them from violence. Many societies, however, fail to have this well-ordered character because private individuals are insufficiently enlightened or insufficiently virtuous. They therefore refuse to accept the restrictions on their own conduct that the collective interest requires. For Rousseau, the lawgiver has the responsibility of inspiring a sense of collective identity in citizens. Rousseau makes a key distinction between sovereign and government. The sovereign, composed of the people as a whole, promulgates laws as an expression of its general will. The government administers the state within the bounds set by the laws and issues decrees that apply the laws to particular cases. Rousseau's conception of democracy rejects the view that the people should exercise sovereignty via a representative assembly. He holds that they should make the laws directly, which would effectively prevent the ideal state from becoming too large.

2.2.4 Charles Montesquieu

The aristocrat Charles-Louis de Secondat, Baron de La Brède et de Montesquieu, is an eighteenth-century political philosopher who had profound influence on America's Founding Fathers. James Madison drew upon Montesquieu's theory of the separation of powers when drafting the US Constitution (Bok 2014). In his treatise *The Spirit of the Laws* (1748),

Montesquieu proposes three types of governments: republican governments, monarchies, and despotisms. He promotes the view that in a democracy, the people are sovereign and govern through ministers. Consistent with empowering the people in democracies, voters must have the power of choosing their ministers and senators for themselves.

For Montesquieu, protecting democracy requires a constant preference for choosing the public interest over the private interest. He further developed the intellectual underpinning for a constitutional system of government with separation of powers and protection of civil liberties. In addition to separation of powers, major concepts outlined by Montesquieu include due process, the right to a fair trial, presumption of innocence, proportionality in the severity of punishment, freedom of speech, and freedom of assembly. Much of what we recognize as America's system of governing appears in the writings of Montesquieu. For example, he postulates that only the legislative branch should have the power to tax while the executive branch should be able to veto acts of the legislature. He advocates a legislature comprised of two houses, each able to prevent the acts of the other from becoming law. According to Montesquieu, the judiciary should be independent from the other branches and should apply their rulings in a fixed and constant manner (Bok 2014).

The baron Montesquieu defines democracy as a state where the body of people possesses the supreme power. Suffrage or the laws that establish the right to vote are fundamental to democracy. It is therefore essential to regulate in what manner, by whom, to whom, and concerning what government assigns the right to vote. Montesquieu argues that the people are qualified to determine some aspects of governing but not all. Ministers or magistrates must conduct the aspects of governing that exceed the abilities of the people; the people nominate and choose their ministers or magistrates. Montesquieu contends that the people are qualified to determine who might be a capable military general based on battlefield prowess or the people may determine who could be a good judge based on general satisfaction with decisions. The people, however, are less capable of assessing intricate affairs and seizing opportunity at critical junctures. Montesquieu therefore maintains that the people are capable of selecting others for administration, however, are incapable of conducting the administration themselves (Montesquieu 1748, Book II, Ch. II).

Montesquieu distinguishes between the nature and principle of government. Nature of government refers to justification for each form of government. Republican governments rely on the people; monarchical by a single person acting under fixed law, despotic by a single person directing everything by caprice. For a democratic state to function effectively what Montesquieu defines as "virtue" (love of the laws and country) is necessary. Love requires a constant preference of public interest to private interest. It also requires education and example. He states, "Government is like everything else: to preserve it, we must love it.... Everything, therefore, depends on establishing this love in a republic; and to inspire it ought to be the principal business of education: but the surest way of instilling it into children is for parents to set them an example.... It is not the young people that degenerate: they are not spoilt till those of maturer age are already sunk into corruption" (Montesquieu 1748, Book IV, Ch. V).

Scholars view Montesquieu as among the greatest philosophers of liberalism. Liberty, according to Montesquieu, involves living under laws that protect people from harm while leaving them free to accomplish as much as possible. Liberty enables people to feel confident that if they obey the laws, the state will not oppress them. Furthermore, government should construct laws to make it as easy as possible for citizens to protect themselves from punishment by not committing crimes (Bok 2014).

3 Modern Democratic Theorists

3.1 A. D. Lindsay

The Scottish political philosopher A. D. Lindsay was a strong defender of the view that citizens are the best judges of their own interests. In his most significant work, *The Modern Democratic State*, Lindsay argues that leaders should treat the opinions of ordinary citizens with the utmost respect. He asserts that claims to share in governance are justified because the average citizen knows "where the shoe pinches." Lindsay reasons that the common people know their own best interest better than others do. The free expression of people who know their own interests therefore is a check on leaders whose policies are antagonist to the interests of the populace (Koven 2008, p. 19; Lindsay 1947, p. 269).

According to Lindsay, democracy is a revolutionary form of government because its aim is to find a place for continual change. Its laws exist to foster freedom; its power exists to protect the law. There is a prima facie case against interference with free association. Preserving spheres of influence that government does not control relies on belief in the value of experimentation and initiative. Equality and liberty are the marks of the democratic community. It is therefore the task of government to be aware of threats against liberty and equality. Lindsay supports the following minimal conditions for democracies, minimal legal rights, and a minimum standard of economic security.

Lindsay's discussion of the value of "common sense" of ordinary men and women makes a major contribution to democratic theory. He admits that the modern state can do its job only with a lot of expert help, expert legislators, and expert administrators. Lindsay notes that there are two sides to the argument that ordinary men and women are better judges on broad issues than are experts. On the one hand, if the goal of democratic government is to minister to the common life of society and remove disharmony then an understanding of that common life is essential to legislators. He states that the common life is the life lived by most members of the society. Those who do not live it cannot know or appreciate that life. They cannot feel the problems of the common person. Their (average person) shoes pinch and they alone can tell where they pinch (Lindsay 1947, p. 269). Lindsay reasons that without that knowledge the wisest legislators cannot make good laws. Lindsay concludes that the argument about shoes pinching is an argument that justifies expanding suffrage. The key to this contention is that all classes in society must be able to express their grievances.

Limitations of the "shoe pinching" argument are that unless there is power behind the expression of average grievances, leaders can ignore those grievances. Furthermore, Lindsay claims that voting does not imply that the electorate is particularly intelligent or that their judgment is sound. It simply implies that since the aim of government is to promote the free life of all citizens, all citizens "must have their say as to how that free life is actually being hindered and how far the work of government is actually removing those hindrances" (p. 272). Lindsay notes that people who have control over executive and administrative power easily forget that they are only servants of the people. The purpose of popular input is to see that the skills of administrators are used to the right ends.

Lindsay exalts the value of "practical wisdom" in democracies. He claims practical wisdom appears in the most unexpected places. People recognize the democratic leader because he or she shares the life and experience of ordinary men and women. The democratic leader knows, almost unconsciously, "where the shoe pinches" and "what people are prepared to do." Knowledge of the common life and its possibilities is the wisdom most wanted for politics. The state is wisely directed if the final control is in the hands of ordinary men not specialized in a vocation or training. The ordinary people have common sense and "sound judgement" (p. 279).

In a series of lectures delivered in 1929 at Swarthmore College, Pennsylvania, Lindsay asserts that discussion is fundamental to democracy and that the purpose of democracy is to represent differences. According to Lindsay, democracy requires an official opposition, tolerance of others, and strong nonpolitical associations. The purported purpose of democracies is to safeguard and harmonize a common life inspired by voluntary nonpolitical activities. He contrasts the aim of democracy (the discovery by discussion of a common plan that gives scope to differences) to the totalitarian state that uses mass persuasion to make people as alike as possible. Lindsay concludes that the totalitarian state sees toleration as a "mischievous absurdity," independent organizations a "dangerous nuisance," and religious minorities as "a crime" against the state. In totalitarian regimes, the state will use their powers of mass propaganda to back forces that already make people more alike. In totalitarian states, planning attempts to impose an "all comprehensive system" to which there is no rival. Democracies also can engage in planning but they allow for differences (Lindsay 1980, p. 5).

3.2 Dennis Thompson

As a professor of political science, Thompson's scholarship contributed greatly to the literature in the fields of both political ethics and democratic theory. His first book on democratic theory relates contemporary social science to theories of democracy (Thompson 1970). In this treatise, Thompson synthesizes a very large body of theoretical and empirical literature. He discusses citizenship in terms of the capacity of citizen to influence politics. Thompson focuses on what he terms democratic citizenship. According to Thompson, citizenship accepts two basic presuppositions: autonomy and improvability. Autonomy treats each citizen as the best judge of his or her own interests. Improvability holds that citizens are capable of showing better political and social judgment over time. Thompson contributes to our understanding of democratic theory by contrasting citizenship theories that accept the presuppositions of autonomy and improvability with elitist democratic theories. He develops standards by which to judge outcomes and is supportive of citizenship theories. He uses evidence from social science to develop his theories and concludes that social science is relevant in three general ways. It is useful to evaluate the present state of citizenship, it helps to point out possibilities for positive change, and it can be used to suggest what advantages could accrue to citizens if changes take place (Thompson 1970, pp. 181–182).

A later coauthored book has been influential in promoting the idea of deliberative democracy that calls for more reasoned discourse in public life (Gutmann and Thompson 1998). The book received extensive attention from scholars and many general readers. In 1999, Oxford University Press published an edited volume (*Deliberative Politics*), which is devoted entirely to discussion of the earlier book. The debate among scholars of deliberative democracy is continuous. In *Democracy and Disagreement* (1996) and *Why Deliberative Democracy?* (2004), Gutmann and Thompson assert that it is not enough that citizens exercise their power through interest group bargaining, or by voting in elections. They believe government should not decide serious matters by logrolling or referendum. Expressions of will should be justified by reason. Gutmann and Thompson argue that deliberative democracy binds citizens to principles that promote public debate about the merits of positions.

Objectives of deliberative democracy are the achievement of moral agreement and mutual respect. Regulations governing public debate in deliberative democracy seek to find common ground. All arguments about public policy should satisfy six principles. Reciprocity requires that all stated reasons for the policy be mutually acceptable to citizens. Publicity requires that reasons be publicly justified. According to the principle of accountability, respect for the claims of citizens significantly affected by the policy is necessary. Basic liberty requires government to respect individual sovereignty over body and mind. Basic opportunity requires government to help secure the necessities for a decent life. Finally, fair opportunity requires government to guarantee fair access to advanced education and skilled employment.

Gutmann and Thompson (2004, p. 7) define deliberative democracy as a form of government in which free and equal citizens, as well as their representatives, justify decisions in a process in which they give one another reasons that are mutually acceptable and generally accessible. The aim of deliberative democracy is reaching conclusions that are binding in the present but open to challenge in the future. Critics of Gutmann and Thompson assert that they unsuccessfully attempt to bridge the gap between high political theory and messy public policy. Critics claim these political theorists abstract away disagreements (Rosen 1996).

3.3 Robert Dahl

Scholars consider Robert Dahl one of the most influential political social scientists of the twentieth century. Among the many contributions to democratic theory are his elucidation of concepts such as pluralism and polyarchy. A prolific writer, some of his major works include *A Preface to Democratic Theory* (1956), *Who Governs?* (1961), *Pluralist Democracy in the United States* (1967), *Dilemmas of Pluralist Democracy* (1982), and *How Democratic Is the American Constitution?* (2001). A comprehensive discussion of Dahl's contributions is beyond the scope of this review; therefore, comments are limited to descriptions of his pluralist theory of democracy.

According to Dahl's pluralist theory of democracy, political outcomes arise through competition between interest groups. Dahl refers to pluralism as a plurality of relatively autonomous (independent) organizations (subsystems) within the domain of the state (Dahl 1982, p. 5). In *Who Governs?* (1961) Dahl argues that in the city of New Haven, Connecticut, no one group monopolized power. In his argument that political power in the United States is not cumulative, he rebutted power-elite theorists who had described the United States as a country ruled by a small group of interconnected individuals occupying key positions of power. Dahl concludes that the ability to influence policy (e.g. power) was not equal in the city of New Haven. However, groups were able to compete with each other. Different groups exerted more or less power within different policy areas.

Dahl explores power relationships in New Haven prior to reaching the conclusion that the political system of New Haven was one of "dispersed inequality." While Dahl recognizes the presence of inequalities in influence, he finds the inequalities that exist in New Haven "noncumulative." Within a century, the political system dominated by one cohesive set of leaders had given way to a system dominated by many different sets of leaders. Each set of leaders had access to a different combination of political resources (p. 86). Individuals who are influential in one sector of public activity tend not to be influential in another sector. In addition, the social strata from which individuals in one sector tend to come from are different from the social strata from which individuals in other sectors are drawn.

Dahl explored the social and economic standing of subleaders in the three issue areas of party nominations, urban redevelopment, and public education. He did not believe subleaders constituted an interlocking group of business elites. Subleaders in urban redevelopment fit the profile of an executive in a large- or medium-sized company who lives in a good or one of the best neighborhoods. Public education subleaders lived in better than average homes. This subleader is likely to be professionally engaged in education as a teacher or school administrator. Dahl characterizes the subleader involved in political nominations as the epitome of the "average man" who left school during or after completion of high school (p. 178).

In Dahl's system of pluralism, leaders and subleaders possess higher levels of direct influence on public policy decisions. Constituents possess low levels of direct influence. However, Dahl contends that most citizens possess a moderate degree of indirect influence because elected leaders keep the real or imagined preferences of constituents in mind when deciding policies (p. 164). Dahl's pluralist democracy highlights the opportunity for organized minorities to block, modify, or delay a policy that the minority opposes. He believes it is rare for any coalition to carry out its policies without having to bargain, negotiate, and compromise with opponents (Dahl 1967, p. 326).

Dahl's analysis of New Haven leads him to conclude that most citizens exert little direct influence on decisions of public officials. A small band of professionals within the political stratum characterizes pluralistic systems. These professionals organize their lives over politics. They usually have occupations that leave them freer to engage in politics than average citizens. Dahl (1961, p. 311) concedes that the political system of New Haven fell short of the usual conceptions of the ideal democracy. However, he maintains that it is an example of a stable democratic system. High levels of suffrage, relatively high participation in elections, a competitive two-party system, freedom to criticize public officials, and frequent change in office from one party to another characterize this stability. A stable set of democratic beliefs among the bulk of citizens and adherence to a democratic creed supports stability. Formal schooling as well as the mass media reinforces allegiance to the creed (p. 325).

3.4 Carole Pateman

Carole Pateman takes exception to the minimalist view of democracy as a free competition for the votes. She advances a more expansive participatory theory of democracy as an alternative to democracy as a simple struggle to attract voters. Pateman argues that the mere presence of representative institutions is not sufficient for a political system to qualify as democratic. For a democratic polity to exist, Pateman believes it is necessary to create a participatory society. She contends that increased space for citizen participation will empower and educate individuals to be effective, democratic citizens. Participation is necessary for an individual to be a thoughtful, public citizen, and not simply a private, self-interested individual.

Pateman identifies a contradiction between the formal equality institutionalized into law in liberal democracy and the inequality experienced socially by women and the lower classes. The issue of equality emerges strongly in her writings. She is concerned with economic inequality, patriarchy, and other social issues. An egalitarian sensibility informs her criticism of contracts, which she claims are problematic because they institutionalize unequal relationships (Vick 2015, p. 209). Pateman refers to political theorists such as Rousseau, John Stuart Mill, and G. D. H. Cole in establishing a vision of democracy as consistent with a need for creative and interdependent social activity. She asserts that democratic theory needs to have a greater focus on the participation of ordinary people and the development of ordinary individuals (Pateman 1970, p. 104).

Pateman denounces democratic theories that rely on the participation of elites and depend upon apathy of the overall public as a bulwark against instability. According to her, the existence of a participatory society would mean that ordinary citizens are better able to assess the performance of representatives, better able to take up issues of importance, and better able to assess the impact of decisions on their own lives. Participation would allow individuals to become educated, public citizens. Pateman concludes that the theory of participatory democracy is not a dangerous illusion since one can have a viable theory of democracy that retains the notion of participation at its heart (p. 111).

4 Alternative Perspectives of Democracy: Elite Democratic Theory

Elite theorists of democracy criticize egalitarian or deliberative forms of democracy because they feel high levels of participation tend to produce bad legislation designed by demagogues who appeal to poorly informed and emotional citizens. These theorists point to a lack of information and apathy on the part of citizens. They, however, regard apathy and ignorance as highly desirable since they believe a highly motivated population is likely to pursue irrational and emotionally appealing aims. Elite theory rejects the possibility that citizens can participate as equals. Elite theorists believe that the few must rule society and the role of citizens is merely to ensure smooth and peaceful circulation of elites.

4.1 Walter Lippmann

Walter Lippmann (1889–1974) was a highly influential American author, reporter, and political commentator of the early twentieth century. His insights regarding the limitations of average citizens and decision makers are as relevant today as when he wrote his highly influential book *Public Opinion* in 1922. Lippmann is highly acclaimed; his appellations range from most influential journalist of the twentieth century, to the father of modern journalism.

In *Public Opinion*, Lippmann asserts that shrewd individuals can readily mislead a bewildered people. Lippmann is highly skeptical about the ability of elected leaders to make informed decisions. He argues that representative government does not work successfully unless there is an independent, expert organization for making unseen facts intelligible to elected officials who have the power to make policy. Lippmann found it an "unworkable fiction" that all voters acquire a competent opinion about public affairs. For Lippmann, understanding the world is out of reach for the average citizen. Lippmann argued that people, including journalists, are more apt to believe "the pictures in their heads" than to come to judgment by critical thinking. He developed the concept that humans condense ideas into symbols; he thought journalism was an ineffective method of education. Lippmann contends the mass of the reading public is not interested in learning and assimilating the results of accurate investigation. Citizens, he wrote, were too self-centered to care about public policy except as pertaining to pressing local issues. Lippmann states, "Man is no Aristotelian god ... He is the creature of an evolution who can just about span a sufficient portion of reality to manage his survival, and snatch what on the scale of time are but a few moments of insight and happiness" (Lippmann 1922, p. 7).

Lippmann developed the concept of "stereotypes" that he believed limits a fuller understanding of reality. He claims that whatever we believe to be a true picture, we treat as if it were the environment itself. For Lippmann, this "pseudo-environment" is a reconstruction of reality in a simpler model. The pseudo-environments are interior representations of the world that determine thought, feeling, and action. The pictures, however, often mislead people. Factors that limit access to true facts include artificial censorship, the comparatively meager time available for paying attention to public affairs, and the distortion arising because journalists compress events into very short messages. Furthermore, Lippmann claims people do not wish to face facts that threaten established routines of their lives (Lippmann 1922, p. 7). Stored up images, preconceptions, and prejudices interpret messages. These limited messages from outside form into a pattern of stereotypes that relate to self-interest.

Lippmann is suspicious and critical of any model of democracy that placed excessive faith and power in the hands of the public. He argued that participatory democracy was unworkable and that the democratic public was a myth. He advocated delegating governance exclusively to political representatives and their expert advisors. Based on evidence about the efficacy of propaganda to shape people's ways of thinking, Lippmann contended that public opinion was highly shaped by leaders. Lippmann called this process of manipulation the manufacture of consent. Lippmann argues that ordinary citizens had no sense of objective reality. Because their ideas are merely stereotypes manipulated at will by people at the top, he views deliberative democracy as an unworkable dogma or impossible dream. He advances the idea that the most feasible alternative to deliberative democracy consists of a technocracy guided by experts whose objectives and disinterested knowledge go beyond the narrow views and the parochial self-interests of average citizens. Lippmann sees the prospect of participatory democracy as policy advocated by romantic individuals who idealize the role of the ignorant masses to address public affairs. He proposed that this is an unrealistic model for the emerging mass society (Schugurensky and Myers 2001).

Lippmann's issues a further critique of democracy in his book *The Phantom Public* (1925). In this book, he expands upon his earlier pessimistic view of democracy that he expresses in *Public Opinion* (1922). Lippmann's critique of democracy in *The Phantom Public* revolves around his assertion that the electorate is not competent to govern his or her own affairs. Lippmann claims that the ideal of an all-competent sovereign citizen is unattainable. According to the father of modern journalism, the ideal of competent citizens is noble but incorrect; it is impractical—bad in the sense that "it is bad for a fat man to try to be a ballet dancer" (p. 39). Lippmann concludes that average citizens do not know how to direct public affairs, do not know what is happening, why it is happening, and that there is no reason to believe that the "compounding of individual ignorances" can produce a continuous directing force in public affairs (p. 39).

Lippmann disputes the core assertion of democratic theories that government reflects the will of the people. He characterizes the private citizen as a deaf spectator in the back row. This citizen has awareness of the effects of policy on him or her but is largely invisible. For Lippmann, the popular will does not direct continually but it intervenes occasionally. The public can watch only for coarse signs indicating where their sympathies ought to turn. The public discerns only gross distinction, is slow to be aroused, and is quickly diverted. Lippmann notes that instead of describing government as an expression of the will of the people it would be better to say that government consists of officials who professionally handle problems (pp. 64–65, 72).

Scholars consider Lippmann an elite theorist since his view of society puts its trust chiefly with insiders/agents who can act "executively" on their own opinions to address the substance of an issue. These agents initiate and administer. The public intervenes only when there is a crisis of maladjustment. This model asks the public to do as little as possible. It confines the efforts of citizens to initiatives that may help to allay a disturbance; citizens then return to their own affairs (p. 199). Lippmann views the public as a bystander and spectator to the real action. He notes that actual governing consists of actions by particular individuals that rarely become visible to the private citizen (p. 41).

4.2 *Joseph Schumpeter*

Joseph Schumpeter ([1943] 1976, p. 269) proposes that democracies are institutional arrangement for arriving at political decisions where individuals acquire power by means of a competitive struggle for the people's vote. This represents a concise statement of the elitist view. In this view, political leaders can make policy and law with little regard for the demands made by ordinary citizens. Citizens participate in the process of competition by voting but they are not the ruling element of the society. Schumpeter sees the process of election as a peaceful way of maintaining or changing rulers. Citizens exert some reserve power since when politicians act in ways that large numbers see as problematic, voters can replace them. Democracy protects society from the most harmful leaders but the role of ordinary citizens is limited to that of choosing between competing elites.

Schumpeter contends that the inability of common people to make intelligent decisions in areas of politics makes it necessary to limit the role of the general populace to the voting booth. This leaves actual rule to an elite minority. Schumpeter challenges what he calls the classical doctrine of democracy in disputing the idea that democracy is a process by which the electorate identifies the common good, and politicians carry out the common good. He argues that people's ignorance and superficiality mean that politicians manipulate the masses; the politicians set the agenda, the masses follow. Schumpeter claims that even if it were possible to identify a common good, it would still not be clear how to achieve it. He advocates a minimalist model whereby democracy is the mechanism for competition between leaders. Periodic votes legitimize governments and keep them accountable; the role for citizens in policy creation and implementation is limited.

In the classic text *Capitalism, Socialism and Democracy* ([1943] 1976) Schumpeter contends that democracy means only that the people have the opportunity of accepting or refuting the people who rule them. Within this framework there exists free competition among would-be leaders for the vote of the electorate. Schumpeter believes that democracy forces politicians to take a short-term, rather than a long-term, look at policy. He equates leaders of democracies with a rider of a horse who is so fully engrossed in trying to keep in the saddle that he or she cannot plan the ride or and a general so fully occupied with making sure that his army will accept orders that the general ignores strategy (p. 287). Schumpeter notes that democracies thrive in certain environments but not in others. He identifies four conditions for success of democracies.

The first condition relates to the quality of government leaders. Individuals of adequate ability and moral character must exist in sufficient numbers. Citizens must choose from those that stand for election. Schumpeter recognizes that the democratic process may create conditions in the political sector that will repel able individuals. Therefore, it is not true that in a democracy people always have the kind and quality of government they want or merit. To assure politicians of sufficiently good quality, polities should create a stratum of politicians that is not too exclusive or too easily accessible for the outsider. According to Schumpeter, politicians should have succeeded in other fields. He believes that England is the only country to fulfill the conditions of quality politicians completely. In contrast, he contends politicians of Germany of the Weimar Republic (1918–1933) were "distinctly below par and in some cases 'pitifully so.'" He states the fact that the Weimar political system met "smashing defeat at the hands of an anti-democratic leader is nevertheless indicative of the lack of inspiring democratic leadership" (p. 291).

A second condition for successful democracy is that the government should not extend its range of political decisions too far. The range of political decisions depends upon the kind and quantity of matters that politicians can successfully handle in the context of their struggle for political survival. It depends on the quality of leaders and public opinion. Under Schumpeter's conception of democracy, legislatures should impose limits on itself. Schumpeter's third condition is of greatest interest for defining the limits of bureaucratic power. Schumpeter clearly notes that democratic governments in modern industrial society must be able to command the services of a well-trained bureaucracy. This bureaucracy should have a strong sense of duty and esprit de corps.

Schumpeter sees the strong bureaucracy as the only answer to the assertion that democratic politics is unable to produce decent city government. He goes further in stating, "It is not enough that the bureaucracy should be efficient in current administration and competent to give advice. It must also be strong enough to guide and, if need be, to instruct the politicians who head the ministries" (p. 293). In order to carry out their assigned responsibilities, bureaus must evolve their own principles with sufficient independence to assert them. Appointment tenure and promotion should depend on their own "corporate opinion" despite clamor that may arise when politicians or the public find themselves disadvantaged by public organizations. Schumpeter claims government can secure the requisite personnel "if there is a social stratum of adequate quality and corresponding prestige that can be drawn upon for recruits" (p. 294).

The fourth set of conditions stipulates that democracy cannot work smoothly unless all the groups that count in the nation are willing to accept legislation and executive orders issued by legally competent authorities. Supporters of the government must accept the government's lead and allow it to implement programs. Political warfare should be contained within certain rules. Habitual violation of rules would "spell the end of a democracy." A right amount of respect for tradition, procedure, and etiquette is necessary. Schumpeter states, "The voters outside of parliament must respect the division of labor between themselves and the politicians they elect. They must not withdraw confidence too easily between elections and they must understand that, once they have elected an individual, political action is his business, and not theirs. This means they must refrain from instructing him about what he is to do" (p. 295).

Schumpeter further contends that effective competition requires a large measure of tolerance for difference of opinion. Every would-be leader should be able to present a case without producing disorder. People may have to stand by patiently while others attack their vital interest or offend cherished ideals. This is not possible without "genuine respect for the opinions of one's fellow citizens amounting to a willingness to subordinate one's own opinions" (p. 295). Schumpeter admits that there are situations in which it is reasonable to abandon competitive leadership and adopt monopolistic leadership. If the monopoly is limited to a definite time or duration of an emergency, the principle of competitive leadership is suspended. However, if the monopoly is not limited there is abrogation of democratic principles and dictatorship emerges.

Schumpeter grounds his view of democracy in his belief that there is no such thing as a common good that all people could agree on by the force of a rational argument. He concludes that to different individuals and groups the common good means different things. Second, even if a common good is identified people will disagree on ways to achieve it (pp. 251–252). Schumpeter's views on democracy therefore are more limited than the views of others. He claims, "Democracy does not mean and cannot mean that the people actually rule … Democracy means only that the people have the opportunity of accepting or refusing men who are to rule them" (pp. 284–285). Furthermore, contemporary society does not always meet Schumpeter's conditions for the success of democracy. Polities do not always have high-quality candidates, legislatures do not always impose limits on their deliberations, and not all groups accept legislative measures or resist the temptation to embarrass opponents. Most relevant for the issue of bureaucratic discretion, Schumpeter endorses the creation of a class of bureaucrats as the main answer to government by amateurs (p. 293). He does not concern himself with the danger of a self-contained bureaucracy becoming a force inimical to the rights of average citizens.

4.3 William Domhoff

If one defines democracy as a relatively equal distribution of political power then, according to William Domhoff, it does not exist in the United States. The basic thesis of Domhoff's first book, *Who Rules America* (1967), is that an elite ownership class dominates the United States both politically and economically. Domhoff posits that the real rulers of America are owners and managers of large income-producing properties such as corporations, banks, other financial institutions, and agri-businesses. Domhoff argues that the enormous economic resources of the corporate community give them the ability to dominate the federal government through lobbying, campaign finance, appointments to key government positions, and a policy-planning network made up of foundations, think tanks, and policy-discussion groups. Chief executive officers of corporations, owners of corporations, top executives of foundations, think tanks, and policy-discussion groups work together as a leadership group to exert influence (Domhoff 2018).

In opposition to the pluralist view of dispersed power, Domhoff argues that rule by the wealthy few occurs despite free speech, regular elections, and organized opposition. He identifies a "power elite" as the leadership group of the upper class. This group consists of a social upper class at the top of the wealth, income, and status ladders; corporate executives who gradually socialize into the upper class as they move up the corporate ladder; and nonprofit organizations that play an important role in framing debates over public policy and in shaping public opinion. Domhoff claims nonprofits portray themselves as "nonpartisan" or "bipartisan" because they do identify with politics or with either of the two major political parties. In reality, however, he asserts they are the real "political party" of the upper class in terms of ensuring the stability of the society and the compliance of government. Ideas of foundations and think tanks go out to the public through pamphlets, books, local discussion groups, mass media, and public relations departments of major corporations.

According to Domhoff, members of the power elite directly involve themselves in the federal government through three basic processes: (1) the special-interest process, (2) the policymaking process, and (3) the candidate-selection process. In the special-interest process specific families, corporations, and industrial sectors are able to realize their narrow and short-run interests in their dealings with congressional committees, regulatory bodies, and executive departments. In the policymaking process, elites develop policies in nonprofits and bring them to the executive and legislative branches of government.

Elites influence the candidate-selection process by means of campaign donations to political candidates. The special-interest process relies on gifts, insider dealing, friendship, and promises of lucrative private jobs in the future for compliant government officials. The network of foundations, think tanks, and policy-discussion organizations also develops policies that reach the federal government through reports, news releases, and interviews that elected officials and their staffs read.

The candidate-selection process operates through the two major political parties. Domhoff believes candidates are free to abandon campaign pledges once elected. This contributes to confusion and apathy among the electorate. Campaigns are often relatively devoid of issues; images and personalities dominate. Domhoff postulates that campaigns can be in good part dominated by members of the power elite through the relatively simple and direct means of large campaign contributions. Through donations and money raising the same people who direct corporations and take part in policy networks play a crucial place in the careers of most politicians who advance beyond the local level. The support of elites is especially important in party primaries, where money is a large factor. Elected officials are willing to go along with the policies advocated by those members of the power elite because the officials are motivated by personal ambition far more than they are by political conviction. Domhoff concludes that if "who benefits?" and "who sits?" (on influential bodies) are valid indicators of power then a very strong case exists for the dominant role of the power elite in the federal government (Domhoff 2018).

4.4 Robert Putnam

In *The Comparative Study of Political Elites* (1976, p. 8) Putnam states the reality that some people have more power than others is axiomatic. In all societies, there is a high correlation among interest in politics, political knowledge and sophistication, political skill and resources, political participation, political position and power. Citizens who are interested in politics tend to be more knowledgeable about public affairs and have more education, wealth, and social prestige. Putnam identifies a stratified political system. In this system, individuals at the top of the pyramid are those directly involved in national policymaking. He terms these individuals "proximate decision makers." Just below this group come the "influential" or individuals with substantial indirect influence. Decision makers look to this group for advice and from whom they fear sanctions. This stratum includes high-level bureaucrats, industrialists, financier, interest group leaders, and consultants.

A third stratum consists of a larger group of citizens who take some active part in politics. Reasons for inclusion in this group can include membership in a political party, being a middle-level bureaucrat, local editor, or letter writer. Putnam terms this stratum "activists." Below the activist is the "attentive public" that pays attention politics as a spectator sport. Following the attentive public in Putnam's strata come the masses of ordinary citizens ("voters") whose only impact on national politics comes at the polling booth. At the bottom are "nonparticipants." Putnam views these individuals as politically powerless. He notes that empirical evidence shows that only a tiny proportion of citizens has more than an infinitesimal chance of directly influencing national policy (p. 9).

Putnam (1977, p. 385) found that according to available evidence technocrats such as scientists, economists, and management consultants have gained prominence in public affairs. He views technical training is an important credential for elite recruitment. This shift has implications for society in that the basic orientations of the technocrat differ from that of the democratically elected politician. Putnam does not view technocrats as a cohesive group. His empirical evidence does not support the notion that technically trained experts typically concur on the substance of policy. He believes experts agree that rationality should replace politics. However, on specific practical issues they may disagree. Putnam concludes that the power of technocrats depends on the power of others such as politicians (p. 409).

5 Conclusions

Theories of democracy are of ancient and contemporary lineage. One must look to the Greeks for insights into the advantages of various forms of rule. Enlightenment and contemporary theorists disagree in terms of how much participation by common citizens is advisable. A firm understanding of democracy is helpful for assessing the major questions of whether bureaucracy poses a threat and how to hold government officials accountable. Some of the literature alludes to the technocratic state. The extent to which such a state exists and erodes assumptions of democracy is a subject of concern.

References

Apperley, A. (1999). Hobbes on democracy. *Politics, 19*(3), 165–171.

Bertram, C. (2017, Summer). Jean Jacques Rousseau. In E. N. Zalta (Ed.), *The Stanford encyclopedia of philosophy*. Retrieved March 28, 2017, from https://plato.stanford.edu/archives/sum2017/entries/rousseau/

Bok, H. (2014, Summer). Baron de Montesquieu, Charles-Louis de Secondat. In E. N. Zalta (Ed.), *The Stanford encyclopedia of philosophy*. Retrieved March 28, 2018, from https://plato.stanford.edu/archives/sum2014/entries/montesquieu/

Christiano, T. (2015, Spring). Democracy. In E. Salta (Ed.), *The Stanford encyclopedia of philosophy*. Retrieved March 6, 2018, from https://plato.stanford.edu/archives/spr2015/entries/democracy/

Clayton, E. (n.d.). Aristotle: Politics. *Internet Encyclopedia of Philosophy*. Retrieved March 16, 2018, from https://www.iep.utm.edu/aris-pol/

Dahl, R. (1956). *A preface to democratic theory.* Chicago: University of Chicago Press.

Dahl, R. (1961). *Who governs? Democracy and power in an American city.* New Haven: Yale University Press.

Dahl, R. (1967). *Pluralist democracy in the United States: Conflict and consent.* Chicago: Rand McNally.

Dahl, R. (1982). *Dilemmas of pluralist democracy.* New Haven: Yale University Press.

Dahl, R. (2001). *How democratic is the American constitution.* New Haven: Yale University Press.

Domhoff, W. (1967). *Who rules America?* Englewood Cliffs: Prentice Hall.

Domhoff, W. (2018). *Who rules America?* Retrieved April 26, 2018, from https://whorulesamerica.ucsc.edu/power/

Gutmann, A., & Thompson, D. (1996). *Democracy and disagreement.* Cambridge, MA: Harvard University Press.

Gutmann, A., & Thompson, D. (1998). *Democracy and disagreement.* Princeton: Princeton University Press.

Gutmann, A., & Thompson, D. (2004). *Why deliberative democracy?* Princeton: Princeton University Press.

Korab-Karpowicz, W. J. (n.d.). Plato: Political philosophy. *Internet Encyclopedia of Philosophy.* Retrieved March 14, 2018, from https://www.iep.utmdu/plato-pol/

Koven, S. G. (2008). *Responsible governance: A case study approach.* Armonk: M.E. Sharpe.

Lindsay, A. D. (1947). *The modern democratic state.* New York: Oxford University Press.

Lindsay, A. D. (1980). *The essentials of democracy.* Westport: Greenwood Press Publishers.

Lippmann, W. (1922). *Public opinion.* New York: Harcourt, Brace and Company.

Lippmann, W. (1925). *The phantom public.* New York: Harcourt, Brace and Company.

Marini, F. (1969). John Locke and the revision of classical democratic theory. *Western Political Quarterly, 22*(1), 5–18.

Mill, J. S. (1861 [1991]). *Considerations on representative government.* Buffalo: Prometheus Books.

Miller, F. (2017, Winter). Aristotle's political theory. In E. Zalta (Ed.), *The Stanford encyclopedia of philosophy.* Retrieved March 16, 2018, from https://plato.stanford.edu/archives/win2017/entries/aristotle-politics/

Montesquieu, C. (1748). *The spirit of laws.* Retrieved April 1, 2018, from http://oll.libertyfund.org/titles/montesquieu-complete-works-vol-1-the-spirit-of-laws

Pateman, C. (1970). *Participation and democratic theory.* Cambridge: Cambridge University Press.

Putnam, R. D. (1976). *The comparative study of political elites.* Englewood Cliffs: Prentice Hall.

Putnam, R. D. (1977). Elite transformation in advance industrial societies: An empirical assessment of the theory of technocracy. *Comparative Political Studies, 10*(3), 383–411.

Rosen, J. (1996, December 29). In search of common ground. *New York Times.* Retrieved April 7, 2018, from https://search-proquest-com.echo.louisville.edu/docview/

Schugurensky, D., & Myers, J. P. (2001). *Walter Lippmann and John Dewey debate the role of citizens in democracy.* Retrieved April 24, 2018, from http://schugurensky.faculty.asu.edu/moments/1922lippdew.html

Schumpeter, J. (1943 [1976]). *Capitalism, socialism and democracy.* New York: Harper and Row.

Thompson, D. (1970). *The democratic citizen: Social science and democratic theory in the 20th century.* New York: Cambridge University Press.

Vick, J. (2015). Participatory versus radical democracy in the 21st century: Carole Pateman, Jacques Rancie're, and Sheldon Wolin. *New Political Science, 37*(2), 204–223.

CHAPTER 3

Checks on Bureaucracy, Organizational Accountability, and Organizational Culture

1 Introduction

As discussed in the previous chapters some scholars view the bureaucracy as a potential threat to democracy. This perspective focuses on nonresponsiveness to citizens, the nonelected status of career bureaucrats, lifetime tenure of employees, the discretionary power of officials, their control of information, their aura of expertise, and other factors that insulate bureaucrats from democratic controls. In the extreme, the "bureaucracy" becomes a synonym for a self-serving group of agencies that are accountable only to themselves. Tenure, credentials, inside information, and discretionary power can transform government agencies into independent power wielders. In this scenario, the public does not bend public agencies to their will; agencies dictate to the people. The bureaucrat and the agencies that employ them can make independent decisions based on internal sets of norms that accord with their own worldviews or serve their self-interests. Cabals of experts replace the people and their representatives as creators and implementers of public policy. This scenario obviously is antithetical to democratic theory. It represents a theft of sovereignty by the technocratic elite.

Discussion of replacing democracy with an alternative paradigm based on expertise, autonomy, efficiency, control of information, and allegiance to internal norms of behavior is not novel. It raises perennial questions such as (1) when do the intended servants transform themselves into actual masters? (2) how can governments prevent this transformation? (3) how can polities be more accountable to the public? (4) who will guard

S. G. Koven, *The Case Against Bureaucratic Discretion*,
https://doi.org/10.1007/978-3-030-05779-4_3

the guardians? and (5) can anyone serve as protector of the people without at least occasionally indulging their appetites?

This chapter describes possible checks on bureaucratic power. It reviews the positions of authors who addressed this issue in the past. Context and difference in missions of public organizations are relevant to the question of control over bureaucratic organizations. Because of the divergence in the nature of specific agencies, the chapter also explores organizational cultures that influence bureaucratic attitudes and conduct.

2 Inner Checks on Bureaucrats

2.1 *Technical Knowledge and Professionalism*

The famous Friedrich-Finer debates of the late 1930s and early 1940s describe controls on bureaucratic behavior through internal and external checks. In a lively exchange between the scholars, Carl Friedrich of Harvard University stresses technical knowledge and professionalism as a check on abusive behavior and Herman Finer of the University of London focuses on the need for external oversight. Friedrich argues that administration is dependent on a grasp of technical abilities. He contends that the complexity of many government activities limits political supervision. Increasing professionalism through education increases the likelihood of responsible public action (Jackson 2009, p. 71). Friedrich continuously emphasizes the necessity of technical knowledge for effective administration.

An inner motivation of public officials is also required. Friedrich stresses the need to elicit responsible conduct from officials who act on their own resolve rather than simply respond to rules and regulations. Eliciting the proper degree of motivation is dependent on training, education, and conditions of employment that give independence to administrators (Friedrich 1935, p. 68). Friedrich believes that in order to secure good results leaders must motivate people rather than merely compel them to act under the fear of penalties.

Friedrich notes that the "psychological factor" of government service is essential. He states that the possibility of rising within public service through meritorious service produces responsible behavior. Friedrich states that responsibility to the people "does not require partisans of a particular outlook, whether Republican or Democrat, conservative, progressive, or socialist, but it does require specialists who 'know the ropes' and will therefore effectively execute the general rules decided upon by executive or legislative leadership in accordance with popular preferences" (p. 38).

Friedrich refers to a sense of moral responsibility. He concludes that since public administrators are involved in making policy, and contemporary governmental activities prevent them from submitting all their actions to elected officials for review, accountability of administrators to politicians must be, at best, partial. Friedrich does not completely ignore input from citizens. He posits that administrative responsibility is answerable to two dominant factors: technical knowledge and popular sentiment. Fellow technicians can hold public administrators accountable since administrators are increasingly involved in specialized, highly technical decisions that neither the politician nor the public can effectively monitor and control (Cooper 1998, p. 154). Friedrich's conclusions are similar to those of earlier scholars that focus on the need for an "inner check" based on professional standards and ideals (Gaus 1936, p. 40).

According to Friedrich, the public plays a role. In a democratic society, the public will freely communicate with government officials through inquiries, criticisms, and suggestions ([1940] 1972, p. 325). Administrators are required to be responsive to preferences and demands of citizens. They need to be sensitive to societal trends and to identify probable resistance to new policies. They should adopt policies to fit public preferences.

In contrast, Finer places his faith in external bodies that establish standards of conduct with finality and exactitude; rewards and punishments must be final. For Finer, responsibility requires the existence of a relationship of obedience to an external controlling authority. Finer takes exception to Friedrich's reliance on self-imposed obligation and feelings of responsibility. He argues that it is most important to distinguish the "sense of duty" from the "fact of responsibility, that is, effective answerability" (Finer 1936, p. 582).

The dilemma of discretion is observable in behavior of street-level bureaucrats such as police. In theory, the inner checks of the sense of duty, professionalism, and sensitivity to popular opinion all act to channel behavior in an appropriate direction. Police will respond appropriately because of their training, responsiveness to public sentiment, and inner sense of obligation. Recent high-profile police actions, however, belie the idea that professionalism, a sense of duty, or public scrutiny is sufficient to deter improper behavior.

The Friedrich-Finer debate does not directly address some important issues such as the question of what to do when organizations become indifferent to citizen demands and what to do when they protect personnel that abuse their discretionary authority. The Friedrich-Finer debate is largely silent regarding organizational culture or the question of how to prevent cultures arising that are resistant to oversight. For organizations to be accountable, citizens must be aware of their action. Organizations are empowered when they act in relative secrecy. Some of these organizations can hide or accept transgressions. This allows for a slippery slope of nonaccountable behavior. Supervisors should be able to identify and punish wrongdoers. Without proper oversight, organizations can descend into anarchy. In the extreme, organizations may engage in "rogue" behavior (e.g. My Lai/Abu Ghraib) that is antithetical to the success of their broad missions and antagonistic to the will of the people. If the public and their elected officials do not sanction illicit behavior, organizations threaten to become independent of democratic accountability.

The core of the Friedrich-Finer debate revolves around the questions of how to control bureaucratic behavior and how to enhance democratic accountability. Resolving the issue of how to create organizations that are both efficient and responsive to the people is essential for the health of democracies. One must ask who oversees actions of bureaucrats. Is it the people, their elected representatives, career technocrats, or political appointees? If bureaucrats overstep their authority how are they constrained and by whose authority? Do bureaucrats curb potential abuse by norms of their profession, by an "inner voice" of right and wrong, by their conceptions of personal integrity or by fear of retribution for misbehavior?

2.2 *Responsiveness to Popular Opinion and Elected Representatives*

Finer admits that intellectual integrity or general loyalty to the spirit and purpose of one's function is important for maintaining efficiency. However, Finer questions whether this "inner check" is sufficient to keep civil servants motivated and honest. He states, "Though judicial and quasi-judicial procedures and standards provide some guarantees of fair and beneficial administration, and though the codes of ethics, interior discipline and all the arrangements to make these effective, offer the guarantees of inventiveness, agility and fruitful administration, nothing is more important in our own day than the fundamentality of political control" (Finer 1936, p. 583). Finer contends it is idle to put too much faith in tools such as staff discipline, promotion criteria, or efficiency rating. He believes the consumers of policy massed together as the electorate and operating through a representative body must control civil servants.

Finer notes that public servants are not autonomous actors but they are responsible to the elected representatives of the people. Elected representatives determine the broad course of action that is feasible. Bureaucrats should eschew independent action; they should guard against imposing their views on others. According to Finer, both politicians and public employees should work for what the public wants, rather than their perception of what the public needs.

Elected institutions (such as Congress) play a vital role. Elected leaders are aware of public desires; they have the power to exact obedience to orders. Finer takes a dim view of reliance on the administrators' conscience or subjective moral sense of responsibility. He believes such reliance will result in the abuses of power that accompany monopolies. Finer states without external punitive controls employees of the public sector will inevitably fail to perform acts required by law, engage in wrongdoing, or undertake duties beyond what the law and custom oblige (Finer 1941, p. 329).

According to Finer, sensitivity to public opinion and professional standards only play auxiliary roles. Legal sanctions are necessary. A basic problem of auxiliary approaches is they rely on the exercise of discretion by public officials. Auxiliary approaches have no power to compel and control conduct. Officials are likely to give themselves the benefit of the doubt in questions of what they believe to be right for the people. In contrast, the directives of legislatures are definitive (p. 343). Finer states that due to the weakness of internal controls, the primary concern of defenders of democracy should be improving legislative control over public servants, along with strengthening legal sanctions. Discipline in the hierarchy through career prospects, pay raises, promotions, and recognition of distinction might exercise some control, yet legal and political sanctions are primary levers of accountability.

Finer's position is consistent with that of Max Weber and the traditional theorists that contend administrators must obey elected masters who have the legitimate power. Administrators only deal with judgments about how to deliver with efficiency what politicians decide. For Weber, administrators should execute the orders of the superior authorities regardless of whether the administrator agrees with the order. The honor of the civil servant resides in his or her ability to execute orders of superiors. Thompson (1975) also advances the argument that the public is the owner of government agencies; intrusions of bureaucrats into this relationship represent a theft of sovereignty (Thompson 1975).

Thompson views government bureaucracies as machinelike instruments that the proper authority (the public) can use. The agencies are artificial systems with prescribed rules and roles. Problems arise when bureaucrats develop their own systems to make informal decisions about the goals and ends of the organization. "Natural systems" of formal organizations may not be responsive to the wishes of the people. The issue of how democracies can control the "natural systems" of public organizations is an ongoing concern. Officials within bureaucratic organizations silently can make policy by enacting directives, unknown to the apathetic public.

Sometimes scrutiny occurs years later. Other times it never occurs at all. Elected US officials did not authorize the killing of women and children in the village of My Lai during the Vietnam War. The "street-level bureaucrat" platoon leader Lieutenant William Calley allegedly ordered troops in his command to push about 80 old men, women, and children into a drainage ditch and shoot into the ditch. Allegedly, the company commander, Ernest Medina, urged his troops to be "extremely aggressive" the night before the assault on My Lai, suggesting that they had a chance to avenge the deaths of their fellow GIs (Koven 2008, p. 144).

At times, actions are independent of and even contrary to popular opinion or the views of elected representatives. For example, behavior at the Abu Ghraib prison complex in Iraq did not depend on public approval or a vote of elected officials. The secretary of defense (Rumsfeld) played a role in getting the military to apply the same interrogation techniques at Abu Ghraib as the "harsh interrogation" techniques used at Guantanamo Bay. The US commander for Iraq signed a memo that authorized interrogation techniques that went beyond those listed in the Army Field Manual without much public awareness or debate (p. 154).

Officials at both high and low levels make policy during the course of their official capacities. According to the nonprofit organization Human Rights Watch, the US Justice Department, in a series of legal memos written in late 2001 and early 2002, helped build a framework to circumvent international law. Justice Department memos argued that the Geneva Convention did not apply to detainees from Afghanistan because they were not fighting for a legitimate government and were not prisoners of war but illegal combatants. A memo from the Department of Justice's Office of Legal Counsel concluded that neither the Geneva Convention nor any of the laws of war applied to the conflict in Afghanistan. A subsequent memo, primarily authored by Assistant Attorney General Jay Bybee (i.e. Bybee memo), provided sweeping authority for harsh interrogation.

The memo defines torture as acts carried out with the intent to inflict severe pain or suffering. In essence, the memo excuses interrogation practices if the intent is to gain information rather than inflict pain (p. 169).

The impact of the bureaucratic decision authored in the Bybee memo was profound. McCoy (2006, pp. 122–123) states that through linguistic legerdemain, the Justice Department granted the CIA de facto authority to use torture techniques, excepting only the most heinous acts that brought maiming or death. The Bybee memo issued a virtual license for torture that would remain in effect during two years of the most aggressive counterterror operations, August 2002 to June 2004.

Bureaucratic discretion occurs at local as well as higher levels of government. Decisions of local elected officials at times run counter to national law. Kim Davis gained international attention in 2015 when she defied a US federal court order to issue marriage licenses to same-sex couples following a US Supreme Court decision to do so. Davis began denying marriage licenses to all couples. Citing religious opposition to same-sex marriage, Davis stated that she was acting under God's authority. She continued to defy the court order and ultimately was sent to jail for contempt of court. The court released Davis five days later under the condition that she would not interfere with the efforts of her deputy clerks, who had started issuing marriage licenses to all couples. Davis then modified the Kentucky marriage licenses used in her office so that they no longer mentioned her name. Davis pledged not to interfere with any deputy clerk who issues marriage licenses; however, she did not personally issue or authorize any of the forms. In 2015, the newly elected governor of Kentucky, Matt Bevin, promised to remove the names of the county clerks from the marriage form in order to protect the religious beliefs of officials who are opposed to gay marriage (Mark 2015).

3 Outer Check on Bureaucrats

3.1 President

Bureaucracies are not autonomous island to themselves. A host of institutional actors (presidents, governors, and mayors) influence the behavior of entrenched government officials. Elected chief executives can work to either bolster or undercut the morale of bureaucrats and the outcomes of their organizations. In the past, elected champions of limited government appointed officials to government agencies that did not support previous initiatives of the organizations. The election of Ronald Reagan in 1980 offers a prime example of how new administrations can inhibit action or completely reverse policies of career officials.

The Reagan administration endeavored to find nominees who were ideologically compatible with the administration's goals. The general intent of these appointments was to ensure the hiring of people who were committed to the political philosophy and policy agenda of the president. During the Reagan administration, subcabinet appointments came under more control by the White House Office of Presidential Personnel (OPP) Office. According to the head of the OPP, in the Reagan administration to succeed in his job it was necessary to understand the president and his philosophy, what he wants to accomplish, what his goals are. Such understanding aids in choosing personnel who will carry out the president's agenda, his approach, and philosophy (Pfiffner 2001, 2013). Presidents often believe that having ideologically simpatico people in place throughout the government will give them the advantage they need to be responsive to the electoral wishes of the people.

Patronage serves as a rough connection between the will of the people (through elections) and the actions of government organizations. In theory, when government organizations and chief executives fail to sufficiently satisfy the wishes of the people new chief executives replace the old. These new executives have at least some ability to shape the orientations of public agencies. They do so through appointing people in the bureaucracy whose ideological orientations are more in line with the mind-sets of the elected officials.

Examples illustrate both the possibility for change through presidential appointment and the ability of the permanent bureaucracy to outlive or resist executive directives. In 1981, the US Senate confirmed President Reagan's appointment of James Watt as his first secretary of the interior. Watt came to the administration from a position as founding president of the Mountain States Legal Foundation (MSLF), a group that acted on the behalf of oil, timber, development, and mineral corporations. The MSLF identified closely with an anti-environmental movement called "Wise Use" and promoted so-called "takings" legislation. This legislation requested the government to compensate private and corporate landholders for having to comply with the government's environmental laws.

As secretary of interior, Watt gained a reputation as one of the most blatantly anti-environmental political appointees in American history. Environmental groups accused Watt of reducing funding for environmental protection, easing regulations of oil and mining, directing the National Park Service to draft rules that would eliminate some national parks, and recommending lease of lands to harvest natural resources. Watt favored speeding the sale of public lands to private interests at relatively low prices. He resisted the idea of donating private land for conservation; Watt suggested opening vast swaths of undeveloped land for drilling and mining. The area leased to coal mining quintupled during his term as secretary of the interior. Watt openly advocated mining more, drilling more, and cutting more timber.

In 1983, Watt resigned in the face of growing support for a resolution in the Senate calling for his ouster. Reagan "reluctantly accepted" the resignation stating that Watt had done an outstanding job in his stewardship of the natural resources of the nation. Prior to his resignation Watt came under fire after characterizing members of a coal advisory commission as follows: "We have every kind of mixture you can have, I have a black, I have a woman, two Jews and a cripple. And we have talent" (Weisman 1983). His insensitivity to minority groups combined with his opposition to environmental preservation generated sufficient public opposition for his ousting.

Limits on the formal power of presidents to mold public bureaucracies to their liking are evident. When contemplating General Eisenhower winning the presidential election in 1952, departing President Harry Truman surmised that Eisenhower would order people to "Do this! Do that! And nothing will happen." Truman notes that the presidency is nothing like the army and Eisenhower will find it very frustrating. Career officials may not be responsive to presidential decisions. Bureaucrats may believe that their conception of what is in the national interest is correct and resist efforts to do things that they feel are contrary to the national interest, their personal interest, or the organization's interests. Halperin et al. (2006, p. 246) note that because presidential decisions are seldom formulated in a way that conveys in detail what should be done and because the president seldom carries out the decision, only in very special cases are presidential decisions self-executing. Usually presidential decisions only begin a process. Problems can arise from multiple directives that are in conflict with each other. For example, the State Department failed to remove American missiles from Turkey in 1961 after President Kennedy had ordered them removed. Officials on the ground felt themselves to be operating under a more general presidential directive to strengthen the North Atlantic Treaty Organization (NATO) alliance. The career officials concluded that the president did not order the missile removal with the intent to contradict the order to strengthen NATO. They raised the issue with the Turkish government. When the Turkish government registered strong objections to removing the missiles, the bureaucrats held off obeying the presidential order (p. 251).

Former Secretary of State Henry Kissinger notes that departments of the bureaucracy become pressure groups for a point of view. If their views differ from that of the president, they may become convinced that some evil influence worked on the president and that they know better. In his memoirs President Harry Truman states, "The difficulty with many career officials in the government is that they regard themselves as the men who really make policy and run the government. They look upon the elected officials as just temporary occupants. Every President in our history has been faced with this problem: how to prevent career people from circumventing presidential policy" (p. 255).

3.2 Congress

Congress possesses various means of influencing actions of administrative officials. It exercises oversight power largely through its congressional committee system. Oversight also occurs through activities such as authorization, appropriations, investigative, and legislative hearings by standing committees. Special investigations by select committees and studies by congressional support agencies also can transpire. Congress' oversight derives its authority from implied powers in the Constitution and is an integral part of the US system of checks and balances. The Supreme Court as well as legislative statutes has legitimated Congress' investigative power.

According to the US State Department, the oversight power of Congress has helped to force officials out of office, change policies, and provide new statutory controls over the executive branch. There are numerous examples of congressional influence on public agencies. For example, in 1949, probes by special Senate investigating subcommittees revealed corruption among high officials in the Truman administration. This resulted in the reorganization of agencies and the formation of a special White House commission to study public sector corruption. The Senate Foreign Relations Committee's televised hearings in the late 1960s helped to mobilize opposition to the Vietnam War. Select committee inquiries in 1975 and 1976 identified abuses by US intelligence agencies and initiated new legislation to control certain activities. In 1987, congressional oversight disclosed violations in the executive branch's secret arms sales to Iran and the diversion of money to anti-government forces fighting the leftist regime in Nicaragua. Congressional findings resulted in proposed legislation to prevent similar occurrences in the future. Senate hearings in 1996 and 1997 uncovered instances of abuse in the Internal Revenue Service (IRS). In 1998, Congress passed IRS reform legislation that expanded taxpayers' protections, which included shifting the burden of proof in tax disputes from the taxpayer to the IRS (United States Department of State n.d.).

In recent times, congressional investigation revealed the tendency for partisan politics to become the dominant driver. Conservatives became highly critical of alleged IRS abuses in the 1990s. Conservative Republicans in Congress criticized IRS actions in targeting certain groups. Liberal Democrats in Congress admitted to bureaucratic failings but claim they were not politically motivated. Political overseers of bureaucratic agencies allege they are only upholding the rule of law. However, congressional overseers tend to move to their own corners during investigations or hearings. This is true for the IRS investigation as well as for the congressional investigation into Russian meddling in the 2016 election.

Background information of the IRS scandal indicates that beginning in 2010, the IRS more closely scrutinized certain organizations applying for tax-exempt status. IRS employees in Cincinnati, Ohio, developed a "BOLO" (be on the look-out) list whereby IRS agents were to give more intensive scrutiny to applicants with names related to a number of political causes. Applications to receive special attention included referenced words such as "Tea Party," "Patriots," "progressive," "government spending," "government debt," "taxes," "making America a better place to live," "the Constitution," and the "Affordable Care Act (Obamacare)." Between 2010 and 2012, the IRS essentially placed on hold the processing of applications for tax-exempt status received from organizations with key words (i.e. Tea Party) in their names. The IRS did not deny conservative-named applications but approved very few. During the same general period, the IRS approved applications from many more liberal-sounding groups whose names included terms such as "progressive," "liberal," or "equality." Liberal and conservative groups received different treatment because line agents could approve liberal groups for tax-exempt status but could not approve conservative-sounding groups. Conservative-sounding applicants were bundled together for further review.

Beginning in 2012, some groups seeking tax-exempt status complained to various members of Congress. In response, a congressional committee asked the IRS commissioner about the allegations of selective treatment. After the commissioner denied that the IRS was unfairly targeting conservative groups, the congressional committee ended the 2012 phase of the investigation. Following a report by the Treasury Department's inspector general, the House Committee on Oversight and Government Reform began a new investigation. The House Committee on Ways and Means also investigated the IRS political targeting allegations. In a 2013 appearance before the House Oversight Committee, Lois Lerner (director of Exempt Organizations Unit of the IRS) invoked her Fifth Amendment right against self-incrimination and refused to testify.

In addition to the House investigations, the Senate Permanent Subcommittee on Investigations began to look into IRS behavior and released its report in 2014. The subcommittee's majority report, authored by the subcommittee's Democrats, concluded that the IRS used inappropriate screening criteria but that there was no intentional wrongdoing or political bias in the actions. The subcommittee's Republican minority submitted a dissenting report and accused the majority of minimizing bias against conservative groups, noting that most of the groups targeted for additional scrutiny were conservative. In 2015, the Senate Finance Committee also issued separate reports. The Republican report stated that the IRS had targeted Tea Party groups for politically motivated reasons, while the Democratic report blamed the agency's failures on gross mismanagement that treated groups in the same poor manner regardless of ideology. Some Democrats in Congress characterized Republican explorations into the IRS as a witch-hunt and political grandstanding on behalf of special interests. Republicans claimed bureaucrats at the IRS arbitrarily and haphazardly administered the tax code and targeted taxpayers based on political ideology.

3.3 Courts

The courts have the power under the US Constitution to limit bureaucratic and executive power. The courts can declare executive or bureaucratic actions void if they fail to meet constitutional requirements. The courts generally apply two standards to administrative action. First, the judicial branch of government can question whether specific actions of agencies are consistent with legislative intent. Second, the courts can overrule an administrative agency if it has violated proper procedures (Meier 1993, p. 162). Despite its legal authority, Lowi (1969) argues that the courts have been ineffective in controlling administrative action since the legislative branch of government delegates its power to bureaucratic agencies without clear guidelines.

The justice system represents a final check on illegal activities of bureaucrats. Judicial action can apply to obvious transgressions such as embezzlement, perjury, fraud, or sexual assault. Ethics laws that apply to federal employees carry criminal penalties for noncompliance. Criminal violations include bribery (receiving or soliciting anything of value in exchange for influence), conflict of interest (participating in matters where one has a financial interest), and salary supplement (receiving income for services one is expected to perform as a government employee). Ethics regulations also require employees to recuse themselves from participating in an official matter if their impartiality comes into question.

The line between criminal behavior and incompetence or overzealousness in performing official duties, however, is not always clear. Juries often give government employees the benefit of the doubt in criminal misconduct cases. For some government agencies (such as police departments), it may be difficult to secure information from other officers. Several notable court cases illustrate that it is possible to prosecute government representatives for their misdeeds but that it may be difficult to secure convictions. One of the most infamous criminal cases of government wrongdoing involved the leasing of oil production rights in Montana (Teapot Dome Scandal). In 1922, Interior Secretary Albert Fall leased federal land to two large oil companies without competitive bidding. Fall had received a no-interest loan in November 1921 and other gifts. In 1927, the Supreme Court invalidated the leases and ordered a return of the land to the government. A jury convicted Albert Fall of accepting bribes. He was sent to jail for one year and became the first former cabinet officer sentenced to prison because of misconduct in office.

During the Watergate period, various Nixon administration officials received prison sentences for different crimes. John Mitchell served as the attorney general for the United States from 1969 to 1972. In 1975, Mitchell was found guilty of conspiracy, obstruction of justice, and perjury. At his trial, the prosecutors charged that Mitchell had approved the plan that led to breaking into the Watergate complex and then had played a central role in the cover-up. The New York State Supreme Court disbarred Mitchell from practicing law in the state. According to Justice Department officials, never before had the courts banned a former attorney general from practicing law. Mitchell initially received a prison sentence of two and a half to eight years. He served 19 months at a minimum-security prison before the courts released him on parole for medical reasons.

Another figure of the Nixon administration, E. Howard Hunt was a career intelligence officer of the Central Intelligence Agency (CIA) (1949–1970) prior to becoming a member of a covert White House Special Investigations Unit known as "the Plumbers." The task of the plumbers unit was to stop the leaking of classified information. Along with former FBI agent G. Gordon Liddy, Hunt plotted the Watergate burglaries and other clandestine operations for the Nixon administration. The courts convicted Hunt of burglary, conspiracy, and wiretapping. He served 33 months in federal prison. Liddy served nearly 52 months in federal prisons following convictions for burglary, conspiracy, and refusing to testify to the Senate committee investigating Watergate.

During the Reagan administration, the assistant administrator of the US Environmental Protection Agency (EPA) for solid waste and emergency response (Rita Lavelle) went to prison on various charges. After an investigation based on whistleblower evidence, evidence showed that Lavelle was involved with misuse of the EPA's $1.6 billion "Superfund" money. In 1983, the courts found her guilty of lying to a House subcommittee investigating toxic waste cleanup programs. Lavelle served three months of a six-month prison sentence, paid a $10,000 fine, and was placed under probation for five years. The courts sentenced James Watt (secretary of the interior from 1981 to 1983) to five years of probation and fined him $5000 for perjury and obstruction of justice.

Other high-profile government officials were subjects of scrutiny by the legal system. In 1998, President Bill Clinton agreed to settle a sexual harassment lawsuit by an employee (Paula Jones) of the Arkansas Industrial Development Commission. In 2001, Clinton agreed to a five-year suspension of his license to practice law and agreed to pay $25,000 to the Arkansas Bar Association. In 2015, a federal judge sentenced former army general and former Director of the CIA David Petraeus to two years' probation plus a fine of $100,000 for providing classified information. In 2017, former Marine general and former National Security Advisor Michael Flynn pled guilty to lying to the FBI. Each of these cases illustrates that the courts can impose clear penalties on wrongdoing of administrative or elected officials.

3.4 Media

The mass media can play an important role in exposing abuses of bureaucrats and then generating support for corrective action. Media coverage can be sketchy since bureaucratic malfeasance is not always the highest-priority narrative for local or national news. Violent crime often occupies the attention of local media. Issues of international relations, economic growth, cultural dissonance, or elections engage the interest of the national media. Occasionally, narratives that involve the misbehavior of government employees dominate the print, television network, Internet, and other media. Part of the literature on public administration asserts that the mass media is responsible for the somewhat negative popular image of administrative agencies. Through negative reporting about civil servants, the media shapes stereotypes in the collective mind of the citizens.

The media plays a role in transmitting framed messages. Political candidates use message framing, symbols, and the media to fuel the public belief that the bureaucracy is in crisis. Language is particularly important in framing messages such as the view that government is the problem, the bureaucracy is too large, and that bureaucrats are lazy or incompetent. Criticism of the bureaucracy during the Reagan administration has received a great deal of scholarly attention. Reagan advanced the imagery of federal bureaucrats as loafers, incompetent buffoons, good ole boys, or tyrants (Garrett et al. 2006).

Fostering the negative image of bureaucracy both preceded and followed the Reagan administration. "Bureaucrat bashing" accompanied Ross Perot's 1992 presidential campaign and the 1994 Republican "Contract with America." Politicians on both sides of the aisle use media effectively to convey their messages that often blame government officials for misdeeds. Politicians recognize that messages focusing on negativity evoke more powerful responses than messages that emphasize benefits or successes. Neatly packaged symbols fit in with the media's coverage (Garrett et al. 2006). Images fostered by the media create an environment of suspicion and hostility. Media attention may demoralize employees to the point that they may not effectively manage programs.

At the same time that media coverage produces negative images, media coverage can enhance accountability of bureaucrats. For example, in 1991 an African-American taxi driver (Rodney King) received international attention as the victim of Los Angeles Police Department brutality after a civilian filmed his beating by police from a nearby balcony and sent the footage to the local news station. The footage clearly shows the police repeatedly hitting King with their batons. At the hospital, doctors found King to have suffered a fractured facial bone, a broken right ankle, and multiple bruises and lacerations.

Following the release of the videotape, Los Angeles district attorney charged four Los Angeles police officers with use of excessive force. At their trial, three of the officers were acquitted; the jury failed to reach a verdict on one charge for the fourth officer. After the acquittals by the Los Angeles courts, the US Department of Justice sought indictments of the police officers for violations of King's civil rights. Trial of the four officers began in 1993 in the US District Court for the Central District of California. The jury found two officers guilty, and they received a sentence of 30 months in prison; the court acquitted two officers of all charges. The city of Los Angeles awarded King $3.8 million in damages. Without the media attention, it is doubtful that there would have been any consequences for the police actions.

The video recording of Rodney King's arrest represents an early example of modern surveillance where civilians with the aid of increasingly sophisticated and affordable video equipment record police actions. In 2014, a videotape surfaced of the shooting of 12-year-old Tamir Rice by a Cleveland police officer. Rice did not receive any first aid after the shooting. The incident received national and international coverage, in part because of its coming shortly after the police shootings of several other black males. In 2017, the city of Cleveland fired the police officer who shot and killed Rice; the city suspended another officer after investigations of the incident. The police chief announced that the officer was fired for having lied on his job application and not disclosing that he had resigned from his previous position to avoid being fired for insubordination, emotional immaturity, dishonesty, and mishandling his gun. The city suspended a second officer involved in the shooting for ten days and ordered him to attend tactical training classes. It was determined that tactics of the second officer during the shooting violated department policies. The city of Cleveland settled a lawsuit brought by Rice's family for $6 million. As in the case of Rodney King, the media played a significant role in holding street-level bureaucrats accountable for their actions.

4 Organizational Accountability: Missions and Public Interest

4.1 Missions

Missions and mission statements help assure accountability to broad legislative mandates as well as to executive directives. Mission statements remind employees of their overall purpose and long-term goals. They guide and direct the actions of public servants; they serve multiple purposes, not least of which is the motivation of public servants. Organizations with strong missions imbue their workers with a sense of purpose that transcends a paycheck or obligation to family. In the public sector mission often links to grandiose and noble ends such as preserving safety, protecting the environment, advancing knowledge, or ensuring economic stability. Missions differ agency to agency. For example, the mission of defense agencies such as the US Marine Corps differs qualitatively from that of knowledge agencies such as the National Science Foundation (NSF) or economic oversight agencies such as the US Federal Reserve Service (Koven 2015, pp. 115–128).

Every new group or organization must develop shared conceptions of core mission, primary task, or reason for being (Schein 2004, p. 89). These shared conceptions focus the attention of workers and provide them with encouragement as they go about their day-to-day activities. Missions of government agencies differ from those of business organizations that concern themselves with profit and market share. Leaders of government agencies must work toward conceptions of the public interest. These conceptions often are vague and allow for wide-ranging interpretation on the part of agencies.

Basic orientations differ across organizations within the public sector. The Marine Corps holds dear values such as honor, courage, and commitment summed up in the motto Semper Fidelis or *Semper Fi*. Semper Fi (Latin for always faithful) guides Marines to remain faithful to the mission at hand, to each other, to the Marine Corps, and to the country. The website of the Marine Corps states the corps exists to ensure the future of the nation. Therefore, it is necessary to build both outstanding warriors and upstanding citizens. In contrast, the mission statement of the NSF focuses on the need to promote and advance scientific progress in the United States. The organization commits itself to build the nation's research capability through strategic investments that support excellence in research and education. It strives to provide an integrated strategy to advance the frontiers of knowledge, cultivate a world-class, broadly inclusive science and engineering workforce, and expand the scientific literacy of all citizens. Finally, the mission of the Federal Reserve (Fed) Board is to provide the nation with a safer, more flexible, and more stable monetary and financial system. Values of the Fed board include efficiency, integrity, high-quality analysis, and independence. The values expressed by the Fed provide assurances about its ability to deliver economic stability through guidance and oversight (p. 126).

Bart (1997, pp. 9–11) notes that mission statements serve numerous purposes. First, they provide a sense of purpose and direction. This limits confusion and distraction. Second, they ensure allegiance to the interests of key stakeholders. Organizations serve the interests of more than one group such as employees and the public. Third, mission statements sharpen an organization's focus; they help to control and inspire employees. Finally, mission statements promote shared values and behavioral standards. They unify those who buy into the mission and drive out those who do not. Those who remain in the organizations are more likely to be dedicated to preserving and protecting its principles. Bart describes mission statements as the "sex drive" or "libido" of organizational life since they inspire passion and pleasure (p. 11).

The best mission statements are clear, memorable, to the point, and short. For example, the mission statement of the Smithsonian Institute is only six words: "The increase and diffusion of knowledge." Other pithy mission statements include those of the Forest Service (caring for the land and serving people), New York Public Library (to inspire lifelong learning, advance knowledge, and strengthen our communities), and Public Broadcasting System (to create content that educates, informs, and inspires) (Koven 2015, p. 93). Mission statements define what sets an organization apart from others. Defining the essence of the organization helps to mold the culture.

Goodsell (2011, p. 1) asks how society moves toward a state of affairs where men and women are "turned on" by the work they are doing such as stopping child abuse, fighting forest fires, battling epidemics, building safe highways, or helping children learn. He concludes that the answer is in the notion he terms mission mystique. This construct focuses attention on the importance of developing belief systems for agencies and the value of a compelling public mission. A fuller description of Goodsell's views on mission appears below.

4.2 *Public Interest*

Public interest represents an ideal that public administrator and political scientists endlessly discuss. This discussion is as relevant as ever, especially when inquiring into the behavior of street-level public servants. Important questions are unresolved. These questions include the following. Do bureaucrats and bureaucracies serve their personal interests or those of the broader public? Do bureaucrats have a realistic or distorted conception of the public interest? Can the public hold bureaucratic organizations accountable to them? How can the public hold these organizations accountable? What remedies are necessary for greater accountability? Is there a present danger that public bureaucracies will evolve into unresponsive power to themselves? Do "red flags" indicate that street-level bureaucrats inevitably morph into masters rather than servants of the people? Can the unorganized majority exert influence on entrenched agencies that often operate outside of public purview? These questions go to the heart of the question of accountability. They go beyond the simple discussion of efficiency and effectiveness that dominates mainstream public administration. These questions relate to core issues of arbitrary power of bureaucrats and civil liberties of individuals.

In the broad sense, public interest refers to the policies that serve the many, rather than the few. To serve the public interest, government organizations have a responsibility to protect the majority, not only the well-funded minority. In theory, public organizations are accountable to the people. The people hold the power and can elect individuals that in turn appoint directors of specific agencies. The public has the option to "throw the bums out" or to try to install a new group. Widespread change can occur when disenchantment reaches a tipping point. "Realigning" elections demonstrate that throughout American history peaceful change transpires. The people hold power since, as stated by Thomas Paine in the 1776 pamphlet *Common Sense*, "the law is king" and elected representatives make the law. The idea of empowering the people appears not only in the US Declaration of Independence but also in the writings of political philosophers such as John Locke, Jean-Jacques Rousseau, and Charles-Louis Montesquieu (Koven 2008, p. 18). These ideas form the bedrock of the American constitutional republic.

Perspectives of the public interest vary by author. Many theorists focus on enhancing the participation of citizens. They tend to believe that the average citizen is the best judge of his or her interests and is capable of showing better judgment over time. Others are highly skeptical of the ability of average citizens to make wise decisions. These authors contend that the demagogue of the day tends to sway the masses away from their true interests. These demagogues use false rhetoric and manipulation of the passions of the public. Some of the different perspectives of public interest can be placed into three categories: rationalist theories, idealist theories, and realist theories (Schubert 1960).

Rationalist theories of the public interest embrace a hierarchical model where the people are at the summit, they elect representatives, political parties help to define the public will, legislators translate the public will into law, executives oversee execution of the law by administrators, and judges enforce the law. The job of administrators is to translate people's desires into specific rules. Delegates of the people serve the public interest when they enforce the public will. The delegates promote the public interest when they minimize or eliminate discretion of administrative officials. Behavior of officials flows smoothly from the will of the people. Private and special interest is subordinate to the preservation of the common interest. This is a traditional view of how the system should work and how it works. It conforms to the system laid out in the US Constitution.

Idealist theories adhere to precepts of natural law. Idealist public interest theorists contend that leaders can accurately interpret by themselves what is in the best interest of the public. These interpretations may not coincide with the public majority view but the interpretations correspond with a "higher" or "natural" law that leaders identify. According to Schubert (1960), under the idealist perspective leaders interpret higher law through their own perceptions. The public interest becomes whatever the consciences and minds of officials believe it to be. Public officials listen to an "inner voice" that guides their actions. This inner voice relies upon their view of reason in making assessments.

The realist view of the public interest is associated with group theory. Government mediates disputes between various interests in society. The public interest is the equilibrium point between competing interests. Conflicts and compromises among groups occur as the groups compete for influence and material rewards. Public officials automatically take into consideration the power of various groups as the officials formulate and implement policy. The potential groups defend the concept of "fair play" and become active only when they believe behavior crosses a line into the unacceptable. In general, conceptions of the public interest include the views that people can check abusive power, representatives of government must act in the interests of the people, and that the average citizen is capable of making independent and wiser decisions over the long run. Each of the perspectives of public interest recognizes that the public may not be all knowing but in the end, they hold the degree of wisdom. This view is consistent with Abraham Lincoln's widely quoted saying, "It is true that you may be able to fool all of the people some of the time, you can even fool some of the people all of the time; but can't fool all of the people all of the time" (Koven 2008, p. 26).

5 Organizational Cultures and Missions

5.1 Herbert Kaufman

In his classic study of administrative behavior in the US Forest Service (USFS), Herbert Kaufman describes cohesive organizational culture (Kaufman 2006). Kaufman provides an explanation for how the US Department of Agriculture Forest Service ensured compliance from field staff despite the large size and decentralized nature of the USFS. According to Kaufman, the USFS has an organizational culture that elicits high levels of compliance. Various factors contribute to the organization's compliance and subsequent cohesiveness.

Kaufman notes that decentralization is at the core of the USFS' administrative philosophy. The organization relies upon delegation of responsibility that, in theory, could eviscerate cohesiveness since decentralization can lead to an unhealthy autonomy. Kaufman contends, however, that various techniques of integration act to overcome or at least neutralize the pressures for independent action. Among the techniques that Kaufman describes are (1) procedural devices for decisions, (2) detecting and discouraging deviation, and (3) developing the will and capacity to conform. In total, these integrating forces help to mold individual as well as group behavior.

Procedural devices refer to formal authorizations, directions, and prohibitions. An authorization permits an action by guaranteeing that others in the organization will not impose sanctions for its implementation. Direction ordinarily leads to action. Prohibitions establish penalties. Also important is the desire of organizational members to observe official requirements "on the feelings of guilt-the pangs of conscience" or "intra-psychic sanctions" that arise in members who violate norms (p. 94). In essence, members of the USFS internalize their responsibility to abide by official dictates and feel a sense of dishonor if they fail to comply.

Procedures for detecting and discouraging deviation by the official dogma reinforce proper behavior. Procedures include formal reporting and regular inspection. Most reports comprise statistical summaries of activities. Personnel submit reports routinely. Falsification of reports is not feasible because misrepresentation in one report would produce contradicts in the many other required accounts. Inspections provide opportunities to find out what is happening in the field. Inspections also train forest officers in organizationally approved methods of resource management. The atmosphere of inspection is not one of trial or competitive examination. When the work is completed and notes written up, inspectors and inspected gather socially to discuss personal and organizational affairs (p. 145).

Perhaps most essential for creating a cohesive organizational culture is what Kaufman terms developing the will and capacity to conform. Willingness to conform is an initial criterion for selection into the USFS. Those who become employees attend conferences, schools, and training camps. On-the-job training is also of great importance. In the many years that it generally takes a probationary forester to command a district, the forester is subject to close supervision. This supervision is not relaxed until the forester knows what the supervisor wants and is capable of performing the desired duties. Training focuses on the "how" of the immediate job rather than the "why" of the USFS (p. 173). Those that avail themselves of programs the agency sponsors indicate that they choose to fit themselves into the agency norms in order to advance in the organization.

The USFS conscientiously builds allegiance to the group. Kaufman states that the environment of the USFS promotes identification with the well-being of the entire organization. Employees link their own welfare with those of the agency. This "sets them apart from all people 'outside' the organization" and "binds them intimately with other organization members." The feeling of commonality with other USFS members increases the probability that each member will make decisions in accord with organizational desires. Without realizing it members of the USFS "internalize the perceptions, values, and premises of action that prevail in the bureau; unconsciously, very often they tend to act in the agency-prescribed fashion" (p. 176).

The USFS enhances identification with the organization through the use of symbols. The purpose of symbols (such as a uniform and badge) is to differentiate the wearers from everybody else. The USFS resembles a closed system that clearly inculcates its values on employees. It is a career system relatively removed from partisan politics. The merit system provides protection; the organization fills vacancies by internal promotion and transfer, rather than by lateral entry. The organization measures excellence on the job by proven predisposition to behave in the agency's desired fashion rather than by technical proficiency (p. 183).

Kaufman concludes that the cohesiveness of USFS personnel has both positive and negative implications. Cohesiveness can heighten enthusiasm and morale of personnel. These workers uniformly align against outside interests such as lumbermen seeking to cut more heavily or stockmen seeking to graze more animals. A high degree of conformity, however, also presents risks. Kaufman states that manipulation of mental images may stifle flexibility that is necessary if an organization is to survive and prosper. Individuals imbued with the spirit of an organization, indoctrinated with its values, and dedicated to its traditions are not likely to experiment or bend with the prevailing winds (p. 235).

5.2 *Charles Goodsell*

In *Mission Mystique*, Goodsell (2011) tries to explain how government agencies can install greater senses of purpose in their organizations. The culture that permeates organization as well as the sense of mission plays vital roles. Goodsell outlines his conception of a "mission mystique belief system" that endows workers with a sense of purpose, passion, commitment, and attributes that sustain the institution over time. This belief system helps to instill a common culture in the organization. The shared feelings of a cohesive culture energize the organization. The ideal culture induces enthusiasm for the purpose of the mission, reinforces employee motivation, conveys a sense of work importance, and supports a willingness to recognize agency shortcomings (p. 20).

Goodell describes organizational cultures in various federal, county, and state organizations. He describes divergences that suggest variegated personas. For example, Goodsell characterizes the culture of the US Peace Corps as anti-bureaucratic, rejecting rigid structure, lifelong careers, and narrow specialization. The culture is such that it allows everybody to do their own thing to a degree, as long as it is within the orbit of practical overseas service and collaborative. A spirit of common dedication prevails. In contrast, he characterizes the Virginia State Police as a paramilitary organization that does much to socialize newcomers. Newcomers endure many weeks of strenuous training. They reinforce their skills and socialization during retraining visits to the state headquarters. The culture embeds itself by daily comradeship in the field and supportive interaction through and beyond retirement.

The culture of the US National Weather Service revolves around the applied science of meteorology, forecasting, disseminating warnings, and weekly training. Unlike the Virginia State Police and the US National Park Service, the agency culture does not depend on social markers such as uniforms, flags, or ceremonies (p. 94). A culture of expertise and professionalism prevails.

Goodsell indirectly addresses the classic issue of whether bureaucratic forces of the modern state endanger democracy. He concludes that agency autonomy can lead to bypassing elected policymakers, but in most instances will not. The danger of such an "end run" occurring is greatest in areas where administrative actors are prone to secrecy and where coercive action comes into play. This characterizes agencies that involve themselves in police, intelligence, or national security activities. The FBI under J. Edgar Hoover from 1924 to 1972, the CIA in the George W. Bush administration, and the New York Public Authority headed by Robert Moses from the 1930s to the 1950s represent examples of individual bureaucrats or agencies bypassing elected leaders. Goodsell does not detect overt disobedience to political superiors. Rather, he claims something more subtle can emerge in the ability of agencies to dominate policy discourse based on an assumed monopoly of scientific correctness (p. 271). Goodsell surmises that America is not a dictatorship where administration is the "instrument of suppression." He sees America as a "populist republic where bureaucracy generally is scorned, checked, investigated and cut back" (p. 24).

5.3 *James Q. Wilson*

The former Harvard University Professor James Q. Wilson notes in *Bureaucracy* (1989, p. 91) that every organization has a culture or a persistent, patterned way of thinking about the central tasks of and human relationships within an organization. He parallels the culture of an organization with the personality of an individual. According to Wilson, human personality consists of traits among individuals that lead them to respond differently in similar situations. For example, when faced with aggression, some people may retreat, some fight back, and some become paralyzed with fear. Similarly, Wilson expects organizations to respond differently when faced with the same stimuli. When faced with a changing environment, some organizations persist in traditional ways while other organizations adopt new ways of behaving. Wilson views all organizations as having one or more cultures. Factors that produce these cultures include predispositions of members, the technology of the organization, and the situational imperative that confronts the organization (p. 93).

Through the discussion of concrete examples, Wilson identifies distinct organizational cultures. For example, Wilson asserts that the culture of the State Department values diplomacy above all else. This implies a prevailing climate of communication and openness. Professional diplomats dominate the culture of the State Department. The diplomat or Foreign Service officer places high value on subtlety, skill in negotiation, cultural sophistication, and good manners. In contrast, an alternative federal agency the Tennessee Valley Authority for a long time possessed an engineering culture. This organizational culture values efficient power production over regional planning and environmental protection. Other agencies also prioritize one type of behavior over others. This is a norm. The culture of many university departments rewards academic research more than classroom teaching (p. 95). The army prioritizes combat arms specializations; the air force prioritizes aviators.

Within organizations, competing cultures exist. For example, Wilson notes that the CIA has two dominant cultures. One emphasizes the analysis of intelligence and focuses on the intentions as well as capabilities of other nations. The other places emphasis on the clandestine gathering of intelligence and the conduct of covert operations. The clandestine culture dominates. According to Wilson, the US Navy has at least three organizational cultures each symbolized by the kind of shoe officers wear. The navy of battleships, cruisers, and destroyers are the "black shoe" navy. The "brown shoe" navy is the navy of aircraft carriers and carrier-based aircraft. Navy aviators wear brown shoes. The "felt shoe" navy consists of the world of submarines. Felt shoes are worn to reduce noise and defeat enemy listening devices. The three cultures of the navy are in greater balance than rivalries in other organizations. For example, Wilson claims that for many years the culture of the US Air Force most highly valued the experience of bomber pilots.

Wilson raises the core issue of this book, namely, how can government delegate and still maintain accountability. He concludes it is a mistake to foster an ethos that encourages every bureaucrat to "go by the book." Wilson also questions the other extreme of allowing zealots to engage in "mission madness," charging off to implement their private versions of some ambiguous public goal (p. 370). Wilson is sanguine in his observation that public bureaucracy in the United States is not as rational and predictable as Weber hoped it would be nor as crushing and mechanistic as Weber feared. He views bureaucracy as "rule-bound without being overpowering, participatory without being corrupt." He concludes, "Our constitutional system, and above all the exceptional power enjoyed by the legislative branch, makes it impossible for us to have anything like a government by appointed experts but easy for individual citizens to obtain redress from the abuses of power" (p. 378). As shown in the previous chapter, many theorists are not as positive as is James Q. Wilson regarding the ability of the US political system to control the actions of bureaucrats and their organizations.

6 Controlling Bureaucracies

6.1 Judith Gruber

Gruber (1987, p. 5) contends that controlling bureaucracies takes on special meaning in democracies because unaccountable power is antithetical to democratic norms. Gruber outlines five broad approaches to controlling bureaucracies. These approaches include (1) control through participation, (2) control through client relations, (3) control through pursuit of the public interest, (4) control through accountability, and (5) self-control. Each approach implies a different perspective on the reason and method to control bureaucracy.

According to the participatory approach, the problem with public bureaucracies is that they are isolated from the public. They are closed and relatively unaccountable. In order to counter this problem, advocates of this approach seek procedural changes such as greater community participation. Prescribed changes focus on increasing direct citizen involvement. Advocates believe procedural changes will produce changes in the nature of policy. Substantive change in policy, however, is not the primary focus; the essence of the approach is in soliciting greater input from the citizenry.

In contrast, the clientele relations approach is more concerned with the nature of decisions. Under this perspective, public agencies are undemocratic because their decisions inadequately serve the needs of citizens. In order to counter this problem, administrators should consult representatives of the groups most affected by government decisions. This consultation can occur through advisory groups or panels. The client relations approach does not value involvement for its own sake (as does the participatory approach) but seeks agency-citizen contacts to transmit information about the needs of client groups.

In what Gruber terms the public-interest approach, one assumes that the decisions of bureaucrats serve the collective interest; they do not simply serve the interests of narrow interest groups. This perspective holds that it is desirable to extend the reach of elected officials into bureaucracies. Bureaucrats must be responsive to the initiatives of elected officials.

The accountability approach assumes that bureaucracies threaten democracy when they abuse their power by acting corruptly, inefficiently, or unfairly. This approach assumes safeguards on bureaucrats will minimize abuses. Safeguards include means of oversight such as freedom of information, ombudsmen, and oversight boards. Codes of ethics, civil service systems, and hearings represent other means of ensuring accountability. The primary focus of this approach is with the process of decision making with only peripheral concern for the content of the decisions.

The self-control approach assumes that democratic control lies primarily with the administrators themselves. This approach does not rely upon strong external controls but on more of an "inner check" on behavior. Control emerges from a process in which bureaucrats interpret the limits of behavior the public will tolerate and then act within those limits. Proponents of the self-control approach posit that often bureaucrats alone are in the best position to determine how to serve the public. Professionalism of bureaucrats, their sense of personal fulfillment, or their background protects democracy.

Gruber recognizes that people differ in their perspectives of how bureaucrats should behave. She proposes four idealized perspectives of bureaucratic behavior. The bureaucrat as "autonomous actor" may be competent but a problem with democratic exists in that actions of the bureaucrat result from his or her choice, not the choice of citizens. The bureaucrat as "end achiever" views his or her role as that of securing specific goals using whatever procedures are necessary to reach the goal. The "clerk" has little or no discretion. All actions flow directly from democratically made legislative decisions. Finally, the "procedure follower" focuses on the importance of due process to the exclusion of other concerns (p. 17).

Gruber asserts that controlling bureaucracy should improve the democratic quality of government. From the perspective of democratic theory, bringing bureaucratic power under the control of the people is highly desirable. Controlling bureaucrats, however, has costs. It may result in declining effectiveness in one of two ways. First, those who control the bureaucrat may unknowingly direct them to behave in a way that will not achieve desired goals. For example, elected school board officials may impose curriculum that is not effective for teaching children. Second, elected officials may impose unduly restrictive constraints. This prevents bureaucrats from doing their jobs successfully. For example, tight restrictions on extra homework assignments may harm high-achieving students of the ability to reach their full potential. Difficulty in enforcing the rules promulgated by elected officials represents another problem. Gruber notes that telling a bureaucrat to behave in a certain way does not guarantee compliance (p. 63). To assure compliance monitoring is necessary. If bureaucrats become deceitful, monitoring costs increase. If controllers punish bureaucrats for factors beyond their control (such as failing to have all their students read at grade level) then bureaucrats may become demoralized and seek other employment. Bureaucrats can also distort their behavior to conform to narrow standards (teach to the test), neglect other responsibilities, or artificially achieve the standard. Controls on bureaucrats become costly when bureaucrats become demoralized, distort behavior, neglect their responsibilities, or quit (p. 68).

Gruber concludes that democratic control of bureaucrats has many faces and there are many ways to reconcile bureaucracy with democracy. Would-be controllers must decide how to exercise control, what values to pursue, and what costs to tolerate. They must make choices in the context of different policy arenas. Gruber notes that those who would enact controls on bureaucrats must come to grips with how capable they think citizens are in governing themselves.

Gruber recognizes that while elected officials have the legal power to constrain behavior of others, bureaucrats possess critical resources. These resources include responsibility for day-to-day decisions, information about the affairs of their agency, and expertise (p. 202). Citizens need the expertise and undivided attention of career workers to conduct the business of government. Bureaucrats are in a privileged position to know what is going on in their agencies. In contrast, democratic controllers may be unable to determine accurately what kinds of constraints on behavior will produce desired ends. Gruber opts for a model of "exchange" as a method for control of bureaucracies. She rejects the traditional conceptions of control based in an authority relationship where bureaucrats are subservient to elected leaders. In Gruber's model, "control results not from political actors telling bureaucrats what to do but from constructing conditions in which bureaucratic behavior is constrained in exchange for resources bureaucrats seek. Such control emanates from a process of interaction, not from one of orders from above" (p. 211). In this exchange model, control is mutually determined.

6.2 *Kenneth Meier and Lawrence O'Toole*

Meier and O'Toole (2006, p. 2) declare that one of the most persistent challenges of modern government is how to reconcile democracy with bureaucracy. A recurring issue of public bureaucracies is to determine how to use its expertise and judgment in determining the political outcomes of who gets what, when, and how. Bureaucrats are unelected and insulated decision makers, yet they make decisions that have political consequence. Meier and O'Toole conclude that excising discretion from bureaucrats is impossible. Because of this discretionary power, bureaucracy poses a threat to democracy. The authors reject both "top-down" and "bottom-up" democratic ideas as a satisfactory picture of how to control bureaucrats. They view the top-down model as incomplete. This model focuses on coercion and socialization as tools of control. Socialization inculcates bureaucrats with the agency mission, emphasizing responsiveness to political authority, and socializing into the mores of democracy. The authors also view the bottom-up model as incomplete with its focus on checking the bureaucracy through direct popular oversight such as citizens' review boards monitoring police departments or by institutional arrangements that incorporate incentives for bureaucrats to pay attention to popular preferences. Meier and O'Toole address the bureaucracy-democracy debate through empirical analysis of bureaucratic responsiveness to external political and internal street-level actors.

The authors note that the ability of political actors to control bureaucratic agencies is limited because programs imbed in networks of public, private, and nonprofit organizations. No single unit has the clear ability to coerce others into taking a given action (p. 67). Political institutions have trouble controlling widespread networks. They can monitor activities but monitoring without the ability to take corrective action is of limited value.

Empirical investigations of school districts in the state of Texas reveal that bureaucratic actors in schools possess extensive powers. School districts vest a great deal of discretionary power in their teachers who function as street-level bureaucrats. Teachers may adopt different pedagogical techniques and teacher influences can spread throughout the school system as colleagues adopt their practices. Teachers might also be able to influence education by providing special support and encouragement for at-risk students.

Teachers can advocate changes in school policy such as more open recruitment into advanced placement classes as the case of Jaime Escalante, who taught mathematics at Garfield High School in East Los Angeles. The 1988 movie *Stand and Deliver* immortalized Escalante's efforts to motivate low-income Latino students through a combination of "pricks and prods." Escalante mixed stringent discipline with humor and affectionate banter to spur math achievement on Advanced Placement exams (Koven 2015, p. 170). Meier and O'Toole's empirical analysis finds that the influence of street-level bureaucrats (Latino teachers) had more impact on performance than the influence of Latino school board officials. The authors concluded that actions of street-level bureaucrats such as classroom teachers should receive greater attention in studies that look at the implications of discretion.

Meier and O'Toole conclude that control of individual bureaucracies is difficult because these organizations act consistently with their own values rather than by direction from electoral institutions. To assume that organizations with discretion, policy preferences, expertise, and lengthy timeframes (e.g. bureaucracies) do not act strategically is not realistic. Analysis of Texas schools that faced demands for improved performance (higher scores on a standardized exam) shows that they engaged in "shirking" and "cheating" as strategies (Meier and O'Toole 2006, p. 96). The concept of "shirking" reveals the enormous power of organizations to achieve ostensibly positive results by abiding by letter of directives but ignoring the larger spirit of their mission.

When confronting pressures by political superiors bureaucratic organizations can choose from a range of options from outright defiance to enthusiastic compliance. Bureaucracies are often interested in responding enough to keep the principal (outside overseer) happy but not so much as to jeopardize their other activities. An example of a subtle form of shirking is for a doctor to treat a patient's symptoms rather than the disease itself. The doctor uses the patient's lack of technical understanding to his or her advantage by making the patient feel better in the short run. The doctor, however, does not address the long-term illness. The pain pill that cancer patients may receive can alleviate the discomfort but not cure the cancer. Bureaucracies can present an appearance of success by identifying what indicators political overseers use to assess behavior. Bureaucracies then focus their attention on the measurable indicators to the exclusion of others. They can use their discretionary power to "game the system" to their benefit.

Public organizations such as school systems might generate positive "numbers" but still fail to address underlying problems. Meier and O'Toole (p. 97) state that a rational organization can do this in one of two ways: (1) continue to operate as in the past but make an effort to improve overall levels of performance and (2) strategically manipulate the output measure. The authors term this strategic manipulation of outputs as "cheating."

Cheating is one form of shirking. Bureaucracies can cheat by determining what indicators political institutions use to judge performance and use the lack of technical understanding of others to their advantage.

Organizations can choose from three options in shirking. These options are lying, cutting corners, and generating biased samples. Lying is relatively simple; the organization simply reports numbers that make it look good such as the use of body counts during the US war in Vietnam. An example of lying in a more recent period is the false reporting of the number of tanks destroyed by the US Air Force in Kosovo between 1998 and 1999. In the international context, Soviet bureaucracy has a reputation for making up numbers to meet announced plans (p. 98). Lying is a high-risk strategy that exposes a bureaucratic unit to increased controls from electoral overseers, more intrusive monitoring, and reduced discretion on decisions where bureaucratic values previously have been influential.

Cutting corners occurs when resources produce more outputs of lower quality. An example of cutting corners is for an Occupational Safety and Health Administration inspector to reduce time spent on an individual site visit but make more site visits. Similarly, law enforcement agencies might generate a large number of arrests for trivial violations and ignore serious offenses. Cutting corners gives the appearance of greater productivity without a more holistic assessment of outputs. Sampling bias occurs when bureaucrats purposely select the cases that generate the most positive results. For example, an employment agency might focus their efforts on individuals with the most job skills or a school district might try to test only students with a high likelihood to achieve high scores.

Cheating can be a rational decision of any organization. Meier and O'Toole state, "The decision to cheat rather than comply with the spirits of the principal's demand is not different from any other decision. An organization cheats because the perceived utility of cheating is greater than the perceived utility of not cheating. In some cases this is a management decision and thus establishes a policy" (p. 100). The empirical research of Meier and O'Toole indicates that Texas school districts that use their discretion to exempt students from the statewide mandatory exam (Texas Assessment of Academic Skills) could improve their overall pass rates. Such a strategy could move school district scores from mediocre to better-than-expected performance (p. 106). For school districts with large numbers of minority and low-income students increasing the number of students exempt from testing can result in significant increases in average test scores. The payoff for exempting low-performing students therefore generates an incentive for districts to select out students that are likely to fail the standardized test. The authors conclude that Texas educators are not "rogue agents" but use deliberate decisions to shape outcomes that serve their interests. The decision to limit the number of test takers improves their standing on one metric (standardized test) that political masters and the broad public monitor closely. The goal of a high or adequate education, however, may suffer from undue attention to such "gaming" of the system. Higher scores on standardized tests may poorly assess the overall quality of teaching, especially when teachers purposely use their discretionary power to increase scores.

Based on their research, Meier and O'Toole reach a number of conclusions with respect to the relationship between bureaucracy and democracy. First, they note that classical bureaucracy does not characterize many of the settings of modern governance. Frequent use of networks creates serious problems for democratic controls. Democratic controls rely on a hierarchical chain of command that does not exist in networks. Networks call into question the very notion of bureaucracies controlling the implementation of public policy since a dozen or more organizations of varying type may involve themselves on behalf of a public program. Second, the authors conclude that bureaucratic values are frequently more important than the values of political overseers in driving the results of public policy. They claim that this does not necessarily mean a weakening of democratic governance since the bureaucracy can also perform representative functions. Third is the conclusion that the bureaucracy can exert influence over policy outcomes in significant ways that are unintended by political leaders. Under this perspective, the bureaucracy is capable of acting on behalf of its own agenda and values rather than the preferences of political leaders or the broader public.

The third conclusion of bureaucrats acting as independent agents is perhaps the most damaging in terms of its lack of democratic accountability. The authors observe that existing perspectives on the bureaucracy-democracy debate are limited. They conclude that public administration plays a central role in democratic governance. At the same time, the literature on political control of the bureaucracy reiterates skepticism toward the view that "any bureaucracy, no matter how benign its values or how farsighted its administrative leadership, can substitute for appropriately broad and general direction from political levels" (p. 153).

7 Conclusions

The literature on bureaucratic controls, for the most part, suggests that through their discretion, access to information, and aura of expertise, bureaucrats can exert significant influence on public policy. This is a concern to democratic theorists who fear the rise of an unaccountable cabal of experts. The cultures and missions of organizations intervene and provide direction to public organizations; however, they do not guarantee responsiveness to public sentiment. Numerous examples of government organizations acting contrary to the accepted values of citizens intimate that bureaucracy and democracy may continue to operate on separate tracks. How to bring bureaucratic actors within the orbit of their so-called political superiors remains an issue of great concern. Various authors not only describe how bureaucrats can "end run" public accountability but also offer suggestions for remedial action.

References

Bart, C. K. (1997, November–December). Sex, lies, and mission statements. *Business Horizons*, pp. 9–18.

Cooper, T. L. (1998). *The responsible administrator* (4th ed.). San Francisco: Jossey-Bass.

Finer, H. (1936). Better government personnel. *Political Science Quarterly, 51*(4), 569–599.

Finer, H. (1941). Administrative responsibility in democratic government. *Public Administration Review, 1*(4), 335–350.

Friedrich, C. J. (1935). *Problems of the American public service.* New York: McGraw-Hill.

Friedrich, C. J. (1940 [1972]). Public policy and the nature of administrative responsibility. In F. Rourke (Ed.), *Bureaucratic power in national politics* (2nd ed.). Boston: Little, Brown.

Garrett, R. S., Thurber, A., Fritschler, A., & Rosenbloom, D. (2006). Assessing the impact of bureaucracy bashing by electoral campaigns. *Public Administration Review, 66*(2), 228–240.

Gaus, J. M. (1936). The responsibility of public administrators. In J. M. Gaus, I. D. White, & M. Dimock (Eds.), *The frontiers of public administration* (pp. 26–44). Chicago: University of Chicago Press.

Goodsell, C. T. (2011). *Mission mystique: Belief systems in public agencies.* Washington, DC: CQ Press.

Gruber, J. E. (1987). *Controlling bureaucracies.* Berkeley: University of California Press.

Halperin, M., Clapp, P., & Kanter, A. (2006). *Bureaucratic politics and foreign policy* (2nd ed.). Washington, DC: Brookings Institute.

Jackson, M. (2009). Responsibility versus accountability in the Friedrich-Finer debate. *Journal of Management History, 15*(1), 66–77.

Kaufman, H. (2006). *The forest ranger: A study in administrative behavior* (Special reprint ed.). Washington, DC: Resources for the Future.

Koven, S. G. (2008). *Responsible governance: A case study approach*. Armonk: M.E. Sharpe.

Koven, S. G. (2015). *Public sector ethics: Theory and applications*. Boca Raton: CRC Press.

Lowi, T. (1969). *The end of liberalism*. New York: W.W. Norton.

Mark, M. (2015, November 6). Amid Kim Davis backlash, Kentucky Gov.-Elect Matt Bevin to remove clerks' names from state marriage licenses. *International Business Times*. Retrieved May 21, 2018, from http://www.ibtimes.com/

McCoy, A. W. (2006). *A question of torture: CIA interrogation, from the cold war to the war on terror*. New York: Henry Holt.

Meier, K. (1993). *Politics and the bureaucracy* (3rd ed.). Belmont: Wadsworth Publishing Company.

Meier, K., & O'Toole, L. (2006). *Bureaucracy in a democratic state*. Baltimore: The Johns Hopkins University Press.

Pfiffner, J. P. (2001). Presidential appointments: Recruiting executive branch leaders. In G. C. Mackenzie (Ed.), *Innocent until nominated: The breakdown of the presidential appointments process* (pp. 50–80). Washington, DC: Brookings Institute.

Pfiffner, J. P. (2013). The paradox of President Reagan's leadership. *Presidential Studies Quarterly, 43*(1), 81–100.

Schein, E. (2004). *Organizational culture and leadership* (3rd ed.). San Francisco: Jossey-Bass.

Schubert, G. (1960). *The public interest*. Glencoe: Free Press.

Thompson, V. (1975). *Without sympathy or enthusiasm: The problem of administrative compassion*. Tuscaloosa: University of Alabama Press.

United States Department of State. (n.d.). *The oversight powers of Congress*. Retrieved May 28, 2018, from http://countrystudies.us/united-states/government-14.htm

Weisman, S. (1983, October 10). Watt quits post; President accepts with 'reluctance.' *New York Times*, p. A1.

Wilson, J. Q. (1989). *Bureaucracy*. New York: Basic Books.

PART II

Application

CHAPTER 4

Discretion and Local Policy: Local Law Enforcement

1 Introduction

How much discretion to give to street-level law enforcement agents represents a quandary for democratically elected leaders and law enforcement administrators. In accord with principles of democracy, police should apply the law equally without regard to class, race, religion, gender, or sexual orientation. Representatives of the government should afford similar protection and similar treatment to all. This mandate is especially critical for the field of law enforcement where police historically have not treated all with equal restraint and forbearance. Police action has led many to question police behavior and become more suspicious of their legitimacy. For some residents, law enforcement agents do not represent protectors against criminal elements in society. They represent the antithesis of protectors; they represent agents of an oppressive state; therefore agents to fear. Discretion is associated with random acts of police violence. Citizens viewing police beatings and shootings on video come to distrust the entire law enforcement community. Videos raise "red flags" in the minds of a normally apathetic public that may not have negative experiences with police.

Citizens wonder whether particular segments of the population receive different treatment than others. They ask whether police follow protocol or run amok without clear direction. Various questions are highly relevant to the issue of whether discretion is synonymous with abuse. One asks, are violations of official protocol rampant or anomalous? Does the protocol itself abuse certain segments of the population? Are police departments

S. G. Koven, *The Case Against Bureaucratic Discretion*,
https://doi.org/10.1007/978-3-030-05779-4_4

willing to correct abusive behavior or is such behavior integral to the organization? Can outside authorities (external check) limit abusive actions of police? Is greater adherence to standards of professionalism (internal check) more effective in reducing abuse than the external check? Do local police departments possess too much independence from oversight by other bodies? Are certain segments of the population entirely justified in their fear and animus toward local law enforcement officials?

This chapter revisits the behavior of local law enforcement representatives and reveals numerous truisms. First, it is evident that those in positions of authority can abuse their authority. Second, the dominant culture of organizations can shape attitudes toward abuse. Third, there exists a range of latitude within organizations regarding permissible and impermissible behavior. Fourth, new mobile devices have the potential to create greater accountability. Fifth, media attention and public awareness can produce corrective action in police departments. Sixth, external overseers, internal cues, or a combination of the two can lead to more accountability.

This chapter reviews the history of abusive behavior in local police departments. Contemporary actions of law enforcement officials are examined in detail. These include incidents in Sanford, Florida; Ferguson, Missouri; Baltimore, Maryland; Chicago, Illinois; North Charleston, South Carolina; and New York City. The chapter concludes with a discussion of possible checks on law enforcement abuses.

2 History of Law Enforcement Abuse

Abuse of authority by law enforcement agents is as old as history. At times, locally elected leaders officially encourage abusive behavior. At other times, abusive behavior seems to emanate from the organization. Discretion afforded to law enforcement authorities increases the prospects that organizational superiors will ignore abusive behavior. Colleagues may hide improper actions from public view by a "wall of silence," an unwillingness to denigrate the organization, fear of retaliation by other officers, apathy, or a sense of solidarity with the group. With the proliferation of devices capable of recording misconduct, however, it is more difficult to escape public scrutiny.

Abuse by law enforcement authorities takes at least two forms: (1) abuse that officials in the bureaucratic hierarchy unambiguously approve and direct and (2) abuse that is a result of unsanctioned "rogue" actions of street-level bureaucrats. The line between sanctioned and unsanctioned abuse, however, is not always clear. For example, there are cases of police brutality that is approved by higher-ranking officials. Violence directed at civil rights or antiwar protestors represents actions ratified by officials in the law enforcement hierarchy. It is less clear whether other abuses actually receive approval. A fuzzy area exists between the clearly approved and clearly disapproved forms of police abuse. For example, top officials may encourage "harsh treatment" of suspects but do not establish a clear protocol for interactions. They may continuously look the other way when abuses occur but do not give direct orders. In these instances, high-level officials may give subtle or not-so-subtle signals that direct street-level behavior.

Police abuse can take many forms. Carter and Barker (1991, p. 17) state that officials can never eliminate police discretion; however, written directives in the form of policies and procedures set guidelines. Written directives inform officers of expected standards of behavior, provide grounds for discipline of errant officers, and provide standards for supervision. Despite written directives, officer misconduct occurs. This misconduct can take forms such as malfeasance, misfeasance, and nonfeasance. Officer malfeasance refers to intentional commission of an act that a law or directive prohibits. Misfeasance refers to the performance of a duty that one is obligated to do in a manner that is improper or negligent. Improper completion of reports, improper searches, unsafe operation of a police vehicle, and aggressively reprimanding a citizen for a traffic violation are illustrations of misfeasance. Finally, nonfeasance refers to the failure to perform an act that one is obligated to do by law or organizational directive. An example of nonfeasance is a failure to complete a report about theft because of the perception that it will be difficult to apprehend the perpetrators (p. 24). Abuses range widely in severity and include disregard of civil rights. In some cases, police action can result in law enforcement agents acting as prosecutor, judge, jury, and executioner. Police may ignore due process in the name of swift justice. A historical review of police abuses is instructive in assessing current behavior.

2.1 Pre-1960s Abuse

Champion (2001, pp. 4, 14) notes that police misconduct continues to be pervasive in US society. Cases of egregious brutality are too numerous to comprehensively catalogue. However, a review of some of the more notorious examples illustrates actions in various places of a given time period. Many of the major metropolitan areas of the nation were hotbeds of official corruption in the early twentieth century. Koven and Koven (2018, p. 90) note that at the turn of the twentieth century, the Minneapolis Police Department (under the direction of Mayor Albert Ames and his brother Police Commissioner Fred Ames) became a collection agency for various forms of graft. Gambling went on openly, opium dens and unlicensed saloons flourished, and prostitutes paid protection money to agents of the Ames brothers. Mayor Ames held four nonconsecutive terms from 1876 until the day he resigned in 1902. The "muckraker" journalist Lincoln Steffens castigated Ames; historians note that Ames spent little time behind his desk and long hours with his foot on the bar rail of a popular drinking establishment.

Periodically reformers exposed wrongdoing in law enforcement. In his 1945 campaign for mayor of Minneapolis, future Vice President Hubert Humphrey actively opposed corruption in the city. Humphrey railed against the prostitution, gambling, liquor sales to minors, and after-hours establishments that prevailed in violation of the law. Humphrey claimed that gangsters from Chicago would take over the city if law-abiding citizens did not take a stand against them. Upon election, Humphrey appointed a police commissioner widely thought to be free of corruption, increased the size of the police force, and increased salaries for police officers.

New York City's police have often been associated with acts of brutality. Johnson (2003, p. 19) reports that between 1865 and 1894 the *New York Times* reported more than 270 cases of alleged police brutality. The most common form of police violence during this time was what the press referred to as "clubbing" or the bludgeoning of a suspect with a baton or nightstick. The majority of clubbing cases occurred between a uniformed officer and single unarmed suspect. Injuries and deaths from these beatings were common. Police often used their clubs when suspects posed a challenge to their authority. For working-class residents, winning a case of brutality against a police officer was incredibly difficult; bringing a case up against an officer was risky. In the late nineteenth century, labor groups in New York City viewed police abuse as a by-product of a morally and politically corrupt police system. Labor union officials depicted the police chief as a tool of capitalists and political thieves. Fearful of radical groups, the *Times* and other newspapers generally condoned clubbing of strikers and protesting workers. The *Times* portrayed protesting workers as either drunken rioters or violent agitators (p. 35).

Some forms of police abuse became pervasive in the 1920s. The "third degree" describes a controversial tactic for fighting crime that includes physical violence, torture, prolonged interrogation, food and sleep deprivation, and psychological coercion. Among the tactics of the third degree was the "sweat box" or a superheated jail cell adjacent to a furnace. The intent of this tactic was to "sweat" confessions from uncooperative suspects (p. 122). Vocal criticism of the third degree intensified in 1929 when President Herbert Hoover established the National Commission on Law Observance and Enforcement, also known as the Wickersham Commission. This body issued 14 reports including a devastating critique of police brutality and the "third degree." The Wickersham Commission found that police use of the third degree was both widespread and common.

The Commission concluded that the "third degree" represented unacceptable behavior. They emphasize that the control of the social order must occur within the constitutional and legal framework that the Founding Fathers and legislative bodies established. The Commission identified four specific troubles with the third degree: (1) the danger of false confessions; (2) impairing police efficiency; (3) impairing the efficiency of justice in the courts; and (4) brutalization of the police, hardening prisoners against society, and lowering the esteem held by the public (Palmiotto 2017b, p. 9). The Wickersham Commission noted that third degree not only was unconstitutional but also promoted a negative image of the police. The third-degree methods produced injuries ranging from black eyes to broken limbs. Police most frequently relied on punching and kicking. The Commission condemned police use of rubber hoses and blackjacks. These weapons rarely left marks when soaked in water to reduce the likelihood of abrasions. Other methods of abuse that the Wickersham Commission denounced include choking with a necktie, dragging by the hair, squeezing the testicles, and hanging a suspect from an upper-story window (Johnson 2003, p. 134). Unsurprisingly, the Commission stated that "third-degree" tactics were most likely to be used against the poor and uninfluential. The more affluent suspects were less likely to be detained and more likely to have access to an attorney. In some cases, vengeance was a strong motive in arrests. Police at times beat suspects of heinous crimes.

Police generally opposed efforts to curtail their discretionary use of force. Interviews of the Wickersham Commission revealed that police feared that any effort to limit clubbing of suspects would lead to increases in crime. Retired police officers contended that police need every means necessary to control criminals. However, the Wickersham Commission

Report was highly critical of "third-degree" interrogations. The report noted that use of third-degree tactics was counterproductive since the tactic could inspire vengeance and could turn a boy bandit into a gunman and cop killer. Reformers cited a 1922 case when a 19-year-old suspect reportedly became so fearful of the beating he would receive that he pulled a gun on the steps of the station house and killed two arresting detectives (p. 140). In this case, law enforcement reformers argued that the thought of police violence helped create the hardened criminals they were supposed to suppress.

Chicago police were infamous for third-degree tactics; however, crime in the city remained rampant. The federal courts shed light on both widespread police abuse and efforts to curtail use of third-degree tactics. In the 1936 Supreme Court decision of *Brown v. Mississippi*, the court excluded the confessions of three black murder suspects who Mississippi police had tortured. Police admitted to whipping the defendants and stringing up one of them on a rope to force a confession. The Mississippi Supreme Court condoned the police action. In ruling the confessions inadmissible, the Supreme Court extended due process protections of the Fourteenth Amendment to state and local cases (p. 147).

Race became a focus of police abuse in the 1940s and 1950s. Johnson (2003, p. 193) reports that throughout World War II, the black press ran regular stories of the mistreatment of black soldiers on southern bases and surrounding communities. Johnson notes that in 1942–1943 alone, white military and civilian police killed young black soldiers stationed in Virginia, Louisiana, Texas, Arkansas, Alabama, and South Carolina. Northern blacks stationed at Camp Stewart, Georgia, who ventured into nearby Savannah were subject to harassments and beatings by white police and business owners (p. 193). Black distrust of police precipitated riots in Detroit in 1943. Prior to the US Army restoring order, 34 people died and 433 people were injured. The riot represented the worst civil unrest in the United States since the New York City draft riots of 1863 (Koven and Koven 2018, p. 34). The National Association for the Advancement of Colored People (NAACP) lawyer and future Supreme Court Justice Thurgood Marshall wrote that police clubbed and shot at black looters and bystanders while they took little action in white neighborhoods. In New York, the pastor of Harlem's Abyssinian Baptist Church (one of the city's most influential African-American churches), Adam Clayton Powell, drew parallels between black citizens killed by Detroit police and the victims of the New York City Police Department (NYPD) (Johnson 2003,

p. 198). In 1943, riots erupted in Harlem resulting in six deaths and 185 injuries. The 1943 Harlem riot began after rumors surfaced of a white cop killing a black soldier (p. 199).

Tensions between police and African-American residents continued unabated. In campaigns of 1948 and 1949, New York branches of the NAACP identified police brutality as their top priority. The Manhattan NAACP branch announced the formation of a Committee for Action Against Police Brutality which would receive, investigate, and act on brutality complaints. NCAA leaders, however, recognized the difficulty of indicting police officers despite the many instances of problematic action. New York administrators dismissed anti-police activism as a Communist plot. In the late 1940s, the leader of the Brooklyn branch of the NAACP declared that it was harder to secure an indictment against police officers who have victimized Negro citizens in Kings County (Brooklyn) than it is in some of the most lynch-ridden places of the South (p. 215).

2.2 *Post-1960s Abuse*

Riots in major cities and political activism characterized the 1960s. Early 1960s civil rights clashes in Birmingham and Selma, Alabama, are indicative of approved police responses to perceived threats to their authority. Other high-profile events further polarized citizens and stoked distrust of police. In recent years, specific high-profile instances of police brutality captivated the attention of the mass media and in some instances became the catalysts for widespread destruction.

2.2.1 Civil Rights Protests

Violent clashes in Birmingham and Selma, Alabama, between police and civil rights protestors intensified awareness of police mistreatment. The Birmingham campaign, or Birmingham movement, was a movement organized in early 1963 by the Southern Christian Leadership Conference (SCLC) to bring attention to the integration efforts of African Americans in Birmingham, Alabama. Civil rights leaders developed a plan to desegregate Birmingham, a city notorious for discrimination. The goal of the plan was to use tactics of nonviolent protest to pressure Birmingham civic and business leaders to desegregate. The demonstrations started in April 1963 as Dr. Martin Luther King Jr., Reverend Ralph Abernathy, and local leader Reverend Fred Shuttlesworth led thousands of African-American protestors in Birmingham. The first phase of the campaign resulted in many arrests, including the arrest of Martin Luther King. A circuit court judge had issued an injunction against protest, picketing, demonstrating, and boycotting. This injunction provided the legal grounds for the arrests.

As the campaign continued, SCLC leader James Bevel created plans for a "Children's Crusade." The SCLC trained thousands of children in the tactics of nonviolence and the children marched throughout the city. Police confronted the marchers; on the first day of the protest, police arrested hundreds of children. On the second day, Commissioner of Public Safety Bull Connor ordered police to spray the children with powerful water hoses, hit them with batons, and threaten them with police dogs. Footage and photographs of the violent crackdown in Birmingham circulated throughout the nation and the world, causing an outcry.

The Birmingham campaign produced some of the most iconic and troubling images of the civil rights movement. Fire hoses were set at a level that would peel bark off a tree or separate bricks from mortar. The force of the water pushed young women over the tops of cars; when young students crouched or fell, the blasts of water rolled them down the asphalt streets and concrete sidewalks. While leading a group of child marchers, injuries from the water hoses sent the Reverend Fred Shuttlesworth to the hospital. National media broadcast the events on national television. The 1963 campaign was not an isolated incident. Two years earlier, in 1961, Commissioner of Public Safety Connor reportedly held police back for 15 minutes as a bus of Freedom Riders arrived in Birmingham. A large mob of white Klansmen attacked the Freedom Riders as they attempted to get service at the all-white lunch counter.

The police clash at Selma, Alabama, occurred on March 7, 1965, when around 600 people crossed the Edmund Pettus Bridge to begin a march from Selma to Montgomery. Sheriff's deputies and state troopers attacked the demonstrators as they left Selma. Television crews recorded the incident and brought it into the living rooms of millions of American homes. Previous demonstrations in Selma and surrounding communities resulted in the arrests of thousands. Two days prior to the March 7, "Bloody Sunday" incident, in a nearby town, state troopers clubbed protestors and fatally shot a 26-year-old African-American demonstrator trying to protect his mother, who was being struck by police. In response, civil rights leaders planned to confront Alabama Governor George Wallace on a 54-mile march from Selma to the state capital of Montgomery. Wallace ordered state troopers to use whatever measures were necessary to prevent a march (Klein 2015). At the head of the march was the representative of the

SCLC Hosea Williams and future member of Congress from Georgia, John Lewis.

On "Bloody Sunday," demonstrators marched across the Edmund Pettus Bridge that led out of Selma. At the end of the bridge, the demonstrators encountered a force of sheriff's deputies, deputized "possemen," and dozens of state troopers. Law enforcement agents informed the marchers that they had two minutes to disperse and moments later state troopers advanced. A melee followed, law enforcement authorities spat upon marchers, overran them by horses, and attacked them with clubs and bullwhips. More than 50 marchers, including John Lewis, were hospitalized (Wallenfeld 2018).

2.2.2 *Police Provocation and Urban Riots*

Actions of the police led directly to numerous riots in large US cities. The Harlem riot of 1964 followed a shooting of a high school student by an off-duty police lieutenant. The shooting and killing of the 15-year-old student occurred after a newly created summer school program brought minority students in close proximity to affluent Upper East Side of Manhattan residents. Accounts of the shooting vary. Apparently, in an effort to disperse minority students the superintendent of an apartment complex across from the school began to spray students with a garden hose. Students then pelted the superintendent with soda bottles and garbage cans. One student pursued the superintendent into the building. An off-duty officer emerged from a nearby store and ordered the youth to halt. Some witnesses (mainly white adults) claimed that the youth had a knife and lunged at the officer. Others (mainly black teens) claimed that they did not see a knife and the student did not advance on the officer. The officer killed the student.

Within hours of the shooting at the Upper East Side, the organizations NAACP and the Congress of Racial Equality (CORE) began organizing protests. At the conclusion of one of the protests, the crowd descended upon the local police station. Scuffles broke out with police using batons and protestors hurling bottles. Violence ensued for six days and spread to large areas of Manhattan and Brooklyn. Rioters started fires, looted stores, fought with police, and assaulted white reporters and motorists. The riot resulted in 465 arrests, 1 death, and more than 100 injuries. CORE and the NAACP criticized the aggressiveness of the city's emergency unit that put down the riot (Johnson 2003, p. 236).

Other riots followed, most notably in Los Angeles, Detroit, and Newark. The Watts riots took place in the Watts neighborhood of Los

Angeles from August 11 to 16, 1965. The immediate cause of the disturbances was the arrest of an African-American man by a white California Highway Patrol officer on suspicion of driving while intoxicated. An argument broke out and then escalated into a fight with police. Rumors spread that the police had hurt a pregnant woman; angry mobs formed and six days of looting and arson followed. The riots resulted in 34 deaths and over $40 million in property damage. The riot engulfed a 46-square-mile swath of Los Angeles.

At the height of the riot, there were 16,000 law enforcement personnel patrolling the city. Signs in the riot area threatened residents with the use of deadly force. Law enforcement or National Guard shootings accounted for 23 of the 34 deaths. Rioters tore up sidewalks and bricks to hurl at Guardsmen and police, and to smash police vehicles. Those participating in the riots started fights with police, blocked Los Angeles Fire Department personnel from their duties, or stopped and beat white motorists entering the area. To quell the riots, the Los Angeles chief of police initiated a policy of mass arrest. Hundreds of buildings and whole city blocks burned to the ground. Firefighters were unable to work, because police could not protect them from the rioters (Edy 2018).

Detroit's 1967 riot resulted in 43 dead, 467 injured, 7231 arrested, and $80 million in property damage. A total of 17,460 police and soldiers were involved in suppressing the riot (Koven and Koven 2018, p. 34). The 1967 riots erupted when on July 23, 1967, Detroit Police Department officers raided an unlicensed weekend drinking club and found 82 revelers celebrating the return of two local soldiers from Vietnam. The police arrested everyone present. While the police were arranging for transportation, a sizable crowd of onlookers gathered on the street. Taunts and slurs eventually turned to rock throwing; looting and arson followed. The scale of the riot was the worst in the United States since the 1863 New York City draft riots; in terms of death and devastation, only the 1992 Los Angeles riot surpassed it. Unlike the 1943 Detroit riots, during 1967 there was little interracial violence among citizens. Most of the violence transpired between black citizens and local police or National Guard forces (Galster 2012, p. 184).

Hostile attitudes toward police contributed to the volatile environment of Detroit. Galster (2012, p. 207) notes it is easy to appreciate how many black Detroiters saw the police as an occupying army. In 1967, over a third of the city's population but only 5 percent of the police officers were black. Police brutality and racial profiling were ordinary occurrences in

Detroit's African-American neighborhoods. Police subjected residents to unwarranted searches, harassment, and excessive use of force. Police engaged in well-publicized shootings and beatings of African Americans in the years preceding the riot (Emeka 2018).

The Newark, New Jersey, riots of 1967 arose after an incident where two Newark police officers arrested and beat an African-American taxi driver. After the beating, police took the cab driver to the local precinct and charged him with assaulting the officers and making insulting remarks. Nearby residents of a large public housing project saw police dragging an incapacitated African-American man into the precinct, and a rumor started that officers beat the man while in custody. Some observers stated that the crowd threw rocks through the precinct windows and police then rushed outside wearing hard hats and carrying clubs. Others claim that police rushed out of their station first to confront the crowd, and then they began to throw bricks, bottles, and rocks. Over several days of rioting, 26 people died including black residents and white firefighters. More than 700 people were injured. The riots caused about $10 million in damages and reduced entire blocks to ruins.

2.2.3 *Police and Antiwar Demonstrators*

Police actions during the 1968 Democratic National Convention in Chicago produced widely viewed images of police clashing with demonstrators. While there were no recorded fatalities during the week of the convention, 192 officers were injured, 49 civilians hospitalized, 425 civilians were treated in hospitals and released, and 200 treated on the scene. Many received treatment for the effects of tear gas or mace. During the course of the week of the convention, damage and destruction occurred to 81 police vehicles, and police made 668 arrests. In the aftermath of the convention, many accused police officers of using excessive force in dealing with protestors (Champion 2001, p. 77).

Mayor Richard Daley played a key role in molding attitudes and behavior of police. Daley openly criticized the Chicago Police Department's handling of riots in Chicago in 1967. Daley accused police leadership of exacerbating problems, in 1967, by their cautious approach to unlawful behavior. Daley argued that police officials should instruct street-level police to kill arsonists and maim looters. The general attitude of the powerful mayor was quite evident to ordinary law enforcement officials.

Protestors did not hide plans for disrupting the 1968 Democratic National Convention. There had been incidents of violence at the recent

Republican National Convention in Miami. Mayor Daley was dedicated to assuring law and order during the Democratic Convention in his city. Chicago law enforcement personnel were aware of plans for disruptions. Protest groups such as the Youth International Party (Yippies) and Students for a Democratic Society intended to gather at popular city locales such as Grant Park, Lincoln Park, Soldier Field, and the Chicago Colosseum. Daley ordered that permits for marches and gatherings be restricted; police strictly enforced an 11:00 p.m. curfew and declared that troublemakers should expect a quick and dramatic response.

Skirmishes between police and protestors increased in frequency during the week. These encounters culminated in the "Battle of Michigan Avenue" on August 28, 1968, when thousands of protestors attempted to march toward the site of the convention. Chicago police and National Guard soldiers blocked their path; law enforcement agents attempted to clear the streets using batons and mace. The ensuing encounter escalated into a brawl that news media broadcast nationwide. Following the convention, a grand jury indicted eight officers of the Chicago Police Department. A jury subsequently acquitted all of the charged officers. Mayor Daley urged prosecutors to pursue criminal action against high-profile protestors. Eight protestors (known as the "Chicago Eight") stood trial for conspiracy and intent to start a riot. All were acquitted of conspiracy charges; five were convicted (later overturned on appeal) of incitement to riot (Robertiello 2017, p. 102).

A subsequent report investigated police behavior at the 1968 convention. The report's conclusions (based on statements from thousands of eyewitnesses as well as review of film) were highly critical of law enforcement's response to the Chicago demonstrations. In a controversial finding, the report characterized law enforcement actions as tantamount to a "police riot." The report criticized police for engaging in indiscriminate and unrestrained violence against not only protestors who provoked them but also peaceful demonstrators, onlookers, and large numbers of residents who were simply passing through or lived in the area. The report was also critical of Chicago leaders for fostering beliefs that higher-level administrators condoned violence against demonstrators. Public opinion, however, did not support the spirit of the post-convention report. Nationwide surveys of Gallup, the *New York Times*, and the University of Michigan indicated that majorities of citizens supported the law enforcement response. Respondents expressed the view that law enforcement agents used appropriate levels of force given the difficult circumstances (p. 103).

2.2.4 *Specific High-Profile Cases of Police Abuse*

In addition to the Democratic National Convention, several notorious cases added to the perception that police officers were out of control. Perhaps the most infamous footage of brutal police beatings occurred in 1991 when four white Los Angeles police officers beat Rodney King after pulling him over while driving. An apartment dweller across from the scene recorded several minutes of police officers hitting King with their batons. King had led California Highway Patrol troopers on a 110-mile chase that eventually ended in a Los Angeles neighborhood (p. 157). According to police, King emerged from his vehicle in an aggressive manner suggesting he might have been high on drugs. Numerous officers delivered over 50 baton blows, many kicks, and two 50,000-volt shocks from a Taser stun gun. Twenty other police officers stood by and watched the beating (Birzer 2017, p. 87). King suffered from a broken cheekbone, a fractured eye socket, missing teeth, kidney damage, skull fractures, external burns, and permanent brain damage (Palmiotto 2017a, p. 21). The videotape of the King beating became a focal point of a national conversation. Some describe the videotape as one of the most watched pieces of amateur video in history (Robertiello 2017, p. 157).

In 1992, a jury that included no African Americans acquitted four police of committing crimes against Rodney King. The defense was successful in moving the trial from Los Angeles County to Ventura County, which has a higher proportion of Caucasian residents. After the acquittals, on April 29, 1992, riots broke out and lasted five days. Losses included 40 deaths, 2382 injuries, more than 5000 buildings burned or destroyed, 40,000 jobs lost, and more than $1 billion in property damage (Champion 2001, p. 80). Three days into the rioting King went on television to ask one of the most famous questions in recent history, "Can we all get along?" He sued the City of Los Angeles and won a $3.8 million settlement (Robertiello 2017, p. 157).

The King beating and Los Angeles riots further reinforced perceptions of police brutality. In response to public outrage over the King beating, Los Angeles Mayor Tom Brady announced the creation of an independent commission to conduct an examination of the operation of the Los Angeles Police Department (LAPD). The 1991 *Report of the Independent Commission on the Los Angeles Police Department* (also known as the Christopher Commission Report) stated that within the minority communities in Los Angeles, there is a widely held view that police misconduct is commonplace. The report notes that the King beating refocused attention on complaints by

African Americans, Latinos, and Asians that LAPD officers treat minorities differently than whites (Birzer 2017, p. 88). The Christopher investigation included testimony from more than 50 expert witnesses and heard from more than 150 private citizens. The Commission concluded that one of the problems of the LAPD was officers' use and misuse of force. High-ranking police officials stated that misuse of force on the part of certain officers was a problem well known to supervisors but the department did not address the misconduct (Robertiello 2017, p. 191).

A second notorious case of police misconduct is that of Abner Louima, a Haitian immigrant who police arrested in a Brooklyn nightclub in 1997. Police charged Louima with disorderly conduct and resisting arrest. Apparently, Louima was mistaken for another Haitian man who punched an officer on the scene. According to Louima, police beat him on the way to the local precinct. After a strip search in the police precinct, officers led him to the bathroom where they sodomized him with a broomstick and then forced the broomstick into his mouth. After bleeding in his cell for several hours, officers finally sent Louima to a hospital. Doctors discovered Louima suffered from a ruptured bladder, a perforated colon, several broken teeth, and a number of other injuries. After the incident went public, the Haitian community of Brooklyn offered legal and moral support to Louima and his family. Community and civil rights groups launched a mass protest march on August 30, 1999. Approximately 10,000 protestors marched across the Brooklyn Bridge and assembled outside the City Hall in Manhattan (Johnson 2003, p. 295).

Louima received \$8.7 million in a settlement believed to be the largest police brutality settlement in the history of New York (Robertiello 2017, p. 195). The Brooklyn district attorney's office indicted four officers and turned the case over to federal prosecutors in the hope of winning stiffer sentences. The New York police chief brought immediate changes to the Brooklyn Precinct where the incident occurred. These changes include recruitment of more African-American and Afro-Caribbean officers who lived in the neighborhood. One of the offending police officers received a prison sentence for assault and violation of Louima's civil rights. Four fellow officers testified. Following the conviction of the officer, Mayor Giuliana claimed that the police's blue wall of silence was not absolute and that the Louima case represents an aberration in an otherwise well-run police department. Anti-brutality activists, however, claimed the blue wall fell in this particular case because it represented an extreme case of sadism and violated the norms of police culture. Subsequent brutality cases revealed that the police code of silence was still deep-rooted (Johnson 2003, 26).

3 Contemporary Police Controversies

3.1 Sanford, Florida

The shooting in Sanford, Florida, of 17-year-old Trayvon Martin raised a number of questions regarding the use of volunteers in law enforcement activity. A neighborhood watch guardian, George Zimmerman shot and killed Martin, a young African-American male, on February 26, 2012. The shooting brought national attention to issues of racial profiling, behavior of community volunteers, communities policing, and the reluctance of police to challenge deadly force in states that operate under "stand-your-ground" laws. The basic facts of the case note that Martin was walking back from a convenience store that was close to the home of his father's girlfriend. Zimmerman was the neighborhood watch coordinator for the gated community he patrolled. Zimmerman spotted Martin and reported suspicious activity to the Sanford Police Department. Zimmerman ignored the advice of a police dispatcher to wait for the police and began to follow Martin on foot; the two engaged in an altercation. Zimmerman claimed that he used his weapon as Martin was beating him and that he feared for his life (Robertiello 2017, p. 255). The police did not charge Zimmerman with a crime at the time of the shooting; the Sanford Police stated that there was no evidence to refute his claim of self-defense. Prosecutors later charged Zimmerman with second-degree murder and manslaughter. A jury acquitted him of both charges in July 2013.

The shooting of Trayvon Martin generated a firestorm of media attention. According to the Pew Research Center, the incident received the highest level of sustained coverage with a major racial component for the period January 2007–May 2012. The case became the number one story in the mainstream press the week of March 19–25, 2012. It accounted for 19 percent of the space in print, online, and on radio and television. The shooting became the first story in 2012 to generate more coverage in a single week than the 2012 presidential campaign. Many in the media portrayed Zimmerman as a neighborhood watch "wannabe cop" that racially profiled and ultimately killed an unarmed, black teenager. Critics of this narrative, however, argued that there was more to the story of a frustrated would-be law enforcement officer gunning down a helpless child (Koven 2017).

With the shooting of Martin, concerns grew in the African-American community about stereotyping and shooting of young males by either regular police or neighborhood vigilantes. The shooting by a resident who was not a regular officer brought up memories of citizen lynching of the past. Pressured by the media, the US Justice Department began an investigation into the Zimmerman shooting. In February of 2015, the Justice Department closed its investigation without filing hate-crime charges against Zimmerman. After interviewing many witnesses federal investigators concluded that there was not enough evidence to prove that Trayvon Martin's death was racially motivated. The Trayvon Martin shooting, however, heightened awareness of police abuse. Rallies, marches, and protests across the nation followed Martin's death. In March 2012, hundreds of students at his high school held a walkout. An online petition calling for a full investigation and prosecution of Zimmerman garnered more than two million signatures.

3.2 Ferguson, Missouri

The shooting death of Michael Brown in Ferguson, Missouri, focused national attention on police actions in minority neighborhoods. Some of the facts surrounding the incident are widely contested; others are not. What is not under dispute is that on the morning of August 9, 2014, the Ferguson Police received a call regarding a robbery. Within minutes, police officer Darren Wilson came upon Brown and a friend; Wilson subsequently fatally shot Brown. Accounts differ regarding the details of the shooting.

According to Officer Wilson, on his way to get lunch he encountered Brown and his friend walking in the middle of the road. Wilson ordered Brown to walk on the side of the road; Brown became confrontational, Wilson tried to exit his police vehicle; Brown prevented Wilson from exiting the car and began to punch Wilson on the side of the face. Wilson claims that he was fighting for his life and fearing for his safety when he attempted to draw his weapon. Wilson and Brown struggled over the weapon; two shots emerged, one grazed Brown's thumb. Following the shots, Brown and his friend fled from the police car. Wilson exited the vehicle and called for the two men to stop running and get on the ground. In sworn testimony, Wilson claims that Brown did not comply with the order and Brown began to advance toward him. Wilson states he then saw Brown reaching for something under his shirt. Wilson then fired ten shots; seven shots hit Brown killing him. The dead body would remain on the street for several hours in the summer heat before removal.

The account of Brown's companion differed dramatically. According to the companion who was at the scene, Wilson approached the two men and after a short conversation grabbed Brown by the throat. Two shots emerged from inside the vehicle. In contrast to Wilson's account, the companion stated that when Wilson ordered the men to stop Brown raised his hands in a peaceful manner and never attempted to charge toward the officer (Robertiello 2017, p. 259).

Multiple YouTube videos of Michael Brown's body lying in the middle of the street went viral. After four days of rioting, the Missouri State Highway Patrol moved in with military gear. The governor of Missouri declared a state of emergency and eventually restored order. The Ferguson shooting precipitated large-scale protests around the country in the following months. Protestors coalesced around signs reading "Black Lives Matter" and "Hands Up-Don't Shoot." A grand jury failed to indict Wilson and he left the Ferguson Police Department.

In 2014, the US Department of Justice (DOJ) Civil Rights Division began an investigation of the Ferguson Police Department. The DOJ declined to pursue federal civil rights charges against Wilson but issued a scathing report about policing in Ferguson. One of the primary findings of the report was that the Ferguson Police Department made ticketing of citizens a high-priority means to generate revenue. The department scheduled patrol shifts around the best time to write tickets; officer evaluations focused on how many tickets they wrote. In addition, the monetary penalties disproportionately fell on low- and moderate-income African-American residents. In many vehicle stops, African Americans received multiple citations. In addition, the DOJ investigators concluded that the Ferguson Police Department's use of force was disproportionate against African Americans. Ninety percent of the use-of-force incidents involved an African American (p. 262).

Ferguson exacerbated antipathy between police and the minority community. Some claim that criticism of the police created a "Ferguson Effect" which asserted that police are not enforcing the law because of fear of retaliation or citizen complaints. Those who supported the police claimed that the consequence of the "Ferguson Effect" nationwide would be a dramatic escalation of crime. The data, however, did not support this contention with no increase in violent crime in the immediate aftermath of the Michael Brown shooting.

3.3 Chicago

The release in 2015 of a video detailing the shooting of a young African American, Laquan McDonald, reminded the nation of the reputation for violence of the Chicago Police Department. After a year, a Cook County judge ordered the release of a 2014 video of the shooting taken from a police dashboard camera. The video shows McDonald running and then walking past officers in the middle of the street and spinning when bullets suddenly strike him. As he is lying on the ground, police appear to shoot him several more times. The video shows none of the officers on the scene offering any assistance.

Chicago Mayor Rahm Emanuel and Police Superintendent Garry McCarthy released the video just over a year after police shot McDonald 16 times. The footage clearly shows McDonald stepping slightly away from Officer Jason Van Dyke. Witnesses said McDonald, who was carrying a three-inch folding knife, never spoke to Van Dyke or any of the other officers and did not make threatening moves toward him. Van Dyke fired all the shots; none of at least seven other police officers on the scene fired their weapons (Davey and Smith 2015).

Prosecutors note Van Dyke was on the scene for fewer than 30 seconds, before he began shooting his service weapon. As other officers confronted and ordered McDonald to drop the knife, Van Dyke pulled up alongside other police vehicles. Van Dyke was a decorated officer with numerous awards but records show that the officer had been the subject of many complaints from residents. These complaints included allegations of using excessive force and making racial slurs. At the time of the shooting, Van Dyke was a 14-year veteran of the Chicago police force.

Following the release of the video, protesters marched through the streets of Chicago's Loop, blocking intersections, chanting outside a police station and along a major road to the city's largest highways; protestors unfurled a banner that cited deaths at the hands of the police. The Cook County state's attorney charged Van Dyke with first-degree murder. Since 2014, a team that included the FBI, the US attorney's office in Chicago, and the Cook County state attorney's office investigated the shooting. Van Dyke was the first Chicago police officer in decades to be charged with murder in an on-duty shooting (Davey and Smith 2015).

The shooting of Laquan McDonald was far from an isolated incident. According to some estimates, the City of Chicago paid more than $500 million in settlements and other costs between 2005 and 2015. In 2015, the City of Chicago agreed to pay the McDonald family $5 million. In the aftermath of the McDonald shooting, Mayor Rahm Emanuel created a task force to review the system of accountability and oversight of Chicago police officers. The Task Force's final report found racism and systemic failures in the city's police force. Police shootings still occur with relative frequency in Chicago. While officers in Chicago began to wear body cameras and carry stun guns, shootings have persisted. In 2015, an officer fatally shot a teen wielding a baseball bat as well as an innocent bystander. In 2016, an officer fatally shot an unarmed teen in the back after he ran from the police. In 2018, residents confronted the police after officers fatally shot an armed man in the back (Smith 2018).

On November 24, 2015, the Cook County state's attorney charged Van Dyke with first-degree murder, and he turned himself in to authorities. On November 30, six days later, Van Dyke posted bail. On December 29, Van Dyke pleaded not guilty to the charges. In July of 2018, more than two and a half years after prosecutors charged Van Dyke with murder, a Cook County judge ruled that Van Dyke would finally stand for trial. Lawyers for Van Dyke asked for a change of venue out of concern that he could not receive a fair trial in Chicago (Associated Press 2018). In October of 2018, Van Dyke was found guilty of second-degree murder and aggravated battery with a firearm.

3.4 Cincinnati

The killing of 19-year-old Timothy Thomas by a Cincinnati police officer in 2001 set off several days of rioting in Cincinnati. The riots lasted from April 9 to April 13, 2001. The disturbance represented the largest urban riots in the United States since the Los Angeles riots of 1992. Looting of businesses in and around downtown Cincinnati was extensive. Police arrested around 800 people during the riots. The riots had a lasting impact since the rate of violent crime in the areas increased for several years following the riot. The facts surrounding the shooting are as follows. The victim of the shooting was apparently leaving a local nightclub when police identified him as a person with outstanding traffic warrants from 21 traffic violations. Thomas ran into an alley to avoid arrest. According to the police report, an officer ran into the alley and shot Thomas in the chest; shortly after the shooting, Thomas was pronounced dead (Robertiello 2017, p. 224).

The killing of an unarmed African-American man for unpaid traffic tickets outraged many citizens of Cincinnati. Hostile relations between the police and the African-American community contributed to the ensuing violence. The police officer who shot Thomas reported that he thought Thomas was reaching for a gun. Investigators later determined that he must have been trying to pull up his sagging pants. A local newspaper notes that police seemed to be targeting African Americans for minor offenses. Police in Cincinnati were twice as likely to cite black motorists for driving without a proper license and not wearing a seatbelt. Police were four times more likely to cite motorists for driving without proof of insurance. The reaction of Cincinnati citizens occurred in an environment of mistrust and suspicion of racism. Between 1995 and 2001, Cincinnati police shot and killed 15 African-American men while there were no white deaths at the hands of the police.

On September 26, 2001, a judge acquitted the police officer charged with shooting Thomas; the officer stood trial on two misdemeanor charges of negligent homicide and obstructing official business. If convicted the officer could have served nine months in jail. According to the judge, the officer's shooting was reasonable since it was due to a quick reaction to a dangerous situation, which Thomas was responsible for creating. The police officer was the first from the Cincinnati police department to stand trial for killing a suspect. The judge scolded the police department for initiating charges (p. 227).

Cincinnati residents were generally apprehensive of the police. Residents note that police were extra vigilant in identifying minor violations such as driving without a seat belt or citing motorists for driving without a license or insurance. Residents believed police target minorities for harsh treatment. In one day alone, two months prior to his death, Thomas received four tickets. Problems between motorists and police were not unique to Cincinnati. Deadly interactions between police and motorists occurred in other places such as Miami, where police claimed that a motorist, Arthur McDuffie, died in a crash during a police chase. The coroner in Miami, however, reported that it appeared someone beat McDuffie with a flashlight (p. 228).

4 Contemporary Police Controversies

4.1 Baltimore

The arrest and subsequent death of Freddie Gray sparked protests in Gray's hometown of Baltimore as well as cities such as Chicago, Denver, Miami, Seattle, Philadelphia, Washington, DC, and New York. The Freddie Gray case arose with the arrest of Gray, a 25-year-old African-American man, on April 12, 2015. Bystanders captured the arrest on video recordings showing Baltimore police officers dragging Gray to a police van and Gray stepping into the van under his own power. The local newspaper the *Baltimore Sun* reported that a witness saw police beating Gray with their batons. Upon finding a knife in Gray's possession, police had placed Gray in a restraining position during the arrest. According to court documents, after the apprehension Baltimore police officers placed Gray in a transport van without securing him with a seatbelt. At a press conference, the Baltimore police commissioner acknowledged that officers did not follow protocol that mandated officers to secure arrestees in seatbelts (Robertiello 2017, p. 301).

While transporting Gray the police made various stops prior to arriving at the local police station. When the van arrived at the police station, severe injuries caused Gray to fall into a coma. The media suggested the cause of his injuries was the "rough ride" in the van. The "rough ride" terminology refers to an unsanctioned practice where police place a handcuffed prisoner without a seatbelt in an erratically driven vehicle. According to Gray's family attorney, in the week following the arrest, Gray remained in a coma, suffered from cardiopulmonary arrest, was resuscitated without regaining consciousness, and underwent extensive surgery in an effort to save his life. His family reported that Gray suffered from three fractured vertebrae, injuries to his voice box, and the sorts of injuries that doctors say are the result of serious car accidents. Police confirmed that the spinal injury led to his death; he died one week after his arrest (Koven 2017).

The Gray incident was not an anomaly. Records indicate that many prisoners die every year while being arrested. On May 1, 2015, the Baltimore Attorney Marilyn Mosby announced her office had filed charges against six Baltimore police officers on the grounds that Gray died as a result of a "rough ride." In 2015, after receiving a medical examiner's report ruling Gray's death a homicide, state prosecutors declared that they had probable cause to file criminal charges against the six officers involved in the arrest. Baltimore County State Attorney Marilyn Mosby claimed that the Baltimore police had acted illegally in placing Gray in the van since Gray did not commit any crime. Mosby further alleged that officers had failed to establish probable cause for Gray's arrest and charged officers with false imprisonment because Gray was carrying a pocketknife of legal size. Officials took all six officers into custody and released them as they posted bail.

The legal outcomes of the arrests disappointed minority residents of Baltimore. Mosby charged all the officers with involuntary manslaughter and misconduct. In addition, one officer (the driver of the police van) faced a charge of second-degree depraved-heart murder. Depraved-heart murder refers to an act in which a defendant is aware that his or her actions could result in death. On September 2, 2015, a judge decided to try each officer separately. In the first case, the jury was unable to reach a verdict and the state promised to retry the officer. Following the first trial, all six of the officers waived their right to a jury trial. Bench trials (trial by judge) of two officers produced not-guilty verdicts. Prosecutors dropped charges against the other four officers.

In 2015, Attorney General Loretta Lynch announced that the US DOJ would conduct a review of the practices of the Baltimore Police Department in relation to the circumstances of Freddie Gray's death. The federal review focused on allegations that Baltimore police officers used excessive force, including deadly force, conducted unlawful searches or arrests, and engaged in discriminatory policing. In 2017, the US DOJ announced it would not bring federal charges against the six Baltimore police officers involved in the arrest and in-custody death of Freddie Gray. The Gray family filed a civil lawsuit against the City of Baltimore and received a settlement of $6.4 million (p. 302). Despite the settlement, Freddy Gray's death only solidified perceptions in some people's minds that the police are unaccountable and that the police are engaging in hostile actions toward minorities.

4.2 *North Charleston, South Carolina*

The shooting of Walter Scott in North Charleston, South Carolina, appeared on video for all viewers to witness. An eyewitness recorded police officer Michael Slager firing upon a fleeing unarmed man. The recorder of the video, Feidin Santana, at first did not share the video out of fear of retribution. Santana, however, became angered when the police report differed from his recording of the events. He eventually shared the video with Scott's family and later with the news media.

Accounts of the Scott shooting differ dramatically. According to the police report of Slager and his backup officer, at around 9:30 a.m. on April 4, 2015, the two officers stopped Walter Scott for a broken tail light. Slager then asked Scott for his driver's license, registration, and proof of insurance. The report notes that as Slager walked back to his vehicle, Scott left his vehicle and began to run away. Slager pursued Scott, the two engaged in a physical alteration, Slager unsuccessfully tried to deploy his Taser, and Scott allegedly grabbed the stun gun. Slager alleges that this caused the officer to feel threatened and led him to fire eight shots at Scott. Five shots hit and killed Scott. The backup officer falsely reported that he performed lifesaving measures but it was too late. In contrast to the police version of events, cell phone video shows Slager on top of Scott with Scott on the ground; it appears in the video that Slager had control over Scott and did not fear for his safety. Eyewitnesses report hearing the Taser go off it then it seemed as if Scott was trying to escape being hit a second time. The video clearly shows Slager firing at Scott after hitting him in the back as he fled (Robertiello 2017, p. 303).

Immediately following the shooting, Slager radioed a dispatcher, stating, "Shots fired and the subject is down. He grabbed my Taser." When Slager fired his gun, Scott was approximately 15 to 20 feet away. After the officer shot Scott, he instructed Scott to place his hands behind his back, and handcuffed him. The video shows that Slager ran back toward where the initial scuffle occurred and picked something up off the ground and dropped the object (possibly the Taser) beside Scott's body. Without the video, Slager's account of events probably would have gone unquestioned.

A review of police records indicates that during Slager's tenure on the police force he was involved in 19 use-of-force incidents; 14 of these incidents involved the use of a Taser. Slager never fired his handgun while on patrol until the Scott case (p. 304). The Scott shooting led to further public criticism of the police and claims that they systematically use excessive force and racially biased tactics against African-American males. Protestors called for the resignation of North Charleston Police Chief Eddie Driggers and the indictment of Slager's partner for filing a false report. Protestors began wearing T-shirts with statements such as "Black Lives Matter" and "Stop Killing Us." The FBI, the US Attorney in South Carolina, the US DOJ's Civil Rights Division, and the South Carolina Law Enforcement Division began to conduct investigations.

At the end of the day the video and public outcry proved to be "a bridge too far" even for those who consistently defend police actions. A South Carolina grand jury indicted Slager on a murder charge. After one mistrial, the state dropped their charges and Slager agreed to plead guilty to a federal offense. In 2017, a US district judge sentenced Slager to 20 years in prison. The judge agreed with prosecutors that the appropriate underlying offense was second-degree murder. In an out-of-court settlement, the City of North Charleston agreed to pay $6.5 million to Scott's family.

4.3 New York City

The Eric Garner case in New York City represents one more of a long list of cases that attracted intense media attention. Questionable actions of police include not only the contemporary controversies discussed earlier but also others such as the shooting of 12-year-old Tamir Rice in Cleveland in 2014. Rice was holding a fake gun when shot by police. In another incident, a Texas state trooper stopped an African-American woman for failure to signal while changing lanes. After a verbal exchange, the trooper handcuffed and arrested her. Three days later, she died in her jail cell. The death was ruled a suicide.

The basic facts of the Eric Garner case became widely reported as two videos recorded the events. Without the video of his final struggle, Garner's death may have attracted little notice; many would have accepted the cause of death as attributed to Garner's health problems such as obesity, asthma, and hypertensive cardiovascular disease. The 6-foot 2-inch, 395-pound Garner also had other health issues including sleep apnea and diabetes. Partially due to poor health, Garner quit his job in the New York City Department of Parks and Recreation. He was unemployed at the time of the incident.

The police knew Garner well. Dating back to the 1980s, police arrested Garner 30 times for crimes such as assault, grand larceny, and illegally selling cigarettes. Nevertheless, people in the Staten Island neighborhood of New York City knew Garner as a peacemaker and many community members referred to him as a "gentle giant." At the time of the fatal encounter, Garner was out on bail for misdemeanor offenses including selling untaxed cigarettes and driving without a license. According to witnesses, on July 17, 2014, police arrived at the Tompkinsville neighborhood of Staten Island because of a fight between two men. Officers recognized Garner and accused him of selling loose cigarettes. The business of loose cigarettes is longstanding. One can purchase cigarettes in Pennsylvania, Delaware, or a nearby Indian reservation; return to heavily taxed New York City; and sell packs for $10 or individual cigarettes for $1 or less. Garner was among a handful of men who sold cigarettes in the area (Baker et al. 2015; Robertiello 2017, p. 265).

A video of the confrontation between police and Garner shows Garner arguing with officers who accused him of illegally selling nontaxed cigarettes. When one officer sought to pull Garner's hands behind him, Garner pulled free. The officer then wrapped his arm around Garner's neck, put him on the ground, and continued to hold him in what city officials later acknowledged appears to be an illegal chokehold. The chokehold maneuver includes any action that puts pressure on the throat or windpipe, which may prevent or hinder breathing or reduce intake of air. While on the ground Garner stated 11 times, "I can't breathe." During this time, officers continued to put pressure on Garner's head and body. His body eventually stopped moving and police handcuffed him.

Following the death, the New York City medical examiner announced that Garner died from a chokehold and compression to his chest. The examiner found that the manner of Garner's death was homicide. The medical examiner stated that Garner's poor health was a contributing factor, but was not the primary cause of death. An autopsy indicates that Garner died from compression of neck (chokehold) and compression of chest during physical restraint by police. The death of Garner raised questions about the "broken windows" style of policing, where officers target low-level crimes (Goldstein and Santora 2014). Many believed the broken windows strategy alienated the community and stoked hostility.

Two videos of Garner quickly went viral. Many who witnessed the video were convinced of police criminal wrongdoing. However, much to the dismay of many citizens, a Staten Island grand jury in December 2014 refused to indict any police officers. The decision not to indict was widely criticized. In December of 2014, a man who stated on social media about his desire for revenge ambushed two NYPD officers in their police cruiser. President Barack Obama stated after the funeral of the two officers that police deserve our respect and gratitude. Following the grand jury's decision not to indict, Obama stated that the decision not to indict spoke to concerns on the part of too many minority communities that law enforcement is not working with them and dealing with them in a fair way (Robertiello 2017, p. 268). The Garner family sued the City of New York in civil court. In July of 2015, the city settled with the family and agreed to pay $5.9 million on the condition that the city not admit to any wrongdoing on its part (p. 270).

5 Possible Checks on Police Abuse

5.1 Organizational Reforms

Ideas concerning how to limit police abuse are readily available. Over the last century, reformers have proposed numerous remedies and conducted many studies. Charges of police brutality and abuse, however, consistently reoccur. Robertiello (2017, p. 345) notes that over the years the police have been accused of using too much force and being too quick to pull the trigger. This has exacerbated negative perceptions of the police. There is an assumption that police are overly aggressive to the point they may be violating due process rights. Furthermore, there is the perception that police are brutalizing more minority and poor citizens.

One proposal to limit police abuse is to train officers to de-escalate confrontations. The intent of this plan is to allow people in the community to gain greater respect for officers and not perceive them as the enemy. Some propose requiring higher education standards for employment in the police department. According to the Bureau of Justice Statistics, less than 10 percent of police departments require a four-year degree. Studies indicate that more highly educated officers are less likely to use force and are more creative at problem-solving. Community policing represents another possible answer to improving police-citizen relations. An innovative initiative calls for police giving youths the option of having their parents pick them up at headquarters, or dropping them off at a church or faith-based organization when they violate curfew. Trenton, New Jersey, experimented with this approach. Other ideas for reforming police include increasing the use of body cameras, better data collection, and counseling "bad actors" (p. 351).

Walker (2015, p. 12) states that new strategies and tools can enhance the accountability of police. These strategies embrace a list of best practices that emerged in the 1980s and 1990s and coalesced into a coherent package in the mid-1990s. Strategies in some cases entail new devices and in other instances extend practices that have existed for some time.

The first new accountability strategy involves requiring written policies that govern the use of force and requiring police officers to file official reports each time they engage in a "critical" use-of-force incident. Policies can broadly define such critical incidents to include risk of life, liberty, or dignity of a citizen. Supervisors automatically review reports to ensure compliance with departmental policies. A second tool of accountability is to maintain an open and accessible process for citizen complaints about police conduct. Under the parameters of this reform, police no longer regard citizen complaints as hostile acts. On the contrary, in the new more open framework complaints represent an important source of information for management. Management can use the information to remedy performance problems.

Early intervention (EI) systems represent a third management tool for enhancing accountability. EI systems are a linchpin of accountability because they pull together use-of-force reports and citizen complaint data. In essence, EI systems involve collection and analysis of data for purposes of correcting problems. A database on officer performance allows commanders to identify officers whose records raise concerns. Supervisors then refer problem officers to some kind of intervention such as counseling or retraining. Studies indicate that a few problem officers can account for a large proportion of police abuse complaints. For example, a 1981 report by the US Civil Rights Commission found that in the Houston Police Department, one officer had received 12 complaints and two others had received 11 complaints over a two-year period. In contrast, 298 officers received only two complaints. Officers who received five or more complaints represented 12 percent of the police force but accounted for 41 percent of all complaints (p. 100).

A final proposed tool for enhancing accountability is external citizen oversight. This brings to the police department input from people who are not members of the police department. One form of oversight is the police auditor. In contrast to a civilian review board, which reviews individual citizen complaints, the auditor investigates larger patterns and practices of a police department. The purpose of such holistic oversight is to make recommendations that will address persistent problems. Police auditors have the authority to probe deeply into departmental policies with an eye toward reducing future misconduct. Auditors can also follow up on issues and determine whether recommendations for change have been implemented (p. 136). The basic goal of all the accountability tools is organizational change.

5.2 *Whistleblowing: Case of Frank Serpico*

Another means of reducing abuse of local-level police officers is through the high-risk strategy of whistleblowing. New York City police officer Frank Serpico gained great notoriety when he reported evidence of corruption in the NYPD to the *New York Times*. After receiving that evidence, the *Times* ran a front-page story about corruption in the police force in April of 1970 entitled "Graft Paid to Police Here Said to Run into Millions."

Serpico's whistleblowing led to the creation of the Knapp Commission to investigate corruption in the NYPD. Serpico testified before the Knapp Commission asserting that honest police officers could not act without fear of ridicule or reprisal in the department (Koven 2015, p. 145). Serpico's actions to root out corruption came at a high personal cost. The son of Italian immigrants growing up in the Bedford-Stuyvesant section of Brooklyn, Serpico dreamed of becoming a police officer. At the age of 24, after a stint in the US Army, he achieved his dream of becoming a full patrolman. Disillusionment, however, quickly set in when Serpico became aware of systematic payoffs (known as the "pad") made to New York police officers. Serpico did not wish to participate in the payoffs that encompassed the department. In his mind, crooked cops seemed to have free reign. He subsequently reported the system of payoffs to top officials in the NYPD as well as representatives of the mayor's office. Eventually, Serpico felt compelled to go to the media with his story. On February 12, 1970, Serpico, along with three other officers, took the fateful step of meeting with representatives of the *New York Times* (p. 145).

Testifying in public before the Knapp Commission, Serpico made an emotional appeal to change the status quo of the NYPD. He stated that an atmosphere does not yet exist in which an honest police officer can act without fear of reprisal from fellow officers. He declared that an atmosphere persisted where the honest cop feared the dishonest officer and that police corruption could not exist unless tolerated at higher levels in the department. Serpico concluded his testimony stating that merely uncovering corruption would not resolve the problem and called for basic changes in attitude.

Officer Serpico paid a heavy price for his efforts to reform the NYPD. After going public with his criticism of the NYPD, he became a pariah within the police force and was a victim of a gunshot to the face on February 3, 1971. He did not receive backup from fellow officers who did not even call for an ambulance. Bullet fragments remained lodged just below his brain from the shooting; he became deaf in his left ear and suffered from nerve damage in his left leg. A bullet lodged at the top of his jaw. The 1973 movie *Serpico* starring Al Pacino thrust the police officer further into the spotlight. The film covers the 12 years of Serpico's service on the NYPD from 1960 to 1972 as he moves from a patrol officer to plainclothes assignments and discovers a world of corruption among his colleagues. The idealistic Serpico decides to expose the NYPD corruption, but this leads to harassment, threats, and problems in his personal relationships. After being shot, Serpico testifies before the Knapp Commission and receives an NYPD medal and a disability pension. The motion picture *Serpico* was a major commercial success. The movie received Academy Award nominations for Best Actor (Al Pacino) and Best Adapted Screenplay.

The personal cost to Serpico for his efforts to expose police corruption appears to be exorbitant. Serpico traveled extensively after leaving the police force in 1972 but returned to the United States in 1980. He lived as a nomad out of a camper and settled about two hours north of New York

City, where he lived in a one-room cabin in the woods. Serpico appears to remain bitter from his experience. In a 2010 interview, he stated that he had nightmares, and steers away from what he saw as an American addiction to consumerism and media brainwashing. He complained about his promotion to third-grade, rather than first-grade, detective. The NYPD's museum in Lower Manhattan declined his offer of his uniform and his service revolver. He noted that the leadership of the NYPD never asks him to speak about corruption or reform and did not have a promotion ceremony for him when he became detective. Serpico complained that he did not receive the respect he thought he deserved because he violated the police code of silence. He believes the NYPD still does not acknowledge its internal problems because the leadership's top priority is to avoid scandal (p. 147).

6 Conclusions

Law enforcement represents one of the key institutions of governing. The interface between average citizens and law enforcement representatives helps to establish citizen attitudes and modes of behavior. Attitudes toward police can range from hostility to respect depending upon one's personal experiences. Given the discretionary power of those in authority, it is not surprising that in many instances it appears that police abuse their authority. Stories of police abuse are part of the American narrative. Police abuse is not new but part of an eternal story. Police misbehavior, however, has real consequences. Actual or perceived narratives of excessive police force precipitated many incidents of civil violence.

The anecdotal and other evidence presented in this chapter notes the obvious that police abuse their authority from time to time. A larger question is one of the size and scope of police abuse. Some analysts claim that cases of abuse represent the few "rotten apples" in an otherwise healthy orchard. Others claim that the orchard itself is diseased and produces poisonous fruit. From the broad societal perspective, the relevant question is not whether abuse exists; the question is at what point does the weight of abuse seriously damage legitimacy and accountability. While police will always have a legitimate function, they can threaten the liberties and freedoms of average citizens. This in turn will erode the foundation of American life. Well-publicized cases of questionable police behavior at the local level suggest a serious need for greater scrutiny that can culminate in organizational reforms.

References

Associated Press. (2018, July 17). Judge: Trial in Laquan McDonald shooting to start Sept. 5. *Miami Herald*. Retrieved July 17, 2018, from https://www.miamiherald.com/news/

Baker, A., Goodman, J. D., & Mueller, B. (2015, June 13). Beyond the chokehold: The path to Eric Garner's death. *New York Times*. Retrieved July 16, 2018, from https://www.nytimes.com/2015/06/14/

Birzer, M. L. (2017). Racial profiling: The intersection of race and policing. In M. J. Palmiotto (Ed.), *Police use of force* (pp. 81–111). Boca Raton: CRC Press.

Carter, D. L., & Barker, T. (1991). Administrative guidance and control of police officer behavior: Policies, procedures, and rules. In T. Barker & D. L. Carter (Eds.), *Police deviance* (2nd ed.). Cincinnati: Anderson Publishing Co.

Champion, D. J. (2001). *Police misconduct in America*. Santa Barbara: ABC-CLIO, Inc.

Davey, M., & Smith, M. (2015, November 24). Chicago protests mostly peaceful after video of police shooting is released. *New York Times*. Retrieved July 16, 2018, from https://www.nytimes.com/2015/11/25/

Edy, J. (2018). Watts riots of 1966. *Encyclopedia Britannica*. Retrieved July 2, 2918, from https://www.britannica.com/event/Watts-Riots-of-1965

Emeka, T. Q. (2018). Detroit riot of 1967. *Encyclopedia Britannica*. Retrieved July 11, 2018, from https://www.britannica.com/event/Detroit-Riot-of-1967

Galster, G. (2012). *Driving Detroit: The quest for respect in the motor city*. Philadelphia: University of Pennsylvania Press.

Goldstein, J., & Santora, M. (2014, August 1). Staten Island man died from chokehold during arrest, autopsy finds. *New York Times*. Retrieved July 16, 2018, from https://www.nytimes.com/2014/08/02

Johnson, M. (2003). *Street justice: A history of police violence in New York City*. Boston: Beacon Press.

Klein, C. (2015, March 6). *Remembering Selma's 'Bloody Sunday'*. Retrieved July 2, 2018, from https://www.history.com/news/selmas-bloody-sunday-50-years-ago

Koven, S. G. (2015). *Public sector ethics: Theory and applications*. Boca Raton: CRC Press.

Koven, S. G. (2017). Causes and consequences of crisis. In A. Farazmand (Ed.), *Global encyclopedia on public administration, public policy and governance*. Cham: Springer International Publishing.

Koven, S. G., & Koven, A. C. (2018). *Growth, decline, and regeneration in large cities: A case study approach*. New York: Routledge.

Palmiotto, M. J. (2017a). Police use of force. In M. J. Palmiotto (Ed.), *Police use of force* (pp. 13–34). Boca Raton: CRC Press.

Palmiotto, M. J. (2017b). Use of force throughout history. In M. J. Palmiotto (Ed.), *Police use of force* (pp. 1–11). Boca Raton: CRC Press.

Robertiello, G. (Ed.). (2017). *The use and abuse of police power in America*. Santa Barbara: ABC-CLIO.

Smith, M. (2018, July 15). Chicago police fatally shoot man, and then a crowd confronts officers. *New York Times*. Retrieved July 15, 2018, from https://www.nytimes.com/2018/07/15/

Walker, S. (2015). *The new world of police accountability*. Thousand Oaks: Sage.

Wallenfeld, J. (2018). Selma march. *Encyclopedia Britannica*. Retrieved June 19, 2018, from https://www.britannica.com/event/Selma-March

CHAPTER 5

Discretion and National Policy: National Law Enforcement and Veterans Affairs Abuses

1 Introduction

This chapter reviews actions of law enforcement bodies at the national level as well as egregious violations of bureaucrats, as exemplified by abuses at Veterans Administration (VA) hospitals. The chapter explores the behavior of former Federal Bureau of Investigation (FBI) officials such as J. Edgar Hoover, Mark Felt, and James Comey and contemporary controversies including the interface between federal and local authorities in enforcement of immigration laws. Conflicts between Immigration and Customs Enforcement (ICE) agents and agents of sanctuary cities highlight ambiguities of authority between various levels of government and the unwillingness of local officials to cooperate with national authorities. The whistleblowing of personnel at the Phoenix VA hospital reveals the ease to which government bureaucrats can "game" the system to their advantage. The courageous actions of some whistleblowers highlight both the presence of scrupulous employees and the likelihood of retaliation. Below is a review of the history of the FBI, controversies under the watches of various FBI officials, disputes between levels of government, and abuses of authority within the VA.

S. G. Koven, *The Case Against Bureaucratic Discretion*,
https://doi.org/10.1007/978-3-030-05779-4_5

2 History of the FBI

2.1 Genesis

Historians cite the date of July 26, 1908, as the beginning of the FBI when the US attorney general, Charles Bonaparte, issued an order that the Department of Justice (DOJ) would conduct investigations by their own agents, rather than "borrowing" agents from the Treasury Department (Jeffreys-Jones 2007, p. 39). Prior to 1908, the Treasury Department controlled the use of agents and authority was limited to countering the growth of counterfeiting. Counterfeiting became a major problem beginning in 1865 when the Union began printing paper money or "greenbacks." Under the authority of 1865 legislation to limit counterfeiting, the secretary of Treasury organized the Secret Service, the federal government's first force of detectives. Consistent with the prevailing sentiment of the times, the Secret Service did not possess broad powers to investigate all violations of federal law. Congress specifically narrowed the scope of authority to protecting the integrity of the nation's currency (Powers 2004, p. 41).

The Secret Service expanded their responsibilities over time. In 1867, Congress expanded the mandate, urging Secret Service agents to investigate the Ku Klux Klan, fraud, smuggling, bootlegging, mail train robbery, and public land swindling. Soon after the Civil War, a host of new issues began to burden the US Attorney General's Office. In 1870, the Attorney General's Office changed its formal name to the Department of Justice (DOJ). In 1871, Congress appropriated funds to the DOJ for the detection and prosecution of crimes against the United States. This appropriation became the rationale to create a detective force that eventually evolved into the FBI.

The presidency of Theodore Roosevelt, beginning in 1901, spurred movement toward a fully professionalized federal law bureau. As an unabashed progressive, Roosevelt viewed the country as corrupted by wealth and power. In the mind of Roosevelt big business was despoiling food and exploiting natural resources; employers did not pay their workers in factories and mines adequate wages. Roosevelt believed that for democracy to survive in an era of giant corporations, government had to become powerful enough to defend the public against rapacious special interests. Roosevelt viewed an investigatory body such as the FBI as a necessary tool to root out corruption that was rampant in his day.

In 1906, Roosevelt appointed fellow reformer Charles Bonaparte, grand-nephew of Napoleon Bonaparte, to the office of US attorney general. The new appointee pressured Congress to have the DOJ create an independent force so that it would not be obligated to request agents from the Treasury Department. Many members of Congress, however, were unreceptive to this expansion of authority and feared that Roosevelt wished to create a detective force to monitor congressional representatives. Supporters of Roosevelt argued that the nation needed a national police force. Congressional hearings revealed that the DOJ actually had the power to create its own detective force and did not need new legislative authorization. Eventually, Congress ended the practice of transferring agents between departments and the DOJ began to hire their own agents. This new "Special Agent Force" of the DOJ consisted of 35 investigators (p. 54).

Some congressional members, however, grew suspicious of the new force and raised concerns that still reverberate today. These concerns act as an eerie reminder that some controversies (such as fear of centralized government power) are never fully resolved. These concerns seem to submerge temporarily, only to emerge at another time. In the early twentieth century, congressional representatives expressed anxiety that the new organization of federal agents would serve as a spy system, similar to organizations that predominated in other countries. Many representatives of the time claimed that the creation of a national police force would undermine freedom and erode the independence of free institutions.

Despite the opposition, the Roosevelt administration institutionalized the new "Special Agent Force." With the establishment of the new force, Roosevelt accomplished one of the progressive objectives of moving toward a more scientific approach to solving the problems of modern society. In addition, the creation of the federal force was consistent with Roosevelt's view and the belief of Attorney General Charles Bonaparte that the federal government and only the federal government had the power to bring the forces of wealth to justice (p. 61).

2.2 *Early Successes*

The Special Agent Force changed names to the Bureau of Investigation (BOI) and, in general, succeeded in creating a detective force that was professional, relatively well paid, and disciplined. According to Attorney General Charles Bonaparte, the new force was superior to the older system of relying on private detectives who often came from the criminal ranks.

By 1910, the BOI surpassed Treasury's Secret Service in terms of both appropriations and number of special agents (Jeffreys-Jones 2007, p. 55). Congress retained its right of oversight of the Bureau, assuaging fear of centralized power. Initially the Bureau was purely investigative; its employees did not carry firearms, did not have the power to arrest, and strictly removed themselves from politics.

An array of high-profile cases burnished the image of the BOI and in 1935 the Bureau of Investigation changed its name to the Federal Bureau of Investigation (FBI). Some of the more infamous successes of the FBI transpired in the 1930s. Under the leadership of the Director J. Edgar Hoover, the Bureau established training schools to teach modern techniques, created a centralized fingerprint file, created state-of-the-art crime laboratories, founded the National Police Academy to train local police, and gave local law enforcement agents access to a central computer database (Israel 1986, p. 33). The FBI killed or apprehended a long list of infamous criminals including Bonnie Parker and Clyde Barrow (later immortalized in the 1967 motion picture *Bonnie and Clyde*), Ma Barker and her four sons, Charles "Pretty Boy" Floyd, John Dillinger, and Al Capone. FBI agents gained respect and fame when, according to legend, they cornered "Machine Gun" Kelly in Memphis, Tennessee, as he called out, "Don't Shoot, G-Men." The moniker gained immediate traction and began a glamorization of the FBI (Jeffreys-Jones 2007, p. 89). Movies such as the 1935 film *G-Men*, starring James Cagney, began to portray the FBI in a heroic light as a defender of law and order, fighting against the criminal elements in American society. The image of the FBI as a positive force for society held for decades (Powers 2004, p. 141). Hoover earnestly worked to promote this image. He appeared before civic and religious groups to denounce criminals; he denounced efforts of popular culture to romanticize criminals. Hoover encouraged magazines in the 1930s to carry comic strips and stories that portrayed the FBI as the "good guys" fighting to protect average Americans (Israel 1986, p. 46).

Other FBI successes helped to reinforce a view of the FBI as a defender against the lawless elements of society or foreign intruders. The FBI involved itself in the kidnapping case of the son of Charles Lindberg, the famous aviator who in 1927 completed the first solo transatlantic flight. In the "crime of the century," an unemployed carpenter named Bruno Richard Hauptmann kidnapped Lindberg's infant son on March 1, 1932. Lindberg paid the kidnapper \$50,000 in ransom money; however, 72 days later searchers found the child's body near the Lindberg home. The dead child had a crushed skull. When local police made little progress in solving the case, President Franklin D. Roosevelt ordered the FBI to coordinate the investigation that eventually led to Hauptmann's arrest and execution. Congress then passed legislation (Lindberg law) that made kidnapping across state lines a federal offense. The assistance of the FBI in solving the case was invaluable. An FBI agent reviewed the handwriting of hundreds of suspects before finding a match with the ransom note. The nation cheered the FBI as the courts convicted Hauptmann of murder and sent him to the electric chair (Jeffreys-Jones 2007, p. 88).

The FBI also became popular during World War II in protecting the home front against foreign spies. In 1942, agents of the Bureau captured eight Nazi saboteurs who landed by submarine on the shores of New York and Florida. The men were skilled in demolition of infrastructure such as bridges, railroad crossings, locks, water stations, and hydroelectric stations. With the help of the US Coast Guard, members of the FBI arrested all eight of the saboteurs. A military tribunal condemned all of them to death; however, two of the German saboteurs had their sentences commuted and were pardoned after the war. The capture and execution of the Nazi infiltrators helped reassure the nation that the FBI was successfully fulfilling its mission of protecting the country against threats both foreign and domestic (Powers 2004, p. 183). The 1942 arrests followed closely on the heels of a 1941 roundup of a German spy ring. In the roundup, agents arrested 33 German spies along with their network of support personnel. This operation practically shut down German intelligence operations in the United States (p. 177) and further embellished the reputation of America's "G-men" as protectors against subversion, both foreign and domestic.

The perceived successes of the FBI in the 1930s and 1940s enhanced the image of the Bureau. From the beginning of the New Deal until the end of World War II, the agency rode the crest of their popularity; the organization was adored by the public and seemingly invulnerable within the government. Everybody seemed to love the glamorous "G-men" (Powers 2004, p. 189). At the end of the 1950s, the Bureau still enjoyed good fortune. According to Powers (2004, p. 242) as the decade of the 1950s ended, the FBI was on top of the world, a massive presence on the American scene, dominating security and law enforcement. The Bureau and its director were "American icons, legendary figures." These halcyon days, however, would not last forever. By the time of Hoover's death in 1972 at the age of 77, the Bureau was embroiled in brewing controversy. Its image suffered great harm with revelations of unlawful behavior.

Many who did not consider themselves threats to the United States but people who exercised their constitutional right to dissent began to view the Bureau with fear and alarm. Later investigations of the FBI revealed that people were justified in their concerns about invasion of privacy and other matters.

3 Controversies—J. Edgar Hoover

J. Edgar Hoover is a polarizing figure in American history. In 1975, President Gerald Ford dedicated a new headquarters of the FBI, named the J. Edgar Hoover building. The 2.8-million-square-foot building is testament to Hoover's lasting influence on the organization. His long tenure as director of the organization (1924–1972) cast a deep shadow. Retrospective analysis of Hoover's actions, however, led to some disturbing revelations. Early in Hoover's tenure, the FBI developed a reputation for integrity and freedom from political control. By the 1970s, however, Hoover came under public criticism for his authoritarian leadership style as well as his disregard for constitutional rights. His zealotry led him to overlook guarantees of freedom inscribed in the US Bill of Rights. History seems to judge Hoover from contradictory lenses. On the one hand, one image of Hoover is that of a heroic "G-man" triumphing over lawlessness. On the other hand, a contrary image that seems to be ascendant is that of a secret police chief working to crush political and social change (Israel 1986, p. 34).

Some of Hoover's most controversial actions include his roundup of suspected leftists in the 1920s (Palmer Raids), deportations of radicals that followed the raids, and creation of FBI's Counter Intelligence Program (COINTELPRO) that engaged in wiretaps and illegal entry. Hoover's COINTELPRO engaged in a series of covert, and at times illegal, investigations designed to discredit or disrupt radical political organizations. The COINTELPRO attacked organization or people Hoover considered subversive. These organizations or people included the Black Panthers, the Socialist Workers Party, Martin Luther King, and the Ku Klux Klan, among others. In one of his more controversial investigations, Hoover ordered a round-the-clock surveillance on the civil rights leader Dr. Martin Luther King in hopes to find evidence of Communist influence or sexual deviance. Hoover gathered large files on King and others such as Eleanor Roosevelt, wife of President Franklin Delano Roosevelt. In 1971, Hoover's use of questionable methods (such as infiltration, burglaries, illegal wiretaps, planted evidence, and false rumors) was exposed and caused great embarrassment within the Bureau. In 1975, the Church Committee conducted an investigation of FBI Counter Intelligence operations and castigated the Bureau for their tactics. By the time Hoover died, people had long forgotten the accomplishments of his early tenure. Revelations of the Church Committee greatly tarnished the image of the agency. An environment of oversight and concern for civil liberties had emerged in the post-Hoover years. This environment differed considerably from the milieu of Hoover's early tenure in the Bureau when fear of subversives dominated.

3.1 Red Scare and Early Image of the FBI

Hoover's initial law enforcement experiences occurred in an environment of "Red Scare" apprehension. In 1919, many believed that Russian Bolsheviks were poised to proselytize the world and topple many of the democracies that were in place. In the United States, a wave of angst and unrest swept over the nation. Around this time, there were race riots, stoppages of coal and steel industries, a general strike in Seattle, and a police strike in Boston. Anarchists engaged in a bombing campaign. On June 2, 1919, an anarchist bomb exploded outside the home of Attorney General A. Mitchell Palmer. After the Palmer bombing, J. Edgar Hoover, at the age of 24, received the assignment of heading a new unit (termed the "Radical Division," later renamed the "General Intelligence Division" or GID) to investigate radical activity. Hoover and his men compiled file/dossiers on 200,000 individuals. Based on Hoover's fervent data collection, US officials deported individuals they considered undesirable. These individuals included popular figures of the American left such as Lithuanian-born anarchist Emma Goldman (Jeffreys-Jones 2007, p. 73).

Hoover enthusiastically embraced the idea of mass deportation. He drew up plans for what would become, at the time, the largest dragnet in American history. Hoover wished to build public support for a law that would extend the same prohibitions against sedition in times of peace as in war. On November 17, 1919 (the second anniversary of the Russian Revolution), Hoover orchestrated raids on meetings of the Union of Russian Workers. The Department of Labor had determined that membership in the organization rendered individuals subject to deportation. Raids across the country placed hundreds of aliens in makeshift holding pens. In Hartford, Connecticut, law enforcement officials held 97 aliens incommunicado for five months before transferring them to a federal prison (Powers 2004, p. 112). In general, government agents sought to rid the country of those they considered subversive and therefore threats to the national interest.

Hoover took personal interest in the arrests of Goldman and Alexander Berkman who attempted to murder Carnegie Steel executive Henry Frick. Hoover wrote the deportation briefs for Goldman (known to the public as "Red Emma") and Berkman. To assist in the deportation, Hoover himself discovered a flaw in Emma Goldman's claim that she was a citizen. Hoover declared that her claim was invalid since her marriage to an American citizen had been performed by someone whose authority to perform marriages was not recognized by American law. Hoover personally arranged for the transport of aliens in 1919. The raids and deportations initially were popular with the American public. None of the deportees, however, were found to directly involve themselves in bombings; deportees did not receive proper due process. The only justification for many deportations was an allegiance to the principles of anarchism (p. 114).

Hoover followed up his initial roundup with a more ambitious plan. He directed informants to convene meetings of radical groups (Communist Party and Communist Labor Party) and then directed hundreds of roundup at the meetings. The so-called Palmer Raids took place in 33 cities in 23 states across the country. On January 2, 1920, and the next few days between 4000 and 6000 radicals were placed in detention centers. Treatment of radicals was harsh (p. 117).

Hoover's autocratic methods gained unwanted attention. A backlash began as the head of the Department of Labor (who administered immigration laws) eventually ruled that membership in the Communist Labor Party was not a deportable offense. The assistant labor secretary found no lawful proof for many of the arrests. Many of those arrested were released. The fallout from Hoover's raids shattered Attorney General Palmer's political ambitions; he stepped down from the attorney general's position in 1921. Hoover survived the backlash; however, he earned the enduring enmity of the American left. The American Civil Liberties Union (ACLU) was formed in response to "Red Scare" abuses. In 1920, aided by prominent lawyers such as Felix Frankfurter, the ACLU released their *Report Upon the Illegal Practices of the United States Department of Justice.* The ACLU report concluded that the real threat to liberty in 1920 was not the Communist movement but the assault by Palmer and Hoover on principles of constitutional liberty (p. 119).

3.2 *Later Abuses of the FBI*

The Church Committee exposed egregious violations of civil rights of citizens during Hoover's long tenure in office. Many facts that previously were obscure became transparent because of the Church inquiry. These facts include the following. Beginning in the 1940s, FBI agents began to compile information about the sexual affairs of prominent Americans including members of Congress, Vice President Henry Wallace, First Lady Eleanor Roosevelt, White House aides, and Cabinet officers. Information contained allegations of homosexuality, adultery, and consorting with prostitutes. FBI officials collected derogatory personal and political information about all members of Congress. FBI reports would include all known instances of subversive activity and immoral conduct. Information from reports went into a "summary memorandum." This information proved invaluable in pressuring congressional representatives to support funding for the FBI. Hoover also maintained a folder on the sex life of President John F. Kennedy that he could potentially use to blackmail the president (Theoharis 2004, p. 103).

In theory, the FBI should not have been able to operate as they did, in wiretapping, opening mail, selectively leaking confidential information, monitoring the personal conduct of American citizens, and advancing partisan political interests. As an investigatory arm of the US DOJ, the mandate of the FBI is only to investigate violations of federal law. Congress has authority over the FBI. Congress can oversee FBI operations, hold hearings to evaluate the lawfulness of actions, and subpoena FBI records. The courts represent another check on the FBI and can prosecute abuses. Despite these checks on the power of the FBI, over time the organization amassed tremendous discretionary power over who to investigate, how to investigate, and who to prosecute.

According to Theoharis (2004, p. 106), secrecy inherent in intelligence gathering and deferential treatment contributed to the Bureau's ability to escape accountability. Theoharis posits that the key reason that FBI officials were able to neutralize presidential, congressional, and judicial oversight was a series of procedures that the agency instituted during the 1940s and 1950s. Beginning in 1940, Bureau officials informally authorized agents to install listening devices through break-ins, an unconstitutional practice. Hoover was committed to employing any technique that would enable the Bureau to anticipate subversive activities. By 1942, Hoover was routinely authorizing FBI break-ins. In order to preclude discovery of this illegal action, Hoover devised a special procedure for filing records. Requests for approval of break-ins were to be captioned "Do Not File." This would notify record keepers not to index files in the FBI's central records system; agents routed files to the director's office (Hoover) or the office of a designated assistant director. This procedure enabled the FBI to respond to requests for information about break-ins by affirming that there was "no record" of approving such practices in the FBI's central records system (p. 108).

The FBI was aware that they were engaged in illegal practices. They screened potential recruits to be participants in "break-in squads." FBI agents received monetary reward and special commendations for their illegal activities. In the 1950s, the FBI also began to compile files on candidates seeking election to Congress. Agents then produced a "summary memorandum" of information. The FBI did not file the memoranda in the Bureau's central records system but maintained the records separately. The Bureau could then truthfully deny that they maintained files or dossiers on members of Congress. This system was uncovered in 1972. Hoover's Personal File contained extensive information about members of Congress. FBI agents developed derogatory personal or political information about members of Congress including affairs of wives, drinking, and relations with male or female prostitutes (p. 115). Representatives in Congress recognized that Hoover had tremendous power over their lives, destinies, and reputations.

In 1956, Hoover unilaterally instituted a secret program named COINTELPRO. Initially the COINTELPRO named COINTELPRO-Communist Party oriented itself to undermining the Communist movement. The intent of the program was to limit the ability of members of the Communist movement to create disunity within America and to mold public opinion. Tactics of COINTELPRO-Communist Party included sending anonymous letters intended to provoke factionalism or leaking derogatory personal information about Communist activists. The FBI leaked information to sympathetic reporters as well as members of Congress (Theoharis 2004, p. 120).

The perceived success of the COINTELPRO-Communist Party program led to the expansion of COINTELPROs to other groups such as the Socialist Workers Party, Ku Klux Klan, Black Nationalists, and the New Left. The COINTELPRO-Socialist Workers Party and COINTELPRO-White Hate employed tactics similar to those employed in the COINTELPRO-Communist Party program. These tactics include sowing internal dissent, leaking derogatory information, and promoting hostile public opinion. The FBI instructed agents to expose duplicity of white supremacists. Efforts of

COINTELPRO-Black Nationalist Hate aimed to disrupt, misdirect, or otherwise neutralize the activities of black-nationalist organizations, their leadership, spokespeople, members, and supporters. Aims of COINTELPRO-New Left were to disseminate misinformation in order to disrupt organizations that associated themselves with the New Left. Tactics ranged from promoting dissension among activists, sending anonymous letters to parents, calling attention to illicit sexual activity or drug use, and disseminating derogatory information to friendly news media. Hoover unilaterally authorized the secret COINTELPROs. The FBI morphed from an intelligence-gathering agency that was divorced from politics into an agency with its own political agenda. The FBI moved in the direction of becoming an autonomous agency with officials advancing their own political agenda (p. 122).

Hoover became highly critical of organizations such as the National Association for the Advancement of Colored People (NAACP) for exacerbating racial tensions through what he termed "racial hatred." He associated civil rights activism with Communist influence. To contain the perceived threat of the civil rights movement, the FBI launched a secret program code-named "Racial Matters" to evaluate the influence of Communist forces on civil rights organizations. The FBI became particularly interested in the activities of Reverend Martin Luther King following his leadership role in the Montgomery bus boycott of 1955. The FBI authorized wiretaps of King's residence, office, headquarters of the Southern Christian Leadership Conference (SCLC), and King's hotel rooms during his trips around the country. In 1964, the FBI created a composite of tapes recording King's sexual activities and mailed the tapes along with a cover letter threatening to expose his "hideous abominations." The letter called King a "colossal fraud and an evil," an "evil beast," and "no clergyman." It concluded, "You are done. There is but one way out for you. You better take it before your filthy fraudulent self is bared to the nation" (Powers 2004, p. 246). King, his wife, and close associates listened to the recording and immediately concluded that it was from the FBI. Friends speculated that the purpose of the mailing was to blackmail King, goad King's wife into a divorce, or put the thought of suicide in King's mind (p. 247).

The use of the FBI as an arm of the president reached unprecedented levels under the Nixon administration. The Watergate scandals helped to unravel the secrecy that previously shrouded the Bureau's operations. Subsequent congressional inquiries (such as the Church Committee) exposed the scope and nature of FBI abuses. People learned that in 1969 at the request of the White House, FBI agents began to monitor and wiretap the president's appointees to the White House, National Security Council (NSC) staff, State Department officials, Defense Department officials, and Washington-based reporters (Theoharis 2004, p. 128).

The congressional investigations further scarred the reputation of the FBI. The investigations revealed that on the one hand the FBI's authority derived from the Attorney General and White House. On the other hand, FBI officials operated independently and insubordinately. Disturbing images formed of the Bureau as an organization that violated the law. Some began to view the leadership of the FBI as mostly committed to advancing their own political and bureaucratic agendas. By 1975, only 37 percent of the public held a "highly favorable" rating of the FBI compared to 84 percent in 1966 and 71 percent in 1970 (p. 139).

The various COINTELPROs launched by the Bureau began to place the organization on a slippery slope and descent into secrecy and illegal means of countering what it considered threats to the nation. Hoover, in his desire to suppress urban riots of the 1960s, advocated tactics that differed from those advanced by Johnson administration officials. Hoover perceived rioters as subversives trying to overthrow the government and destroy society. He advocated the use of undercover programs to disrupt protest movements. Others such as Johnson administration Attorney General Katzenbach sought negotiation and open contact with protestors. Hoover launched various disruptive operations against "black hate" groups. He tried to incite confrontations between the Black Panther Party and rivals within the black movement (Powers 2004, p. 274).

By the end of Hoover's long reign, the image of the FBI was in tatters. Its days of G-man glory were a distant memory. It was no longer a force of good; it mutated into a force of evil to forever chip away at civil liberties. Powers (2004, p. 295) states:

> Before the seventies were over, Hoover's successor would be driven from office in disgrace for destroying evidence during the Watergate scandal. The secrets of COINTELPRO would be laid bare in excruciating detail and would, unfairly but understandably come to symbolize the FBI of the Hoover era. The G-man hero, an American icon for decades, would become a popular entertainment villain, the face of a government in conspiracy against its citizens' liberties.... The Bureau would now become something to be resisted and reviled, a scapegoat for the nation's sins of Vietnam and Watergate.

4 Controversies—Mark Felt and James Comey

4.1 Mark Felt

Certain individuals within the FBI helped to promulgate massive changes in American politics. Two such men are Mark Felt of Watergate fame and James Comey, linked to the Clinton email and Russia collusion investigations. The activities of both these individuals seem to extend well beyond the purported investigatory role of the FBI. The activities of both Felt and Comey suggest that FBI agents have begun to play a proactive role in American politics. This role includes leaking Nixon cover-up information to the press ("Deep Throat" intrigue of Watergate), holding press conferences about abuses of a presidential candidate (Clinton email controversy), and creating as well as leaking records of conversations with a sitting president (Comey memos of discussion with Trump). Like Hoover, some FBI figures have become dominant players in the political arena. This is a sharp departure from the original intent of the FBI as more of a staff function, an investigatory arm of the DOJ.

To his family and opponents of Richard Nixon, Mark Felt will always be a hero. Felt, as "Deep Throat," helped enormously in convincing Richard Nixon to step down from the office of the presidency. As a key whistleblower, Felt supplied inside information to *Washington Post* investigatory reporters Bob Woodward and Carl Bernstein. According to First Amendment scholars, whistleblowers such as Felt serve the public by breaking ranks and assisting in the exposure of governmental misconduct. From this perspective, Felt deserves the nation's honor and respect. Without Felt, the public may never have known about abuses of presidential powers in the Nixon White House. Felt's motivations for leaking information, however, are unclear. Felt stated he believed that Nixon had been misusing the FBI for political advantage. He wrote that the president wanted a politician in the FBI who would convert the bureau into an adjunct of the White House. Felt's motives may not have been noble; personal antagonisms with the White House were involved. In 1971, J. Edgar Hoover promoted Felt to deputy associate director of the FBI. Felt expected to become the next FBI director. He was the number three person at the Bureau and his two immediate superiors were aging. When J. Edgar Hoover died in 1972, however, Nixon appointed Assistant Attorney General L. Patrick Gray to be acting director.

According to notes from *Washington Post* reporter Bob Woodward, Felt was not completely honest in their discussions. Former White House counsel John Dean stated that the quality of Felt's information as found in the Woodward and Bernstein book *All the President's Men* is of questionable value. Some express the opinion that Felt betrayed the FBI and the legal machinery that protects the country. According to this view, Felt was no hero; he did everything with one goal in mind: to become FBI director. He did not assist the media for the good of the country; he used the media in service of his own ambition. Despite the cynics, a 2017 movie, *Mark Felt: The Man Who Brought Down the White House*, portrays Felt as a profound patriot and dedicated career public servant (Holland 2017). Felt as the inside source of information for journalists Bob Woodward and Carl Bernstein played a pivotal role in bringing down the presidency of Richard Nixon in 1974. Felt wished to remain anonymous; yet in 2005, reports revealed his identity. His family persuaded Felt to come into the open in order to capitalize on a book deal and other opportunities. Felt died in 2008 at the age of 95.

Felt's legacy is decidedly mixed. To many critics of Richard Nixon, he remains a hero for aiding in the resignation of a feared and despised president. To others he contributed to the dark practices of the FBI and did damage to the Bureau's reputation. In the early 1970s, as a member of the FBI, Felt oversaw operations that collected information about radical groups such as the Weather Underground. Felt authorized FBI agents to break into homes without a search warrant. After revelation of illegal wiretaps, the government prosecuted many FBI agents, including Felt. In 1976, Felt admitted to ordering break-ins; he also expressed the view that the government should not punish agents under this direction since they were merely following his orders. Felt recognized that the break-ins were extralegal but justified them as necessary for protecting the greater good. He noted that he would act in the same manner again.

In 1980, the government tried Felt for violating the civil rights of people thought to be associated with the Weather Underground Organization. At the Felt trial, former president Nixon appeared as a witness and testified that in authorizing the FBI to conduct break-ins to gather intelligence information Felt was acting on precedents established by a number of former presidents. Nixon also contributed money to Felt's defense fund. The jury in Felt's trial returned a guilty verdict. Although the charges against him carried a maximum sentence of ten years in prison, Felt received a fine of $5000. President Ronald Reagan later pardoned Felt, noting that during his long career Felt served the FBI and America with great distinction. Reagan stated that Felt's conviction grew out of his good-faith belief that the actions were necessary to preserve the security interests of America. Felt appealed the conviction and, in 1982, he was able to reacquire his law license (Koven 2015).

Mark Felt is not as notorious as other FBI officials such as J. Edgar Hoover or James Comey. His whistleblowing actions during the Watergate reporting, however, produced a number of revelations. First, the FBI as the nation's lead investigatory organization has inside knowledge about many powerful men and women in the United States. This was true in the time of Hoover and remains true in the time of Felt and Comey. Second, this inside knowledge can and has been "weaponized" through strategic leaks to a media that is always eager to collect "dirt" that might produce good stories and sell more newspapers. Third, the discretionary power of government organizations such as the FBI to reveal or hide information often operates below the radar. Government organizations and officials working within the organizations have great power to discredit political opponents. The unusual actions of FBI Director Comey follow the script of Mark Felt in terms of leaking information to the media and becoming engaged in political intrigue. In contrast to acting at the behest of legitimate authorities for investigating dangerous behavior, civil libertarians fear that the FBI and their representatives may become a power unto themselves with significant influence over elections and even influential in the removal of officials.

The section below reviews James Comey's actions during and following the 2016 presidential election. It appears that Comey's very public pronouncements about Hillary Clinton's emails and his decision not to prosecute her, as well as his decision to "memorialize" and leak conversations with Donald Trump, had a profound effect on both Clinton and Trump. This would appear to go far beyond the mandate of an FBI official and perhaps augur in a new era where the FBI takes a more active role in determining election outcomes.

4.2 *James Comey*

James Comey did not enhance the image and reputation of the FBI in the eyes of much of the American public. Comey probably brought more attention to the Bureau than any director did since J. Edgar Hoover brought. His conduct during the Hillary Clinton email investigation was particularly befuddling to average Americans when after castigating her conduct he declared that no "reasonable" prosecutor would bring charges against her. This conclusion only raised "red flags" to even casual observers of American politics. Did Comey conclude that former Secretary of State Clinton was too important of a person for someone to believe that prosecutors could convict her of a crime? Was the evidence weak? Why did Comey present a public spectacle of describing a series of potentially criminal acts only to declare that he decided not to take action? Is the role of the FBI to publicly castigate high-level politicians and then proclaim their exoneration? Is the proper role of the FBI to investigate potential crimes and turn matters over to the DOJ for prosecution, not to inform the public about misbehaving politicians while at the same time saying the action does not reach a level high enough for prosecution? It appears that Comey's announcement about Hillary Clinton did not instill confidence in the Bureau but further stoked antipathy toward the organization. The FBI became a target of Clinton supporters who blamed him for her 2016 defeat. Later, Comey earned the wrath of Trump supporters with his efforts to appoint a special prosecutor by leaking contents of a discussion with President Trump.

Hoover and Comey bear some similarity. Both used the media to generate attention. Both were convinced about the righteousness of their actions. Both seem to have stretched the law at times in order to attain their goals. Notable differences, however, exist. In the 1970s as the Church Committee uncovered illegal practices of the FBI, civil libertarians attacked the FBI for illegal methods of obtaining information about perceived subversives. Supporters of "law and order" tended to be more forgiving and justified some FBI action in the name of protecting America from dangerous dissidents. In contrast, attacks on Comey and the FBI came from both liberal Democrats and conservative Republicans. Comey stirred the anger of both Clinton and Trump loyalists. This is unusual for the head of a government agency supposedly detached from the quagmire of politics.

In her book *What Happened*, Clinton noted that James Comey's interventions in the investigation of her emails sapped her momentum and allowed Donald Trump to paint her as "Crooked Hillary." The former secretary of state contended that the FBI was a hotbed on anti-Clinton fervor while at the same time they did not confirm the existence of a Trump-Russia investigation (Landler 2017). Longtime Clinton supporters openly criticized Director Comey. Clinton's former economic advisor

Jared Bernstein stated that the damage Comey did to the country by his role in the 2016 election far surpasses any credit he gets for investigating Trump. Clinton ally Lanny Davis called Comey a "renegade narcissist" who thought he was above the law. In one of his many tweets, Donald Trump claimed that Comey had disclosed classified information, lied to Congress, was not smart, and was the worst FBI director in history, by far (Shear 2018).

In a May 10, 2017, memo addressed to Attorney General Jeff Sessions, deputy director of the DOJ, Rod Rosenstein, delineates reasons for his disapproval of James Comey's conduct. In the memo titled "Restoring public confidence in the FBI" Rosenstein states that it is "deeply troubling to many Department [FBI] employees and veterans, legislators and citizens" that the FBI's reputation and credibility have suffered "substantial damage." He notes that Comey is "an articulate and persuasive speaker about leadership and immutable principles of the Department of Justice." Nevertheless Rosenstein concludes that he "cannot defend the Director's handling at the conclusion of Secretary Clinton's emails, and I do not understand his refusal to accept the nearly universal judgment that he was mistaken." Ironically, the deputy director notes that Comey's "serious mistakes" represent "one of the few issues that unites people of diverse perspectives."

In a stinging rebuke to Comey, Rosenstein writes that it "was wrong to usurp the Attorney General's authority" and announce that the case "should be closed without prosecution." Rosenstein points out that "it is not the function of the Director [Comey] to make such an announcement. At most, the Director should have said the FBI had completed its investigation and presented its findings to federal prosecutors." Comey defended his decision by asserting his belief that former Attorney General Loretta Lynch had a conflict. Rosenstein rebuts this assertion noting, "The FBI Director is never empowered to supplant federal prosecutors and assume command of the Justice Department.... We do not hold press conferences to release derogatory information about the subject of a declined criminal investigation.... The Director laid out his version of the facts for the news media as if it were a closing argument, but without a trial. It is a textbook example of what federal prosecutors and agents are taught not to do." In the memo, Rosenstein states that his perspective on Comey's "wrong" actions is shared by former attorney general and deputy attorney general from different eras and both political parties. He concludes, "I agree with the nearly unanimous opinions of former Department officials. The way the Director handled the conclusion of the email investigation was wrong. As a result, the FBI is unlikely to regain public and congressional trust until it has a Director who understands the gravity of the mistakes and pledges never the repeat them. Having refused to admit his errors, the Director cannot be expected to implement the necessary corrective actions" (Rosenstein 2017).

People of all political stripes described the damage they believed Comey did, not only to the FBI but to the credibility of the election system. Democrats said the findings of a Bureau's investigator general report made it clear that the FBI had effectively helped elect Trump by damaging Hillary Clinton. House Judiciary Committee ranking member Jerry Nadler of New York and Oversight Committee ranking member Elijah Cummings of Maryland stated that Comey had a double standard; he spoke publicly about the Clinton investigation while keeping secret from the American people the investigation of Donald Trump and Russia. The Democratic leaders were angered that Comey talked so much and so often, about a case that he ultimately had concluded should not result in any prosecution. The Democratic leaders surmised that the FBI should not have revealed that they had reopened the case just days before the election. Those actions violate guidelines designed to protect citizens from unfair attacks and avoid influencing elections. New Bureau Director Christopher Wray pledged to take immediate remedial actions to reinforce the importance of maintaining a work environment free from the appearance of political bias (Johnson 2018).

Conservative commentators were equally critical of Director Comey. Fox News contributor Gregg Jarrett (2018, p. 244) claims that Comey cultivated a public image of himself as a grown-up Boy Scout, honest and morally straight. However, Jarrett maintains that the truth is quite different because records show that he was less than honest, engaged in acts of questionable legality, and abused his power to further his ambitions. During testimony to the Senate Intelligence Committee in June 2017, Comey admitted that he deliberately leaked contents of his conversations with Donald Trump to Daniel Richman of Columbia University Law School. He then directed the law professor to leak the information to the *New York Times* with the objective of triggering the appointment of a Special Counsel to investigate Trump. Jarrett concludes, "Far from the image of an honest and honourable Boy Scout, the evidence is compelling that James Comey sought to mislead, deflect, and deceive. He also appears to have abused the powers of his office to exact punishment on the president who fired him. His plan to convert presidential memos for his own use, then leak them to the media to damage Trump suggests a willingness to defy rules, regulations, and federal laws with impunity" (p. 252).

Jarrett further asserts that Comey contorted the law to clear the path for the election of Hillary Clinton and abuse the power of his position to bring a case against Donald Trump to defeat him in the election. When Trump was elected, Jarrett claims that Comey and other "Washington insiders" sought to frame the new president for crimes he did not commit (p. xiv). Jarrett observes that it became evident to him that "the FBI, as well as the Department of Justice, had become cesspools of corruption that played a direct hand in attempting to influence the election and subvert the democratic process" (p. xv). He surmises that top officials in the FBI misconstrued the law to absolve Hillary Clinton of felony statutes and "weaponized other laws" to investigate Trump in an effort to destroy him. In so doing Comey and others "breached their duty to uphold the law" (p. 282).

5 Jurisdictional Conflict—ICE and Sanctuary Cities

5.1 ICE

US Immigration and Customs Enforcement (ICE) agency was formed in 2003 following Homeland Security legislation. In 2018, its budget was $7.6 billion with more than 20,000 employees. The organization has two primary responsibilities: Homeland Security Investigations (HSI) and Enforcement and Removal Operations (ERO). ICE's mandate is to enforce approximately 400 federal immigration and labor-related statutes, primarily in the nation's interior, and work to remove people for immigration violations. An additional duty includes monitoring businesses for undocumented workers. Patrolling the US border is the responsibility of Customs and Border Protection, another agency that was formed in 2003.

Upon ICE's creation in 2003, various agencies moved entirely or partially merged into the new organization of ICE. ICE acquired the investigative and intelligence resources of the US Customs Service, as well as the criminal investigative, detention, and deportation resources of the Immigration and Naturalization Services. The ERO branch of ICE identifies and apprehends removable aliens, detains individuals when necessary, and removes illegal aliens from the United States. ERO manages aliens in custody and provides access to legal resources. A mission of the ERO is to identify, arrest, and remove aliens who present a danger to national security or are a risk to public safety including those who enter the United States illegally.

The HSI branch of ICE represents an investigative arm of the Department of Homeland Security. It is committed to combating criminal organizations who exploit America's travel, trade, financial, and immigration systems. HSI has broad legal authority to enforce an array of federal statutes. It investigates all types of cross-border criminal activity, including money laundering, theft of intellectual property, human smuggling, document fraud, narcotics trafficking, and other activities. ICE has become a lightning rod for controversy, particularly regarding the activities of enforcement and removal.

Presidential directives highly influence operational guidelines for ICE. In 2016, Donald Trump ran on a platform that promised to deport millions of undocumented immigrants. In January 2017, he issued an executive order that prioritized removal of anyone who had entered the country illegally. This, in essence, marked a return to a policy that Barack Obama originally embraced but ultimately repudiated. For the first six years of his presidency, Obama oversaw a program under which ICE picked up undocumented persons who were booked into jail on any criminal charges. In 2014, Obama altered the policy to focus on immigrants guilty of "serious" crimes. In contrast to the Obama policy of prioritizing "serious" crimes, during the Trump administration ICE agents expanded their mandate and used decades-old misdemeanors as grounds for arrest. ICE critics claim that agents have arrested undocumented immigrants seeking redress at family and small claims courts. Immigrant advocates allege that domestic violence complaints in immigrant communities have decreased as a result (Hinkle and Levinson-Waldman 2018).

The precise rationale for targeting individuals is unclear. The Trump and early Obama administrations focus on any undocumented immigrant while the later Obama administration prioritizes those linked to "serious" crimes. Under Obama, it appears that prosecutors had wide discretion in pursuing immigration cases. Under Trump, ICE agents could select people for deportation even if they had committed minor violations.

The ICE narrative is part of a broader debate in the United States about immigration policy. Lawmakers calling to abolish ICE have framed the issue in moral terms, claiming that the agency's widespread use of deportations for undocumented immigrants without criminal records is inhumane, and detracts from its more important function of investigating drug smuggling and human rights abuses. Sean McElwee has been a leader in the effort to eliminate ICE. According to McElwee, the Abolish ICE movement is fundamentally an anti-deportation movement and after the agency is gone, the central aim has to be ensuring that mass deportation is not housed somewhere else in the government.

Polling from Gallup in 2018 shows that most American adults generally oppose deporting all undocumented immigrants. Critics of immigration policy depict ICE as a personal deportation force for Donald Trump. A number of lawmakers such as Democratic Representative Pramila Jayapal of Washington and Representative Mark Pocan of Wisconsin called for the total elimination of ICE. Pocan introduced legislation to dismantle the agency. Congressman Pocan did not state that authorities should stop pursuing undocumented immigrants altogether but was highly critical of what he perceived to be the indiscriminate, random use of deportations. Many Democrats believe deportations should still happen, but are unclear about the criteria for deportation. Immigrant policy observers note that there has not been a broader conversation about which undocumented immigrants they would remove and which they would not (Godfrey 2018).

ICE is among the many law enforcement agencies that evoke fear and distrust among residents of the United States. During the Trump administration, the perceived discretionary power of ICE has increased as the approximate 11 million undocumented immigrants have become subject to arrest and deportation. Many believe that it is unrealistic politically and practically to deport 11 million people, many of whom have lived in the United States for decades. Therefore, ICE might act arbitrarily and capriciously to choose who to arrest rather than apply one standard uniformly. This will likely exacerbate fear and charges of "unfair" application of rules. Foer (2018, p. 68) notes that under Trump's executive order that repealed the policy of prioritizing deportation of illegals that committed "serious" crimes, every undocumented immigrant was unsafe. Trump officials later claimed that they would use some prioritization mechanism for removal.

The more aggressive nature of ICE's actions during the Trump administration is evident in the number of arrests and the places of arrest. Prior to the election of Donald Trump, ICE officials did not move into "sensitive locations" such as schools, places of worship, and hospitals. Anecdotal evidence reveals a change in this policy as ICE more frequently operates in those "sensitive locations." ICE increasingly conducted raids in sanctuary cities where local police decline to hand over information about undocumented immigrants to federal authorities (p. 68). Evidence exists that immigrant families are altering their life routines by driving less, keeping children indoors, and declining to report domestic abuse. Local newspapers in Los

Angeles and Houston report sharp decreases in Latino use of health clinics and declines in allegations of Latino domestic abuse.

ICE actions feed into the narrative of law enforcement abuse that is prevalent in low-income and minority communities. ICE may already have accomplished the goal of limiting immigration. According to the Pew Research Center, there were 1.3 million fewer undocumented Mexican immigrants in the United States in 2016 than in 2007. Even with the increase in migration from Honduras, El Salvador, and Guatemala, illegal border crossings in 2017 were a fraction of what they were in the 1980s and 1990s (p. 69).

5.2 *Sanctuary Cities*

There is no single definition of what is a sanctuary city. The phrase is often recognized as a representing a jurisdiction that limits its cooperation with federal immigration enforcement agents in order to protect immigrants from deportation. How localities limit cooperation varies. Some sanctuary cities refrain from alerting federal authorities about undocumented immigrants; others have laws that prohibit law enforcement officers from asking people about their immigration status or implement unofficial practices that help protect immigrants from deportation. In 2018, according to the Center for Immigration Studies, there were about 300 cities, counties, and states with policies that hinder federal immigration enforcement. These jurisdictions include large cities such as New York, Boston, and New Orleans as well as states such as California, New Mexico, and Colorado.

The perception among some Americans that sanctuary cities harbor dangerous criminals helps to fuel fear of immigrants and distrust in the ability of the government to provide safety for law-abiding citizens. Sanctuary cities illuminate noncompliance with national directives and ideological dissonance between levels of government. Sanctuary cities also have become a "hot button" political issue with significant electoral ramifications. Anti-immigrant politicians have leveraged the sanctuary city controversy to their advantage, especially regarding fears of the "other." These politicians maintain that these "others" threaten traditional American norms and values.

Advocates for sanctuary cities point to the image of America as a nation of immigrants, the need for workers, or the good conduct of many undocumented immigrants who have lived in the United States for decades

(Koven and Göetzke 2010). Sanctuary city supporters note that complying with ICE requests to detain arrestees could harm police-community trust and make undocumented people afraid to report crimes. Critics of sanctuary cities, on the other hand, claim that sanctuary cities harbor dangerous criminals, produce needless deaths, make it more difficult to combat gangs, and necessitate spending valuable resources to arrest people after local communities release them. Those who attack sanctuary cities note that it would be chaos to have 3000 differing immigration policies with each locality creating their own rules. They advocate more uniformity in immigration rules with the federal government taking the lead.

The sanctuary city controversy exacerbates perceptions of unfairness in the American judicial system. Rather than the concept of equal justice under the law, sanctuary cities reinforce the view that place matters. The 2015 shooting death of a 31-year-old woman, Kathryn Steinle, along the San Francisco waterfront inflamed the contentious debate over sanctuary cities. In 2015, Obama administration officials accused San Francisco officials of releasing the suspected murderer of Steinle in defiance of national efforts that could have led to his deportation. The murder suspect, Juan Francisco Lopez-Sanchez (also known as Jose Ines Garcia-Zarate), had seven felony convictions and authorities deported him from the United States five times. Despite the criminal background, San Francisco officials released Lopez-Sanchez from custody after a local arrest for a drug offense. The federal Department of Homeland Security requested that Lopez-Sanchez be deported a sixth time to his native Mexico but according to ICE agents, San Francisco officials did not provide them with the necessary information. The Steinle murder became fodder for 2016 Republican candidate Donald Trump who began to describe Mexicans entering the country illegally as "rapists" and "murderers" (Markon 2015). The 2018 arrest of undocumented immigrant Cristhian Rivera in the murder of 20-year-old University of Iowa student Mollie Tibbetts further fueled distrust of immigrants.

Conflicts between higher and lower levels of US government are endemic and originate at least as far back as the conflicting views of Thomas Jefferson and Alexander Hamilton. The sanctuary city conflict reveals not only a lack of consistency with policy but also a willingness of localities to implement policies in open defiance of national directives. The conflict between the various levels of government fuels distrust of police. On one side of the policy debate are politicians such as Oakland Mayor

Libby Schaaf who praise sanctuary cities as the epitome of humane treatment. At the other extreme is former Attorney General Jeff Sessions, who threatened to withhold federal funds from several sanctuary cities and filed suit against California. In 2018, Donald Trump declared that sanctuary cities put innocent Americans at the mercy of hardened criminals.

Federal agents in the past have operated without regard to local sensibilities. Local laws have not deterred ICE raids. In 2017, California passed a law that prevents local jail officials from telling federal ICE agents when they will release a prisoner unless ICE has a warrant signed by a judge. This noncooperation of information sharing, however, does not stop ICE agents from being able to arrest, detain, or deport immigrants. Following the 2017 California law, ICE escalated their arrests raids in California. In 2018, ICE agents engaged in a large immigrant sweep in Northern California and raids on numerous California 7-Eleven franchises (Lind 2018).

The issue of sanctuary cities relates fundamentally to the conception of federalism and the divisions of power between the national level and other levels of government. The courts recognize that immigration enforcement is the prerogative of the federal government; however, Congress has defined specific circumstances under which the federal government may delegate immigration enforcement authority to state and local authorities. Delegation occurs when state and local police departments sign Memoranda of Understanding (MOU) with ICE. These MOUs allow state and local police to enforce civil immigration laws as long as they participate in ICE training, agree to ICE supervision, and abide by certain ICE rules. Undocumented immigrants have less protection against law enforcement agents than American citizens. Immigrants are more susceptible to police action for two reasons. First, immigrants are entitled to fewer constitutional protections. Second, the structure of immigration law, with its multiple overlapping actors, limits accountability (Policing Immigrant Communities 2015).

Federal as well as local agents can abuse their authority. They possess discretion in terms of who to arrest and/or prosecute. The discretionary powers of federal organizations such as the FBI or ICE are significant but limits exist. Whistleblowing on the part of government employees, in the past, have exposed major violations within some large federal organizations. The narrative of the VA indicates that individuals still come forward to expose and take actions that may lead to corrective behavior.

6 Possible Checks on Agency Abuses—Whistleblowing

6.1 Sam Foote, the Doctor Who Launched the VA Scandal

The whistleblowing actions of Dr. Sam Foote further reinforces the belief that the actions of concerned professionals can have immense impact on remedying problems in a large government bureaucracy. When Foote filed a complaint with the VA Office of Inspector General (OIG) in 2013, it directly led to nationwide investigations, congressional hearings, political speeches, and the resignation of a Cabinet secretary. Foote's internal moral compass forced him to investigate what turned out to be gross abuses of power by national-level bureaucrats that impaired veteran care.

Foote became concerned in August 2013 when a colleague informed him that veterans were dying while waiting for treatment. Scheduling clerks who made reminder calls to veterans learned that in at least ten cases patients had already died. Foote then became aware of the fact that his employer, the Phoenix VA hospital, was "cooking the books" in a variety of ways in order to cover up wait-time delays. Foote discovered for himself that veterans died waiting for care and began to raise concerns. Foote realized that VA administrators were earning promotions and bonus pay by fraudulently stating that patient access had improved dramatically. Foote's concerns, however, did not generate remedial action. In early 2013, he lodged a formal complaint against a VA executive; soon after supervisors retaliated against him by increasing his caseload. The longtime employee then moved up the date for his retirement and began to collect information for an OIG complaint. The complaint would allege that up to 40 veterans died while awaiting care from the Phoenix VA system. The VA responded by dispatching an inspector general team to Phoenix to begin investigating (Wagner 2014).

At the same time as the OIG team began investigating, Foote contacted the local media (newspaper *The Arizona Republic*) and agreed to cooperate on an investigative project. In February 2014, a former Maricopa County attorney advised Foote to go national with the story. Foote then mailed a second letter to the VA inspector general with copies to Sen. John McCain (R-Ariz.), Rep. Ann Kirkpatrick (D-Ariz.), and the US Attorney's Office. In the letter, Foote complained that VA investigators had failed to protect Arizona veterans despite evidence of "gross mismanagement of VA resources and criminal misconduct" that had caused "systemic patient-safety issues and possible wrongful deaths."

The Arizona newspaper located additional whistleblowers, including Dr. Katherine Mitchell, a physician at the VA who corroborated Foote's information. Initially, Foote felt that politicians were ignoring his complaint but his assertions gained traction when the staff director of the oversight subcommittee of the House Committee on Veterans' Affairs took notice. On April 9, 2014, during a House Veterans' Affairs Committee hearing, Florida Representative Jeff Miller announced evidence showing VA officials were falsifying records of care for veterans in Arizona. Miller then stated delays in veteran care could have caused as many as 40 deaths (Wagner 2014).

On April 23, 2014, CNN interviewed Foote, who told the network that the Phoenix VA hospital had a "sham list" showing the VA was providing medical appointments within 14 days, a national goal. The hospital reached the goal by allowing a patient to remain on the secret list until he or she had an appointment time that was less than 14 days. This process would give the appearance that the hospital was sharply reducing waiting times, when, in reality, the wait to see a doctor had been 6, 9, and, in some cases, 21 months. Foote described other means the VA used to distort reality. He noted that if a veteran requested an appointment and the first available slot was five months away, if the veteran agreed to that wait time a VA scheduler could mark the wait as zero days.

"Tricks" employed in the Phoenix VA hospital included reducing caseloads by having staff make appointments for people who were dead and calling a patient the night before an appointment, requesting additional paperwork, and reschedule appointments for a later date. Foote's narrative of abuse at the VA hospital went viral. Veterans' organizations held town halls, House and Senate Committees convened hearings, and more whistleblowers came forward. VA Secretary Eric Shinseki ordered audits of the department's more than 900 medical facilities. The OIG confirmed Foote's accusations and launched probes in at least 42 other VA locations. Many members of Congress demanded the resignation of VA Secretary Shinseki who subsequently resigned. Following Shinseki's resignation, Foote stated that he could not celebrate his vindication. He speculated that former Secretary Shinseki was a good man duped or overmatched by a monolithic bureaucracy (Wagner 2014).

7 Additional VA Whistleblowers

Dr. Katherine Mitchell, a colleague of Sam Foote, became a whistleblower who publicized numerous problems at the VA Medical Center in Phoenix, Arizona. The Department of Veterans Affairs failed to protect her confidentiality, reassigned her to a different department, and left her open to retaliation by fellow employees. The VA transferred Mitchell after she filed complaints with hospital administrators about patient-threatening problems in the hospital's Emergency Department (ED). She later became the object of an investigation and reprimand after raising serious concerns about veteran suicides. Along with Foote, Mitchell provided detailed information to Congress, the VA inspector general, and the local newspaper about delayed care, falsified appointment data, mismanagement, and other issues.

In written testimony submitted in 2014 to the Senate Committee on Veterans' Affairs, Mitchell stated that the VA involuntarily transferred her to a defunct VA clinic in retaliation for repeatedly identifying dangerous ED patient safety deficits. She claims that after years of having her reports of life-threatening conditions ignored by the Phoenix VA she publicly became a whistleblower in April of 2014. Mitchell alerted both the public and Congress to unsafe conditions in the Phoenix VA ED, facility scheduling irregularities, and other issues such as the hospital's retaliation against her. After she accepted another position in the VA, VA officials informed her that she could not actively address the dangerous conditions that exist at the Phoenix VA (Mitchell 2015).

In her testimony before Congress, Mitchell referred to an Office of Special Counsel(OSC)/VA Office of Medical Inspector report that admitted to substandard nursing care, a significant lack of nurse training, and inadequate nursing protocols. She notes that training to remedy identified deficiencies did not convey necessary symptom knowledge or imply a mastery of necessary skills. Mitchell stated that the Phoenix VA misled the public into believing that training resolved safety deficits while, in fact, there had been no significant training to give nurses the knowledge to evaluate patient symptoms effectively. Mitchell was not satisfied with the government response to her revelations. She states, "Since the Phoenix VA access scandal erupted there has been no significant change in the dysfunctional institutional culture of the Phoenix VA Medical Center or sister VA facilities. In Phoenix and elsewhere administrators who are known to retaliate still occupy positions of leadership.... VA employees today still risk backlash for bringing up patient care problems, identifying misuse of facility resources, and questioning violations of VA policies and procedures" (Mitchell 2015).

According to Mitchell, dangerous conditions still existed in the Phoenix VA. She identified the potential of dangerous condition in VA Emergency Rooms and Mental Health clinics. Mitchell concluded that the purpose of her written testimony was to cite examples of Phoenix VA patient care delays potentially contributing to veteran deaths. She also highlighted the persistent culture of retaliation against whistleblowers at the Phoenix VA and other VA facilities.

Paula Pedene served for 20 years as chief spokesperson for Phoenix Veterans Affairs Hospital. She was one of the first whistleblowers at the Phoenix Veterans Affairs Health Care System, where, along with Sam Foote, she reported mismanagement of funds and a hostile work environment. Pedene suffered retribution from her supervisors and spent two years in the hospital basement as a clerk in the library before receiving a settlement in a whistleblower case against the VA. After reporting on financial abuses, VA officials moved Pedene from her building to a place where they could more closely monitor her activities. Officials removed her staff and funding but kept her duties the same. Officials told her to perform some of her responsibilities on personal time at her own expense.

The VA seemed to go out of their way to accuse Pedene of improper activity. One such example is when as an organizer for the hospital's annual Veterans Day Parade, Pedene asked her husband to help upload some parade photos onto her work computer. Having a nonemployee use a VA computer for such an activity represents an infraction of VA policy. Following this minor violation of VA rules, Pedene was demoted multiple levels. Supervisors reassigned her to a desk in the basement library, forced her to surrender a phone, and stripped her of her position as hospital spokesperson. Previously the VA lauded Pedene for her public relations expertise and role as a community leader. Following her whistleblowing, Pedene spent her days assisting people with tasks such as running the copier. The VA lodged several unsubstantiated investigations against Pedene before she filed a retaliation complaint. After investigations by the House Veterans' Affairs Committee and VA's OSC, Pedene eventually reached a financial settlement with the VA (Interview with Paula Pedene: Triumph of a PR Hero and Whistleblower 2016).

Pauline DeWenter was the scheduling clerk at the Phoenix VA who reported that supervisors ordered her to manage and handle the so-called "secret waiting list." This list recorded the names of veterans who were seeking medical care but did not receive care for months or did not receive care at all. DeWenter changed records to hide how many people died while waiting for care at the hospital. She removed deceased citations to make the hospital's statistics look better so that others could receive performance bonuses. DeWenter reported that records indicating wait delay deaths were physically altered, and written over by people other than herself.

DeWenter stated that she stuffed new requests by veterans wanting treatment into a drawer, to make the books look better. She hid the requests at a time when the VA was paying bonuses to senior staff. In early 2013, the wait list at the Phoenix VA included the names of 1700 veterans; many veterans could not get an appointment for as much as nine months, or longer. DeWenter surmised that hospital administration was totally focused on meeting the goal of shorter wait times and did not really care about patients. DeWenter concluded that there simply were not enough doctors to handle new patients, backlogged patients, and even very sick patients. She attempted to schedule appointments for the veterans who were in most dire need of care. Frustrated with the situation they confronted, DeWenter and Dr. Sam Foote eventually went to the VA's OIG with their concerns. DeWenter complained that even after going to the OIG nothing happened until Foote exposed the story to the media (Bronstein et al. 2014).

8 Conclusions

Discretion in law enforcement includes decisions about which laws to enforce and against whom to enforce them. According to research published in the *Harvard Law Review*, federal law includes more than 3000 crimes; states criminalize thousands of additional acts. It therefore requires some degree discretion to determine how officers will interpret and enforce the many laws on the books. In addition to the task of determining which laws to enforce against whom, law enforcement agents often must make instant judgments about the amount of force that is necessary in circumstances that are uncertain, and rapidly evolving. The job of law enforcement agents therefore is both difficult and susceptible to abuse. This is true at the local level (as described in the previous chapter) and at the national level as identified in abuses of the FBI. Law-abiding citizens may at times suffer the consequences of law enforcement abuse. In controversial cases, the benefit of the doubt often resides with law enforcers. For example, there are no comprehensive analyses of police killings in the United States; however, voluntary databases reported 2600 police homicides between 2005 and 2011. This number likely undercounts actual police homicides. Officers rarely faced trial; out of the 2600 homicides, there were 43 charges of murder or manslaughter (Policing Immigrant Communities 2015).

Noncitizens possess fewer rights and are subject to deportation and indefinite detention. The disparity in legal rights between citizens and noncitizens permits differential treatment. Officers enforcing immigration law can raid work sites and target day laborers. During raids, officers can make arrests without individual probable cause. This greatly empowers immigration officials. Deportations often occur without a hearing. The precarious situation that undocumented immigrants face leads to conflicts between local and national officials. The conflict between agents at different levels of government only enhances perceptions of unfairness in the immigration system. Unequal treatment (depending upon where you live) seems to defy the mandate carved into the Supreme Court structure—equal protection under law (Policing Immigrant Communities 2015).

Immigration is not the only area where national law enforcers exercise great power. The history of the FBI is replete with narratives of wiretaps, salacious files, and infiltration of groups thought to threaten the United States. The line between national law enforcement as protectors of legitimate threats to US security and national law enforcement as a danger to individual rights is vague. Similar to the narrative of local law enforcement, national-level agents can abuse their authority and act in a manner that arouses more fear than security in the minds of citizens.

Actions of FBI heads from J. Edgar Hoover to James Comey suggest that in theory, the FBI is solely an investigatory body that makes recommendations to others. In reality, agents can independently take on the responsibility of securing outcomes they perceive to be in the best interests of the nation. This can take the form of collecting dossiers on leaders such as Martin Luther King or Donald Trump. In the extreme, the danger is that law enforcement agencies could morph into tools of a police state whose job is to crush political opponents. Congressional hearings in 2017 and 2018 of FBI officials James Comey and Peter Strzok suggest that agents of the FBI had considerable discretion regarding when to open or close investigations, what information to collect, and how to use the information.

The example of VA whistleblowers reveals that abuses deeply offended some government employees. The example suggests that not all federal agents are "bad apples" and that there is hope that representatives within the government structure can effect meaningful reform. Skeptics declare that whistleblowers such as Foote are anomalies and pay a high price for their actions. This price is too high for many average government employees to bear.

References

Bronstein, S., Griffin, D., & Black, N. (2014, June 24). VA deaths covered up to make statistics look better, whistle-blower says. *CNN*. Retrieved August 23, 2018, from https://www.cnn.com/

Foer, F. (2018, September). How ICE went rogue. *The Atlantic*, pp. 56–70.

Godfrey, R. (2018, July 11). What 'Abolish ICE' actually means. *The Atlantic*. Retrieved August 15, 2018, from https://www.theatlantic.com/politics/archive

Hinkle, H., & Levinson-Waldman, R. (2018, July 30). The abolish ICE movement explained. *Brennan Center for Justice*. Retrieved August 15, 2018, from https://www.brennancenter.org/

Holland, M. (2017, September 10). The myth of deep throat. *Politico Magazine*. Retrieved August 6, 2018, from https://www.politico.com/magazine/story/

Interview with Paula Pedene: Triumph of a PR Hero and Whistleblower. (2016). Retrieved August 23, 2018, from http://www.irispr.com/blog/

Israel, F. L. (1986). *The FBI*. New York: Chelsea House Publishers.

Jarrett, G. (2018). *The Russia hoax*. New York: HarperCollins Publishers.

Jeffreys-Jones, R. (2007). *The FBI: A history*. New York/New Haven: Yale University Press.

Johnson, C. (2018, June 14). *Report condemns FBI violations in 2016 Clinton probe but finds no political bias*. Retrieved August 4, 2018, from http://www.npr.org

Koven, S. G. (2015). *Public sector ethics: Theory and applications*. Boca Raton: CRC Press.

Koven, S. G., & Göetzke, F. (2010). *American immigration policy: Confronting the nation's challenges*. New York: Springer.

Landler, M. (2017, September 7). Hillary Clinton, in book, regrets not striking back at James Comey. *New York Times*. Retrieved August 2, 2018, from https://www.nytimes.com

Lind, D. (2018, March 7). *Jeff Sessions's lawsuit against California's "sanctuary" laws, explained*. Retrieved August 20, 2018, from https://www.vox.com/

Markon, J. (2015, July 6). California killing inflames debate on illegal immigrants, 'sanctuary cities.' *Washington Post*. Retrieved August 19, 2018, from https://www.washingtonpost.com/

Mitchell, K. (2015, December 14). *Written testimony of Dr. Katherine L. Mitchell.* Retrieved August 23, 2018, from https://www.veterans.senate.gov/imo/media/doc/
Policing Immigrant Communities. (2015). *Harvard Law Review, 128*(6), 1771–1793. Retrieved December 22, 2018, from https://harvardlawreview.org/2015/04policing-immigrant-communities/
Powers, R. G. (2004). *Broken: The troubled past and uncertain future of the FBI.* New York: Free Press.
Rosenstein, R. (2017). *Memo for the Attorney General.* Retrieved August 4, 2018, from https://www.bbc.com
Shear, M. D. (2018, April 16). Nursing election grievances, Hillary Clinton supporters curse Comey. *New York Times.* Retrieved August 1, 2018, from www.nytimes.com
Theoharis, A. G. (2004). *The FBI & American democracy: A brief critical history.* Lawrence: University Press of Kansas.
Wagner, D. (2014, May 31). The doctor who launched the VA scandal. *AZCentral.* Retrieved October 8, 2018, from https://www.azcentral.com/

CHAPTER 6

Discretion and Foreign Policy

1 Introduction

This chapter reviews the history of discretion in the foreign policy bureaucracies such as the Central Intelligence Agency (CIA) and the National Security Agency (NSA). In addition, this section describes the loss of accountability in secret or "black budget" operations. Controversies such as false body counts in Vietnam, CIA "harsh interrogations" in Abu Ghraib, and massive surveillance programs of the NSA provide illustrations of the dangers posed by these organizations. A review of the Iran-Contra controversy identifies the threat that "rogue" operations pose to America's standing as a force for morality. The chapter supplements the earlier reviews of policing/law enforcement activities at the local (Chap. 4) and national (Chap. 5) levels with explications of behavior at the international level. It highlights the observation that many of the law enforcement agencies such as local police, the Federal Bureau of Investigation (FBI), and foreign policy–focused organizations (such as the CIA and the NSA) may become forces unto themselves, operating largely out of public view. These agencies therefore may move in the direction of making their own policy with limited oversight or input from elected representatives.

Strict oversight of national security agencies is often constrained because in many cases the benefit of the doubt resides with the authorities. These authorities can then exercise their discretion in identifying actions that are necessary to carry out their security responsibilities. The unintended

S. G. Koven, *The Case Against Bureaucratic Discretion*,
https://doi.org/10.1007/978-3-030-05779-4_6

consequence is the loss of personal freedom and liberty of US and other citizens of the world. The security mandate therefore may dangerously empower those that work beyond the cleansing light of accountability.

2 History of CIA and NSA

2.1 Creation of the CIA

From the beginnings of recorded time, societies were in need of accurate information about their adversaries. Leaders had great discretion in how to collect information, on whom to collect information, and how to use the information. Ransom (1970, p. 83) characterizes the intelligence failure of Pearl Harbor as the stimulus for creation of the CIA. The surprise attack at Pearl Harbor brought attention to a number of issues. First, information about potential adversaries is essential to mitigate future attacks. Second, a lack of preparedness can become an open invitation for attack. The United States seemed to be "napping" and ill-informed prior to the Japanese attack. When Secretary of the Navy Frank Knox received notice on December 7, 1941, that Pearl Harbor was being bombed he did not believe the message. In their collective wisdom, military officials perceived Hawaii as too distant from Japan for the Japanese to launch an attack. The military thought the Japanese Navy was technically incapable of such action, Japanese aviation was insufficiently skilled, and the risks of failure were too great. Political and military officials expected an attack in Thailand, Malaysia, or the Philippines. The flawed intelligence proved to be very costly; the results were devastating. After two hours, the US Navy suffered more than 2000 fatalities and 710 wounded. Together 327 army and Marine Corps were killed and 433 wounded. The attack disabled half of the aircraft on the island of Oahu and sunk many ships of the Pacific Fleet (p. 58).

In retrospect, analysts place blame for the failed intelligence on interservice rivalries that prevented full sharing of information. There did not exist a single high-level joint intelligence group for sharing and interpreting information or a joint intelligence group to evaluate, analyze, synthesize, and disseminate information. The deficiencies in intelligence sharing were not a surprise. Prior to the attack on December 7, 1941, President Franklin D. Roosevelt acted to improve communication between branches of the military. In June of 1941, Roosevelt appointed Colonel (later Major General) William J. Donovan as "Coordinator of Information" with instructions to collect and analyze intelligence information and furnish the results to the president and other agencies. Donovan's intelligence organization was formed in June of 1942 and fell under the aegis of the newly created Office of Strategic Services (OSS). The OSS along with other organizations (such as the Department of State, Navy Intelligence, and Army Intelligence) formed a Joint Intelligence Committee, an agency of the military Joint Chiefs of Staff.

The OSS as the precursor of the CIA became a combined research, foreign espionage, and special operations agency. Its creation marked for the first time active US involvement in strategic intelligence research, extensive espionage, and political action operations on a world scale (p. 66). The OSS placed espionage agents all over the world, except for Latin America which became the province of the FBI. The OSS gained a reputation for being an eclectic group that included college professors, Hollywood stuntmen, Wall Street bankers, Chicago bartenders, football players, and missionaries. Some members of the OSS did careful scholarly work while others accepted more dangerous missions; the organization became best known for its special operations. These operations covered espionage, counterintelligence in foreign nations, sabotage, propaganda, commando raids, and guerrilla activity (p. 71).

In the aftermath of World War II, President Truman ordered the disbanding of the OSS. For Truman and others international spying and secret operations organizations in peacetime seemed un-American. Donovan, a Congressional Medal of Honor recipient for his service in World War I, continued to pressure Truman for establishment of a central body to collect intelligence information. On January 22, 1946, Truman issued an Executive Order establishing the Central Intelligence Group (CIG), the forerunner to the CIA. The CIG consisted of secretaries of state, war, navy, and the president's personal representative; it coordinated the work of the various existing departments. The CIG began to brief the president daily on important international intelligence and was formally dissolved with the creation of the CIA in 1947.

The CIA was to be only one of several intelligence agencies of the federal government. It as well as other intelligence agencies grew significantly in size and scope after 1947. In its initial form, the CIA was an intelligence agency with no other assigned responsibilities. The National Security Act of 1947 specifically assigned to the CIA five functions to be performed under the direction of the National Security Council (NSC). These functions include:

1. to advise the NSC on intelligence matters related to national security
2. to make recommendations to the NSC for coordination of intelligence activities
3. to correlate and evaluate intelligence and provide for appropriate dissemination within the government
4. to perform for intelligence agencies additional services as the NSC determines can be efficiently accomplished
5. to perform other functions and duties related to national security intelligence as the NSC may direct.

Precise directives for the CIA are left to the president and the NSC. While Congress intended that CIA functions relate to intelligence, its activities have expanded over the years. Scholars such as Ransom (1970, p. 86) note that today CIA actions go well beyond that of intelligence gathering. By distorting the meaning of the term "intelligence," the organization justifies its expanding responsibilities. Today the elastic interpretation of its mission allows the CIA to engage in functions never specifically authorized by Congress. Much of the early growth of the CIA stems from deep anxiety about the spread of communist governments. From the perspective of anti-Communism, CIA operations represent a defensive reaction to Soviet expansionism (Daugherty 2004, p. 41). The Soviet leaders provided Truman with ample justification for an intensification of intelligence operations.

In 1946, Soviet leader Joseph Stalin in a speech to the Communist Party elites declared that democratic capitalism and Communism could not live together peacefully and that Communism eventually would triumph. The Soviet Union solidified control over six countries of Eastern Europe in violation of America's interpretation of the 1945 Yalta agreement. In Italy, France, Turkey, and Greece, clandestine Soviet intelligence support began to work with local communist parties to gain control. Some estimate that by the late 1940s the Soviet Union had established in Europe the most skilled collection of covert operations in the history of the world (p. 114). In 1947, Soviet leader Joseph Stalin initiated a road and air blockade of West Germany. The Soviets also placed significant numbers of clandestine operations officers in key Western capitals such as London, Rome, Paris, and Washington. The total of these and other events (such as the Soviet detonation of an atomic bomb) led President Truman and his advisors to initiate the first of numerous programs to contain Soviet advances. Advisors to Truman stressed the need for political and propaganda actions. Truman became the first modern president to endorse programs to counter subversive political activities by giving assistance to nations and groups which opposed Communist aims (p. 115).

Truman signed into law the National Security Act of 1947 that established the NSC and created the CIA. A 1947 NSC policy document (NSC-4A) provided funds for the CIA to initiate and conduct "covert psychological operations designed to counteract Soviet and Soviet-inspired activities which constitute a threat to world peace and security, or are designed to discredit and defeat the United States in its endeavors to promote world peace and security" (p. 118). NSC-4A authorized operations such as propaganda, sabotage, demolitions, subversion of adversary states, and assistance to indigenous, anti-Communist underground movements. Over time, the CIA assumed responsibilities for Soviet-style intelligence tactics such as bribery, recruitment of newspaper editors, coopting labor unions, purchasing politicians, and printing election-oriented posters. An NSC policy document (NSC-10/2) signed by Truman in 1948 states that it was desirable to place all responsibility for covert operations on the CIA. Soon after the signing of NSC-10/2 the CIA operations expanded beyond Europe to the Middle East, South Asia, the Far East, Latin America, and sub-Saharan Africa. A subsequent document (NSC-10/5) assigns additional authority to the CIA by giving it responsibility for paramilitary (guerrilla) warfare (p. 123).

2.2 Early Successes and Evolution

The CIA and its predecessor organizations supplied vital information for US decision makers. Intelligence successes during World War II include the navy breaking of the Japanese code. The US code-breaking led to the location and defeat of the Japanese Navy's carrier force, an act that conceivably turned the tide for US victory in the war in the Pacific. Intelligence also kept German defenses unaware about the exact place of the D-Day invasion of Europe on June 6, 1944. Wartime intelligence produced reports on Nazi rocket experiments and information about V-2 super bomb bases being set up for attacks on Great Britain (Ransom 1970, p. 64).

All nations need some type of intelligence to assure their survival. It is difficult, however, to assign with complete surety the "victories" and "defeats" of intelligence organizations. Individual intelligence victories may be fleeting. Failures may represent "teachable moments." Some say that every victory sows the seeds of defeat and in every defeat lie the seeds of victory. This aphorism is especially applicable to the complex world of intelligence. Critics of the CIA claim that many of the early "successes" of the CIA produced later problems. For example, CIA funding of Afghan resistance fighters (Mujahedin who opposed the Soviet-sponsored government of Afghanistan) became a detriment a decade later when anti-American groups that the United States previously aided grew in power. Critics of US clandestine operations denounced the decision to provide military aid to Afghan fighters because of the potential threat of these fighters to US interests.

Others criticized the morality of regime change operations such as the 1953 CIA-sponsored overthrow of the government of Iran and the 1954 overthrow of the government of Guatemala. These "successes" were later denounced for placing dictators in power (p. 38). Others attacked the CIA for failing to anticipate the 1950 Chinese Communist intervention in the Korean War, inadequate forewarning of the construction of the Berlin Wall in 1961, and a failure to detect the medium-range ballistic missiles discovered in Cuba in 1962 (Ransom 1970, p. 96). Despite other controversies over possible CIA involvement in the deaths of President Ngo Dinh Diem of South Vietnam in 1963 and President Salvador Allende of Chile in 1973, defenders of the CIA credit the agency with protecting and defending the United States against ruthless enemies.

Daugherty (2004, p. 19) states that it is empirically proven that covert action has its place in American foreign policy by the fact that every president has relied upon it since World War II. Defenders of the CIA argue that covert action has been valuable not only for American citizens but also for government officials who understand its uses and limits. Covert action varies in style and form; it may rely upon the power of the pen, the power of public demonstrations, or the power of arms. Traditional covert operations of the CIA involve (1) propaganda, (2) political action, and (3) paramilitary operations. A fourth type of covert operations involves information warfare.

Propaganda activities of the CIA entail systematic dissemination of doctrines and viewpoints to a chosen audience. Official propaganda organs that the United States established early in the Cold War include dissemination of information through radio outlets such as Radio Free Europe and Radio Liberty. The CIA covertly funded these stations and broadcast the American version of world news to Soviet and Eastern European citizens. CIA activities included "white propaganda" (information presented in a truthful but one-sided fashion), "gray" propaganda (distortion of facts from someone other than the actual author), and "black" propaganda (complete fabrication of messages and source of messages). The use of “black” propaganda is commonly termed “disinformation.” The intent of “black” propaganda was to reinforce rumor and unfounded beliefs. Disinformation campaigns were widely employed by the Soviet KGB. Soviet-inspired propaganda helped propagate disinformation such as the narrative that the United States created the AIDS virus (p. 77).

The second type of covert activity, political action, is more visible and often more aggressive than propaganda. Political action can include secretly funding political campaigns, giving money to influential actors who can destabilize regimes, funding labor strikes, funding rallies, supporting social groups, undermining monetary systems, sabotaging industrial facilities, instigating coups, and infecting computers to manipulate information. As an example of political action, in the early 1960s, the United States supported Japan’s right-leaning Liberal Democratic Party.

The third type of covert actions (paramilitary) is often limited in scope and it often escapes public notice. The CIA’s role in paramilitary action frequently takes the form of organizer, trainer, and logistician rather than actual combatant. At times, CIA officers conducted combat operations. For example, in Laos in the 1960s CIA agents not only trained but also led indigenous people in combat operations (p. 85). Two prominent “successes” of the CIA include the 1948 election of the US preferred party in Italy, and support for the Solidarity Movement in Poland in 1982.

In 1948, an NSC policy document held that a Communist victory in Italy in the coming elections gravely threatened US security interests in the Mediterranean. The document expressed fear that the Communists would follow “a pattern made familiar in Eastern Europe, take over complete control of the government and transform Italy into a totalitarian state subservient to Moscow” (p. 117). To counter the prospect of electoral victory by the Italian Communist Party (PCI), the United States delivered military assistance, economic assistance, and propaganda in order to offset similar Communist efforts. Covert operatives funneled money to Italian political parties of the Center, Right, and selected Left. Operations went to get out the vote for the Christian Democratic Party and to finance anti-Communist literature. In addition to these covert operations, President Truman threatened to reduce or terminate aid to Italy if the Communists won the 1948 election. In the end, the US preferred party, the Christian Democrats, won 54 percent of the vote and blocked the PRI from playing any role in the Italian government (p. 120).

CIA political actions also took place in more recent times. Daugherty (2004, p. 4) argues that the Reagan administration's conviction that a democratic Poland would lead to a free Eastern Europe must be viewed as one of the most successful foreign policies ever formulated. He views the foreign policy successes of the Reagan administration as a combination of skillful overt diplomacy and imaginative covert action. As reported by journalist Carl Bernstein, Reagan met with Pope John Paul II in 1982 and asked the pope to join with the United States to covertly support the Solidarity Movement in an effort to hasten the dissolution of the Communist empire. The US-supported forces were already in place in Poland. Covert assistance given to Solidarity and the Polish underground entailed funds, communication equipment, intelligence, personal computers, fax machines, and training in communications.

Thousands of postcards were printed or smuggled into Poland. Postcards described sermons of a popular Polish priest. Daugherty concludes that covert action in Poland during the 1990s prevented Soviet invasion and occupation. The Reagan administration fervently believed that if Poland became democratic, other Eastern European nations too would follow. In the spring of 1989, Poland became the first Soviet satellite state to hold free elections. In less than one year, all of the other Eastern European nations under the domination of the Soviet Union followed suit. CIA operations cannot take full credit for this result; however, without its operations the final outcome may have been longer in coming and perhaps, not as peaceful (p. 201).

2.3 Creation of the NSA

The lack of cooperation between units of the military provided the motivation for creating the NSA. After years of attempted reorganization of intelligence, disunity in intelligence gathering was omnipresent. By 1951, influential members of government began to demand an overall review of US communications intelligence activities. President Truman then established a committee (Brownell Committee) to make recommendations about how to strengthen intelligence gathering. Ten months after the establishment of the Brownell Committee, Truman issued two directives that led to the establishment of the NSA. Truman assigned the NSA responsibility for both communications intelligence and communications security activities. Truman also ordered strengthening and clarification of the new agency's powers in his NSC Intelligence Directive No. 9. With the new initiative, the NSA centralized authority for communications and at the same time went out of its way to ensure that civilian authorities play a major role in intelligence gathering (Burns 1990).

Truman placed NSA operations within the Department of Defense (DOD), giving the NSA responsibility for cryptographic and communications intelligence. Creation of the NSA arose out of the belief that the importance of communications intelligence warranted an organization distinct from both the armed forces and the other intelligence agencies. The highly secretive NSA was to operate under the supervision of the director of national intelligence. The agency's mission includes the protection and formulation of cryptology for the US military and other government agencies as well as the interception, analysis, and solution of coded transmissions. The NSA intercepts signals around the world; its basic function is that of making and breaking of codes (ciphers).

Creators of the NSA hoped it would improve upon the performance of the prior communications intelligence organization (Armed Forces Security Agency or AFSA). By 1950, a consensus began to emerge that the AFSA needed radical changes to effectively carry out its mission. Officials believed the AFSA lacked the money, personnel, and equipment to function successfully in the modern era of communications gathering. The ineffectiveness of US intelligence became particularly evident on June 25, 1950, when over one hundred thousand North Korean troops backed by Russian-made tanks and artillery crossed the 38th parallel into South Korea. Neither the AFSA nor the three military cryptologic agencies provided any advance warning (Aid 2009, p. 25). Military and civilian leaders pledged to reverse the environment where such a communications breakdown could occur.

Numerous problems such as internal squabbling within the AFSA enfeebled the organization. In addition, the military services refused to cooperate with the AFSA to provide information requested by other government organizations such as the FBI, CIA, and State Department. The Brownell Report stated that the AFSA simply did not produce good intelligence due to their serious management problems. The Report recommended scrapping the AFSA and replacing it with a new agency that would have greater authority to operate a modern, centralized global effort. The official birth of the NSA occurred without fanfare. On October 24, 1952, President Harry Truman signed an eight-page document titled "Communications Intelligence Activities" placing the NSA within the ambit of the Defense Department and outside the jurisdiction of the

CIA. Except for Truman, Director of Central Intelligence Walter Bedell Smith, and Executive Director of the NSC James Lay, Jr., very few people in Washington knew about the creation of the NSA.

2.4 Early Successes and Evolution

As a secretive operation, the successes and failures of the NSA remain shrouded. Commentators, however, provide some indication of perceived successes and failures of NSA programs. Some deficiencies appear evident. Aid (2009, p. 105) notes that after 1962, except for a short period of time, the NSA was unable to read any high-level North Vietnamese and Viet Cong communication. The NSA then shifted its efforts on solving lower-level military codes used on the battlefield of South Vietnam. Failure to forecast the North Vietnamese-Viet Cong 1968 Tet Offensive represents a touchstone of intelligence failure during the Vietnam War. The NSA achieved some success, however, at deciphering battlefield-level communication. Intelligence from the NSA was able to locate virtually every major North Vietnamese combat unit stationed in North and South Vietnam as well as locations of every regiment in the North Vietnamese air force (Aid 2009, p. 109). Despite this success, Tet remains a signature intelligence failure.

NSA's ability to track North Vietnamese and Viet Cong troop movements via signal intelligence led to a number of battlefield successes during the war. Signal intelligence was able to provide advance warning of many enemy offensives. Signal intelligence also provided information concerning the number of North Vietnamese troops coming down the Ho Chi Minh Trail from the fall of 1967 onwards. The NSA also provided the majority of all targeting information for US bombers during the Vietnam War (National Security Agency Releases History of Cold War Intelligence Activities 2008). Nevertheless, some intelligence reporting was ignored, misunderstood, or misapplied. In 1975, the US ambassador to South Vietnam refused to believe intelligence reports of a massive North Vietnamese military buildup around Saigon; reports were ignored even after the South Vietnamese president and most of his ministers fled the country (p. 118).

Despite the outcome of the Vietnam War or as a consequence of the intelligence failures, the budget of the NSA expanded rapidly. Between 1961 and 1969, the NSA grew from 59,000 military and civilian personnel, with a budget of $654 million, to 93,067 personnel and a budget of over $1 billion (p. 128). Many of the NSA employees were stationed at NSA headquarters at Fort Meade, Maryland. In 1969, the NSA was larger than all the other US intelligence agencies combined. The NSA boasted various intelligence-gathering successes during the 1960s and 1970s. They identified Soviet military intensification for the 1968 invasion of Czechoslovakia. The NSA played an important role in negotiations that led up to the 1972 signing of two Strategic Arms Limitation Treaties; they launched into orbit a new generation of satellites to monitor Soviet communications, and according to NSA Director Bobby Inman accurately predicted the Soviet invasion of Afghanistan in 1979 (p. 168).

By the end of the 1970s, NSA cryptology was yielding the best information since World War II. It became a several-billion-dollar-a-year enterprise with thousands of people operating a global enterprise. Growth continued. In the 1980s the NSA expanded from more than 50,000 personnel to 75,000. In 1991, the NSA supported Operation Desert Storm in Iraq. Aid (2009, p. 192) states that the crushing victory by US and coalition forces would not have been possible without the benefit of NSA's intelligence. This intelligence was particularly successful in helping to neutralize the large Iraqi air defense system. In the five-month interval after the Iraqi invasion of Kuwait, NSA satellites, listening posts, and aircraft mapped the locations of all Iraqi missile sites, radar stations, and command centers. Within hours of initiation of US bombing, the Iraqi air defense system was reduced to rubble (p. 193).

Evidence points to NSA success in preventing dozens of terrorist attacks across Europe. A 2014 report published by the Dutch agency responsible for overseeing Dutch intelligence states that, with the aid of the NSA, European officials neutralized 26 attacks that were targeted for European soil. Despite initial denials and condemnation of spying operations, Europe's own intelligence agencies fully cooperated with the NSA in efforts to combat terrorism. Germany is a hub of the NSA's European operations. Cooperation between Germany's foreign intelligence services, the BND, and America's NSA is deep. German intelligence agencies consider their cooperation with the NSA to be indispensable for counterterrorism efforts, for the fight against the proliferation of weapons of mass destruction, and for the battle against organized crime.

The German media news outlet *Der Spiegel* reports that between 2012 and 2013 German officials sent some three million items of intercepted conversations and messages to the United States each month. Investigations reveal that European intelligence agencies were willing to push the limits of their privacy laws in efforts to combat the threat of terrorism. European reports note that international cooperation has allowed Western forces to kill terrorist leaders and effectively fight against Islamic terrorism (Esman 2014).

According to James Bamford (2002, p. 359), much of the growth of the NSA is credited to the work of Louis Tordella, deputy director of the NSA for a decade. Bamford claims that by the late 1960s, NSA was an agency unrestrained by laws or legislative charter and led by a man (Tordella) obsessed with secrecy and power. Tordella transformed the NSA from a sleepy backwater to the largest and most secret intelligence organization in American history. Boundary line became blurred between US citizens and foreign enemies. In the fall of 1967 (at the request of the army), the NSA began to intercept communications of American citizens. Agencies such as the CIA and FBI and Defense Intelligence Agency (DIA) began to use NSA information. Eventually even popular counterculture figures such as folk singer Joan Baez, pediatrician Benjamin Spock, actress Jane Fonda, and Dr. Martin Luther King Jr. were put under surveillance. A domestic watch list program (Minaret Program) observed communications of individuals or organizations thought to be involved in civil disturbances and antiwar movements. The Minaret Program also monitored military deserters involved in antiwar demonstrations.

When the NSA was first established, its headquarters and cryptographic center were in Washington, DC. The agency later moved to Fort Meade, Maryland, because it was far enough away from Washington, DC, in case of a nuclear strike. The NSA is the largest employer in the state of Maryland; two-thirds of its personnel work at Fort Meade. By the early 2000s, the area comprising NSA headquarters, if incorporated, would be one of the largest municipalities in the state of Maryland with more than 32,000 specially cleared personnel (civilians, military, and contractors). At Fort Meade, workers enter one of 50 buildings whose combined floor space totals more than seven million square feet. Between 1982 and 1996 the NSA undertook more than half a billion dollars' worth of new construction. The NSA budget is relatively secret. Some information, however, is available. Bamford (2002, p. 404) reports that NSA's overall budget for 1995–1999 totaled more than $17.5 billion with another $7.3 billion sought for 2000–2001. In the late 1990s, NSA employed more people than the CIA and FBI combined. Another 25,000 that do not count as NSA employees worked in listening posts in various parts of the world. The "invisible city" of NSA headquarters replicates an autonomous city that distributes its own mail, guards and patrols its perimeter, and has its own SWAT team (p. 404).

At the heart of the "invisible city" is NSA's Headquarters/Operations Building with more than 68 acres of floor space. As befitting a first-class code-breaking operation, behind the outer glass of the Headquarters Building is a layer of orange-colored copper, windows with a thick, bulletproof-like outer pane, five inches of sound-deadening space, a thin copper screen, and an inner pane. The objective of the design is to prevent the escape of all sounds and signals (p. 409).

Expenditures of the NSA have remained high, averaging about $10 billion a year from 2011 to 2017. In 2018, President Donald Trump requested $59.9 billion for nonmilitary intelligence agencies and $21.2 billion for military intelligence. Trump's civilian request was 3.8 percent higher than the previous year's request, and the military figure was 2.4 percent higher. NSA data is sketchy, yet former NSA contractor Edward Snowden disclosed some agency figures. Records on the fiscal 2013 budget indicate $14.7 billion in CIA funding and $10.8 billion for the NSA that year (Nelson 2018). By any measure, the NSA is a massive data-collecting organization. The size and scope of NSA operations remain a source of security for some, but a font of anxiety for others. The extensiveness of NSA "snooping" led privacy advocates to attack the organization.

In 2005, a *New York Times* article revealed that for four years the NSA had monitored the communications of Americans without obtaining warrants from the Foreign Intelligence Surveillance Court. Such warrants are ordinarily required to conduct any form of surveillance outside the United States. In 2006, *USA Today* revealed that a number of the largest American telecommunications companies including AT&T, MCI, and Sprint closely collaborate with the NSA in warrantless eavesdropping. In 2013, NSA contract employee Edward Snowden began leaking classified documents to the media that revealed previously unknown details of a global surveillance apparatus run by the NSA. Snowden's stolen computer files indicate that the NSA was harvesting millions of email and instant messaging contact lists, searching email content, and tracking the location of cell phones. The NSA was also secretly accessing Yahoo and Google data centers to collect information from hundreds of millions of account holders. Snowden's disclosures indicate that the NSA tracked the sexual behavior of people in order to discredit them and that the United States spied on world leaders, such as German Chancellor Angela Merkel. Merkel subsequently compared the NSA with the East German Stasi, reputed to be one of the most repressive intelligence and secret police agencies to have ever existed.

3 Foreign Policy Controversies

3.1 Vietnam Body Counts

Questionable body count data accumulated in the Vietnam War served to further erode faith and confidence in the ability of US officials to tell the truth to the American people. This not only undermined the credibility of the military but also eviscerated confidence in all governmental institutions. In a discredited war, questionable "body count" data incentivized fraud while at the same time producing a distorted picture of reality to senior military and civilian officials. Reliance on the "body count" metric underscored a stark difference in Vietnam's war strategy from conventional war strategies such as capturing territory, holding territory, capturing an enemy's capital, killing or imprisoning enemy leaders, and instilling a new government in power. Numerous authors have described the manipulation of data during the war. Numbers were inflated in order to paint a far rosier picture of the situation on the ground. The faulty data illustrates deficiencies in intelligence reporting that supplemented the faulty war strategy.

Daddis (2012) notes that as the war in Vietnam advanced, the military's embrace of pure quantification overshadowed analysis. Daddis states that in the "numbers mill" any chance of finding useful insights became lost in the sheer volume of information reported and processed. Analysts were able to justify anything from the mounds of data collected in Vietnam. Without a coherent strategy, the relevance of the information lost meaning. The fog of unconventional war further undermined data utility. The military simply counted activities and events; they had little knowledge of the impact of events on an ultimate goal. Daddis (2012, p. 90) states that as search and destroy missions gained prominence, interest in killing the enemy thrived. The system of counting, however, "proved inaccurate." Inaccuracies arose because soldiers rarely marked corpses to prevent double counting and there were incentives to claim a high body count. Daddis notes, "Padded claims kept everyone happy; there were no penalties for overstating enemy losses, but an understatement could lead to sharp questions as to why US casualties were so high with the results achieved" (p. 91).

Inaccuracies plagued reporting. Problems in differentiating innocent civilians from enemy Vietcong led many units to classify all dead from an engagement as enemy kills. A survey of general officers after the war revealed that a majority of the high-ranking officers considered body counts either inflated or simply blatant lies. Body counts were inflated because they served as yardsticks of performance for commanders in the field. The military continued to judge commanders by how many enemies they killed, how many operations they launched, and the success of the operations. Miscounting appears to be only one aspect of a larger problem. According to Daddis (2012, p. 97), the larger problem was that the metrics provided a false sense of progress. Measurement failures were symptomatic of a larger breakdown in both how the military fought the war and how they thought about the war.

Body count metrics relate to larger data issues. Murry (2018) discusses how the concept of the "crossover point" (attrition of enemy forces at a rate equal to the capacity to put people into the field) drove operations. A desire to obtain favorable forecast led to political assessments. In 1967, the commander of US forces in Vietnam, General William Westmoreland, delivered a report to the chairman of the Joint Chief of Staff, General Earle Wheeler, showing that the Communist enemy was holding or even increasing the tactical initiative. Wheeler advised Westmoreland not to allow the figure to become public knowledge. The chair of the Joint Chiefs informed Westmoreland that he could not go to President Johnson with such information since Westmoreland's assessments contradicted that of the Joint Chiefs. Following the directive of the Joint Chiefs Westmoreland created new definitions, criteria, and formats to report enemy activity. He then informed President Johnson that it appeared to him that the US military had successfully reached a crossover point.

Faulty body count data in addition to political manipulation of information is indicative of the false narrative of the Vietnam War. In creating a false narrative, American leaders undermined the short-term goal of Communist containment as well as the longer-term goal of maintaining faith in the credibility of US leadership. Furthermore, the metric of body count itself, even if accurate, was of questionable value toward achieving the larger goal of enhancing the durability of the nation of South Vietnam. Strategy seemed flawed at its core. Rather than boosting the legitimacy of the leadership of South Vietnam or capturing an enemy's territory, the military focused on trying to assure that an adversary could not replenish its stock of human capital, a perilous goal in a continent as populous as Asia.

Anderson (2002, p. 57) observes that since a war of attrition could not be measured on a map, the Pentagon under Secretary of Defense McNamara devised a host of statistical measures to ensure success. The most controversial of the measures utilized was that of body count. Body count data, however, proved unreliable and easily falsified; unit commanders reported their own totals and totals were not verified. The military could count any dead Vietnamese including noncombatants, which, according to Anderson, "in effect encouraged indiscriminate targeting of people, especially villagers in rural areas" (p. 59). As the war progressed, air and ground warfare resulted in the deaths of the very people US policy claimed to be defending.

More evidence of fraudulent data management appears in the suppressed analysis of CIA agent Sam Adams. While working for the CIA between 1963 and 1973, Adams was responsible for a daily enemy assessment report. His basic contention was that military officials were fabricating low numbers of South Vietnamese Communist soldiers to demonstrate progress against the enemy. Beginning in 1966, Adams uncovered intelligence suggesting an enemy army more than twice as large (about 400,000) as US government contentions. His information was ignored by superiors and Adams was forced to resign from the CIA in 1973 (Fitzgerald 2006).

3.2 Abu Ghraib Prisoner Interrogations

Exposure of questionable practices at the Abu Ghraib prison complex in Iraq provides one more example of questionable behavior of US street-level bureaucrats. These practices were hidden from public view for a significant period of time. The American public became aware of unlawful CIA interrogations at the prison only through the actions of a Military Police (MP) whistleblower who in 2004 slipped a compact disc (CD) of the photos under the door of an Army Criminal Investigation Division (CID) office. Corporal Charles Graner passed the CD to Specialist Joseph Darby, who, upset with the contents, passed the images on to the investigatory officials of the Abu Ghraib prison complex. Before long, photos appeared on the CBS *60 Minutes 2* television program. In one picture, Private Lynndie England stands with Graner giving a thumbs-up sign behind a cluster of naked Iraqis piled in a pyramid. In another photograph, a kneeling, naked prisoner appears to be performing oral sex on a naked and hooded prisoner. Other images display dogs barking at naked men and Iraqis writhing in pain. A photo of an Iraqi standing on a box with wires connected to his body and a picture of an Iraqi on a leash were widely circulated over the Internet. A Pandora's box of problems for the soldiers in the photos as well as their superiors then ensued (Koven 2008, p. 153).

General Ricardo Sanchez, the US commander for Iraq, placed blame for the apparent breakdown in prisoner treatment on Brigadier General

Janis Karpinski, who commanded the forces that operated Abu Ghraib and other prisons in Iraq in 2003 and 2004. Karpinski, however, asserted that personnel from Military Intelligence (MI) or the CIA usurped her authority at the prison. Various soldiers who testified at court-martial proceedings stated that they were not sure who was in charge at Abu Ghraib. Some believed intelligence officer Colonel Thomas Pappas was in control; others thought another intelligence officer (Lieutenant Colonel Steven Jordan) had authority.

This confusion was emblematic of a loss of accountability. At Abu Ghraib, CIA officials began to interrogate "ghost" detainees, identified as individuals who were not registered as prisoners. CIA and MI agents began to use interrogation techniques that were previously used on "enemy combatants" at Guantanamo Naval Base but according to the US interpretation of the Geneva Convention should not have been applied to prisoners in Iraq. MP soldiers at Abu Ghraib were instructed to "soften up" detainees who were later interrogated by the CIA, MI, and private contractors (p. 163). Abuses appear to be widespread. Mestrovic (2007, p. 3) notes that abuses also took place at other locations, that government and military leaders were aware of the abuses, and that the abuses were not "thought up" by low-level personnel. Blame could not be attributed to a few "rotten apples" but to the "entire orchard."

Behavior at Abu Ghraib led directly to a number of relatively high-profile investigations. A report issued in 2004 by Major General George Fay offers the following conclusions: (1) there was confusion about who was in charge at Abu Ghraib, (2) approaches to interrogation used at Guantanamo were implemented at Abu Ghraib without proper authority, (3) many contract interrogators lacked formal military training as interrogators, (4) CIA interrogation practices led to a loss of accountability, and (5) supervisors ignored objections to the abuses. In addition, the Fay Report declared that there was escalating dehumanization of detainees. External reports by organizations such as the Red Cross and Human Rights Watch supplemented the Fay Report. The external organization Human Rights Watch issued a report in 2005 titled "Getting Away with Torture? Command Responsibilities for the U.S. Abuse of Detainees." Among its many findings, the report concludes: (1) torture took place at Abu Ghraib as well as dozens of other US detention facilities, (2) many detainees were civilians with no connection to terrorism, (3) the only wrongdoers brought to justice were at the bottom of the chain of command, (4) detainees were "rendered" for interrogation to governments that according to the United States engage in torture, (5) White House Counsel Alberto Gonzales and Secretary of Defense Donald Rumsfeld both contributed to changes in the war on terrorism, and (6) language of memos written by Gonzales and techniques for interrogation approved by Rumsfeld violated the Geneva Convention (Koven 2008, p. 165).

Questionable behavior at Abu Ghraib and in regard to the war on terrorism in general was supported by an array of legal justifications. The US DOJ through a series of legal memos written in 2001 and 2002 helped build a framework for circumventing international law. John Yoo of the DOJ coauthored a memo concluding that neither the Geneva Convention nor any of the laws of war applied to the conflict in Afghanistan since Afghanistan was a "failed state" and both the Taliban and al-Qaeda were "illegal enemy combatants." Gonzales and President George W. Bush supported the Yoo interpretation that the Geneva Convention did not apply to illegal combatants. In addition, in January of 2002, Assistant Attorney General Jay Bybee delivered to Gonzales a memo arguing that the Geneva Convention did not apply to Abu Ghraib prisoners. Bybee, aided by his deputy DOJ official John Yoo and Vice President Richard Cheney's legal counsel David Addington, sent to White House Counsel Gonzales a memo providing sweeping authority for "harsh interrogations." The Bybee memo, in essence, excused interrogation techniques if the intent was to gain information rather than purely inflict pain. It defined torture as pain equivalent in intensity to serious physical injury such as organ failure or death (p. 170).

The impact of the Bybee memo was to grant to the CIA de facto authority to use torture techniques, excepting only heinous acts that brought maiming or death. It issued a license for torture that would remain in effect during two years of the most aggressive counterterror operations: August 2002 to June 2004 (McCoy 2006, pp. 122–123). The egregious conduct at Abu Ghraib and the public disclosure of the treatment of prisoners produced a public outcry. By 2004, the Bush administration issued apologies for prisoner interrogations, yet claimed that behavior at Abu Ghraib was the result of abuse, not a systematic strategy. The administration repudiated the Bybee memo. In 2004, the US Supreme Court affirmed the right of enemy combatants to due process of law. However, damage already accrued to the worldwide reputation of the United States as a defender of human rights.

3.3 *Iran-Contra Funding*

The so-called Iran-Contra affair provides further evidence of relatively hidden public officials making policy based upon their vision of action necessary to protect national security. In the case of Iran-Contra the goal was a world devoid of a Communist threat. Iran-Contra, however, raised serious questions about the power of well-placed government officials to make policy and the ineffectiveness of Congress' oversight of foreign affairs. An investigatory body (Tower Commission) investigated Iran-Contra and raised the ancient question of Roman poet Juvenal, "Quis custodiet ipsos custodes?"("Who will watch the watchmen?").

The crux of the Iran-Contra affair revolves around contravening of the Boland Amendment by high-ranking national security officials of the United States. The Boland Amendment describes three US legislative amendments passed between 1982 and 1984, aimed at limiting US government assistance to rebel groups (Contras) that were active from 1979 to the early 1990s in trying to overthrow the Sandinista government of Daniel Ortega in Nicaragua. The US government viewed the Sandinistas as a threat to economic interests of American corporations in Nicaragua and to US national security in general. President Ronald Reagan accused the Sandinistas of importing Cuban-style socialism and aiding leftist guerrillas in El Salvador. The Reagan administration also viewed the Sandinistas as undemocratic despite declarations by foreign observers that the 1984 Nicaraguan elections were generally fair. Furthermore, US effort to support the contras was consistent with one component of the Reagan Doctrine that called for providing military support to movements opposing Soviet-supported communist governments. Despite Reagan's wishes, Congress cut off all funding for the Contras in 1985.

In direct violation of congressional intent, in 1985, the head of the NSC, Robert McFarlane, undertook the sale of antitank and antiaircraft missiles to Iran in the belief that such a sale would secure the release of American citizens held captive in Lebanon by groups loyal to Iran. This and subsequent weapon sales to Iran in 1986 violated the publicly stated policy of refusing to bargain with terrorists or to aid Iran in its war with Iraq. Groups who opposed the Sandinista government in Nicaragua (Contras) received a portion of the money that Iran paid the United States for the illegal weapon shipments. NSC staff member Lieutenant Colonel Oliver North supervised monetary transfers with the approval of McFarlane's NSA successor, Rear Admiral John Poindexter. North and his associates also raised private funds for the Contras. Upon discovery of NSC actions in 1986, controversy ensued. The Reagan administration admitted that it had covertly continued to fund the Contras by diverting money from arms sales. North claimed that both Reagan and his vice president, George Bush, had known about the covert operations, though both denied any knowledge of the details. The Tower Commission established to investigate the affair accused Reagan of a lax managerial style and aloofness from policy detail but they did not directly link Reagan to knowingly breaking the law in order to stifle Communist influence (Mathews 2017).

Iran-Contra demonstrates some measure of accountability in the sense that Congress established a commission to investigate wrongdoing; the commission investigated and prosecuted specific individuals. At the same time, one can argue that perpetrators of serious crimes such as subverting the general will of Congress and the American people did not ultimately receive the level of punishment that they deserved. This in turn sent negative signals about the consequences of flouting the rule of law. When the Iran-Contra dealings became known, many legal and constitutional scholars expressed dismay that the NSC, which was supposed to act solely as an advisory body, had "gone operational" by covertly formulating and independently executing foreign policy.

In January 1987, Congress announced it was opening an investigation into the arms sales and aid to the Nicaragua Contras. Ultimately, the government indicted numerous high-profile individuals including Secretary of Defense Caspar Weinberger, National Security Advisor Robert McFarlane, Assistant Secretary of State Elliot Abrams, and a member of the NSC, Oliver North. Weinberger received a pardon from George H. W. Bush before trial; McFarlane and Abrams received sentences of two years of probation and both were later pardoned; the courts overturned North's convictions because of his receipt of immunity for testifying before Congress.

The consequences of Iran-Contra in terms of establishing accountability of foreign policy officials are unclear. Princeton University historian Julian Zelizer (2018) notes that Iran-Contra did not fatally damage the Reagan presidency. Reagan ended his second term with strong approval ratings. His ratings had declined by 20 percentage points to 43 percent during the five most dramatic months of Iran-Contra but climbed back up to 63 percent by December of 1988. Most of the presidential rankings continually place Reagan in the top ten of commanders-in-chief. While the *Congressional Report* stated Reagan's policies revealed pervasive dishonesty, deception, and disdain for the law, a large number of Republicans stood firmly behind the president. Reagan and his supporters succeeded in shaping the broader narrative; they shaped Iran-Contra as justified in order to check and contain the spread of communism. Republicans focused on the issue of congressional interference in Reagan's foreign policies. When Lieutenant Colonel Oliver North testified before Congress in August 1987, he refused to apologize for his behavior. Reagan termed Colonel North a hero. In a written statement pardoning Iran-Contra participants, George H. W. Bush said that the men had already paid a price that was "grossly disproportionate to any misdeeds or errors of judgment they may have committed." He characterized Casper Weinberger as a true American patriot. Lieutenant Colonel Oliver North ended up a celebrity for talk radio and television.

3.4 Black Box Operations

Black box operations by definition imply a lack of transparency and subsequent loss of accountability. Accountability calls for light (not darkness), transparency (not secrecy), and knowledge (not ignorance) of important government actions. An absence of accountability represents an open invitation for arbitrary action, lawlessness, autonomous behavior, and feelings of omnipotence on the part of opaque officials. Black box operations are consistent with the epithet of "deep state" defined as a body of people, typically influential members of government who many believe are involved in the secret manipulation or control of government policy. The "deep state" suggests that faceless officials within the bowels of large bureaucracies increasingly gain power to the detriment of the public. In an inversion of democratic theory, the masses lose power to a small group who claim to be "experts" or knowledgeable based on career experience. These experts in turn have wide discretion in correcting perceived wrongs or in creating a safer world such as a world unhindered by the plague of Communist aggression.

"Black box" operations are relatively hidden from public scrutiny; they remain in a clouded container, removed from general discussion. Such operations enhance the "secrecy state" and diminish the power of the people to set policy priorities. This secrecy state clearly is antithetical to the construct of governing through consent of the governed. Consent in fact loses all meaning if people are unaware of what they might consent to and from what program they might express dissent. The black box negates debate and enhances the power of well-placed officials who independently create and implement public policy.

The United States maintains a large intelligence bureaucracy; however, historical data on its size and scope is scarce. Estimates in 2008 put the annual cost of the US DOD "black budget" at $30 billion, increasing to an estimated $50 billion in 2009. An article based on information provided by Edward Snowden detailed how the United States allocated $52.8 billion in 2012 for black budget "hidden spending" (Gellman and Miller 2013). The Congressional Research Service (CRS) reported that funding associated with the 17 components of the Intelligence Community is significant. The CRS estimates that for Fiscal Year 2018, the aggregate amount of appropriations requested for national and military intelligence programs totaled $78.4 billion ($57.7 billion for the National Intelligence Program and $20.7 billion for the Military Intelligence Program). Large organizations within the National Intelligence Community include the CIA, the NSA, the National Reconnaissance Office, and the DIA (Devine 2018).

For security purposes, much of the intelligence spending is hidden in the budget of the DOD. Those arguing for more accountability advocate greater disclosure of details of spending projects; however, the leadership in the Intelligence Community argues that disclosure of such figures could damage national security. Annual intelligence spending has remained relatively constant as a percent of annual national defense spending (11 percent) over the decade Fiscal Years 2008–2018. In global terms, US intelligence spending is exceedingly high. Some have asserted that America's intelligence agencies may spend more money on gathering and disseminating intelligence than the rest of the world's intelligence services combined (Devine 2018).

In recent years, spending by the CIA grew to exceed that of every other spy agency. Budgets enhance the power of the CIA. Spending increased after intelligence failures leading up to the 2001 attacks. The United States spent more than $500 billion on intelligence between 2001 and 2013. CIA supporters contend that this outlay has succeeded in its main objective: preventing another catastrophic terrorist attack in the United States. Intelligence spending now supports an espionage network with resources and a reach beyond those of any adversary. Resources for the CIA fund secret prisons, interrogation, and deployment of lethal drones. The CIA also supports a paramilitary force. Expansion of the CIA "covert action program" line item suggests greater spending for drone operations in Pakistan, Yemen, and other places as well as payments to militias in

Afghanistan and Africa, and more vigorous attempts to sabotage Iran's nuclear program (Gellman and Miller 2013).

Throughout American history, the nation required good intelligence and used covert agents to enhance security. However, even the most extensive and expensive intelligence programs are not all seeing. Intelligence has produced some very favorable outcomes such as the World War II breaking of Japanese and German codes. Notable failures also exist. For example, some of the most infamous intelligence failures include the inability to predict the attack on Pearl Harbor, the failed Bay of Pigs invasion of Cuba in 1961, failure to anticipate the 1968 Tet Offensive in Vietnam, inability to predict the 1973 Yom Kippur War in Israel, and the failure to anticipate the Iranian Revolution of 1979. Other intelligence failures relate to a lack of information regarding the Soviet invasion of Afghanistan in 1979, inability to predict the fall of the Soviet Union in 1991, the Indian nuclear test of 1998, the September 11, 2001, attack on the World Trade Center, and the 1990 invasion of Kuwait by Iraq (Friedman 2012).

3.5 Secret Surveillance—NSA Snowden

Edward Snowden helped to reveal the full scale and scope of NSA surveillance operations. Snowden as a disillusioned and idealistic former contract worker for the NSA copied large numbers of top-secret documents and delivered those documents to journalists who in turn revealed the dimensions of various NSA programs. Snowden's background includes dropping out of high school, a stint in the army, employment at Microsoft, employment as a security guard at a building used by the NSA, employment as a cybersecurity expert for the CIA, work as a contractor for the NSA, and additional employment for a private defense contractor. By the time Snowden was 29 years old, he had access to some of the most sensitive secret documents of the US government and was ready to tell his story about secret surveillance operations carried out by the NSA.

In his many jobs, Snowden gained a reputation as a top cybersecurity expert who was more knowledgeable and proficient than most of his older, college-educated colleagues. His proficiency led the DIA's Joint Counterintelligence Training Academy to allow him to teach a course in cyber counterintelligence. Over time, Snowden became very uneasy with his knowledge of government intelligence activities. He came to the realization that the goal of the NSA was to build a system that would eliminate all privacy, globally, to build a system where no one could communicate electronically without the NSA being able to collect, store, and analyze communications. With this knowledge in hand, in 2012, Snowden decided to become a whistleblower, to reveal what he knew to the world. Snowden spent part of 2012 downloading documents. He took a pay cut to work for a company (defense contractor Booz Allen Hamilton) to gain access to documents he felt the world should see (Greenwald 2014, p. 48).

In order to tell his story, Snowden met with journalists and a documentary filmmaker in Hong Kong. Snowden selected journalist Glenn Greenwald as the conduit of information because of Greenwald's reputation as an author of a best-selling book about illegal NSA eavesdropping. Snowden claims he believed Greenwald understood the dangers of mass surveillance and state secrecy, and would not back down from government pressure (p. 2). Snowden only requested that stories appear one by one and there would not be a mass Internet dump of documents. Greenwald agreed to publish stories sequentially and not stop until all the issues in the public interest were covered. Greenwald quickly completed four stories for the British newspaper the *Guardian*.

The first of Greenwald's stories ran under the banner "NSA Collecting Phone Records of Millions of Verizon Customers Daily." The article went on to note that the NSA is currently collecting the telephone records of millions of US customers of Verizon under a top-secret court order. The court order requires Verizon on an ongoing daily basis to give the NSA information on all telephone calls in its system, both within the United States and between the United States and other countries. The NSA collected communication records of millions of US citizens regardless of suspicion of wrongdoing. The Obama administration defended such collection of information as a critical tool in protecting the nation from terrorist threats. In contrast, the American Civil Liberties Union stated that from a civil liberties perspective it is "beyond Orwellian" and proves further evidence of the extent to which people secretly surrendered basic rights to the demands of unaccountable intelligence agencies. The Associated Press confirmed that the NSA program was in place for years and that the NSA directed all US telecom providers, not just Verizon, to hand over records (p. 73).

A second story in the *Guardian* describes the secret PRISM program whereby the NSA collected information directly from the following US service providers: Microsoft, Yahoo, Google, Facebook, Paltalk, AOL, Skype, YouTube, and Apple. The *Washington Post* also published a story about PRISM stating that the NSA and FBI tapped directly into the central servers of nine leading US Internet companies extracting chats, photographs, emails, documents, and logs that enable analysts to track foreign targets. A third article discusses a 2012 directive ordering the Pentagon and related agencies to prepare a list of potential overseas targets for US cyber-attacks. The fourth article prepared by Greenwald describes an NSA data-tracking program that shows the collection, analysis, and storing of billions of telephone calls and emails sent across American telecommunications. The article also raised questions about whether NSA officials lied to Congress when they refused to answer questions about the number of domestic communications intercepted (p. 81). Documents provided by Snowden contained proof that the NSA collected telephone and email information about millions of Americans every day. One graphic indicated that for a 30-day period ending in February 2013, one unit of the NSA collected more than three billion pieces of communication data from the US communication system alone (p. 30).

The release of the four articles immediately produced a firestorm of media attention. Greenwald appeared for interviews on MSNBC (*Morning Joe*) and NBC (*Today* show). He felt journalists should celebrate Snowden for bringing transparency to the national security state. Instead, reporters focused attention on Snowden who fled to China (p. 89). In 2013, US federal prosecutors filed a criminal complaint against Snowden, charging him with theft of government property and two counts of violating the Espionage Act of 1917 through unauthorized communication of national defense information and willful communication of classified information to an unauthorized person. Each of the three charges carries a maximum possible prison term of ten years. Russia granted temporary asylum to Snowden in 2013 and later extended his asylum.

Snowden was under no illusion about the consequences he faced for his actions. He proclaims that his aim was to spark a worldwide debate about privacy, Internet freedom, and the dangers of the surveillance state. He accepted that his life "will likely be over" after his disclosures but states, "I know it's the right thing to do" (p. 18). Snowden contends his only fear was that people see his document and not care. In a letter he placed in a computer file, Snowden declared that many would malign him for failing to look away from society's problems but "citizenship carries with it a duty to first police one's own government before seeking to correct others." He speculates that the US government only grudgingly allows limited oversight and refuses to ensure accountability. He castigates the United States for what he perceives as allowing the most powerful telecommunication providers to commit tens of millions of felonies (p. 32).

4 Possible Checks on Foreign Policy Abuses

Even in the realm of foreign policy, bureaucracies are not completely autonomous agents, working secretly with their own sets of norms and standard operating procedures. Other institutions exist that have the ability to make policy more responsive to the desires and wishes of the American people. A vibrant, independent, free press represents one such institution while public opinion represents a second.

4.1 Media and Public Opinion

Public opinion and the media that helps to shape that opinion play a vital role in checking nonaccountable behavior at all levels of government. Foreign policy is no exception, even though officials in this domain acquire wide discretion. The relative secrecy of many operations often insulates officials from penetrating public scrutiny. Even in the realm of foreign policy, government actions do not receive a perpetual blank check. At some point, the public may simply no longer believe what government officials are saying. Long before Donald Trump presented the construct of "alternative facts" people have long been skeptical of US foreign policy assertions.

The 1968 Tet Offensive in Vietnam undermined faith in the American public that the United States was winning the war in Vietnam and that there was "light at the end of the tunnel" foreshadowing an impending US victory. The administration of Lyndon Johnson became associated with a "credibility gap" as average Americans no longer accepted the pronouncements of White House or military officials. During the Vietnam War, the derogatory phrase "Five O'Clock Follies" characterized daily press briefings that occurred in Saigon, sponsored by the US Public Affairs Office. In later years foreign policy pronouncements would also become discredited. The hype surrounding Iraqi weapons of mass destruction as a legitimate pretext for war in Iraq is refuted today. Revelations of Edward Snowden raise the specter of "Big Brotherism" capable of eliminating any form of dissent. Donald Trump has been particularly critical of the role of the media in shaping perceptions. Trump regularly castigates what he terms "fake" news outlets such as the *New York Times* and the Cable News Network.

A free and active media (termed by many as fourth estate) plays a vital role in shaping both domestic and foreign policy. In theory, the news media is an institution that serves to hold government leaders accountable to the people, publicizes vital issues, educates citizens, and connects people to each other. The media can play an important role in determining elections and the future course of public policy. Changes in information delivery, however, have altered information flows in recent years. The few outlets of yesterday no longer can dominate the agenda. Today the traditional media of the "elite press" is supplemented with social media platforms like Facebook and Twitter, bloggers, and journalists publishing in nonmainstream media outlets. This often produces an "echo chamber" of like-minded people who reinforce their own political preferences.

In regard to the media and public opinion, a review of American history suggests two important points. First, a free media can influence opinion and second, public opinion can affect public policy although it may take a considerable amount of time. A few foreign policy examples are useful. President Harry Truman suffered greatly from the unpopular Korean War of the 1950s. In June of 1945 after the German surrender to Allied forces Truman's popularity reached 87 percent. By February 1952, at the height of the Korean War, Truman's popularity hit a low of 22 percent. Truman did not run for reelection in 1952 when the former war hero Dwight Eisenhower was elected. Eisenhower helped negotiate a formal end to hostilities in Korea. The Korean War Armistice was signed on July 27, 1953. In March of 1964, soon after the assassination of John F. Kennedy, Lyndon Johnson enjoyed an 80 percent approval rating in a Gallup Poll survey. Johnson's popularity subsequently plummeted and by August 1968 stood at 35 percent. Johnson declined to run for reelection in 1968. Soon after his election President Richard Nixon announced his Vietnamization plan (replace US troops with South Vietnamese forces). US troop strength in Vietnam declined from a 1968 peak of 540,000 to 140,000 by the end of 1971. By the end of 1972, US combat troops in Vietnam numbered fewer than 30,000. By 1974, Congress voted to cut off all aid to South Vietnam. Other presidents reversed major foreign policy initiatives as a consequence of negative public opinion. This is indicative of some measure of responsiveness to perceived foreign policy disasters.

George W. Bush possessed a 90 percent approval rating in a poll taken less than a month after the attacks of September 11, 2001, the best approval rating for any post–World War II president. By October 2008, his ratings declined to 25 percent. Some polls from that time showed him with a 19 percent approval rating (Weinstein 2011). Bush's approval declined significantly after the US invasion of Iraq. Immediately before and after the 2003 invasion of Iraq, most US polls showed a substantial majority supporting the war; by December 2004, polls consistently showed that a majority thought the invasion was a mistake. In 2007, surveys generally showed a majority in favor of setting a timetable for withdrawal. The number of US military forces in Iraq peaked at 170,300 in November 2007. On September 13, 2007, President Bush announced that American troop strength in Iraq would be reduced. In November of 2008, the American people elected Barack Obama who as a US senator in 2007 introduced a bill (Iraq War De-Escalation Act of 2007) to begin a phased redeployment of troops from Iraq with the goal of removing all combat forces by March 31, 2008. In 2010, the last American combat brigade withdrew from Iraq. By 2011, President Obama announced the full withdrawal of US troops from Iraq, with the United States retaining an embassy in Baghdad with approximately 17,000 personnel, and between 4000 and 5000 defense contractors (MacAskill 2011).

The major foreign policy alterations discussed above suggest that public opinion has an impact. The process may be slow and cumbersome; however, it appears that when a critical mass of public dissent becomes evident, policy can and does change. This is fully consistent with ideals of democracy and governing by consent. It should be recognized, however, that many decisions can still be made "under the radar" by obscure officials without much public awareness. The few examples of major policy reversal (under intense public outcry) should not imply that the powers of the foreign policy bureaucracy are severely circumscribed with little likelihood for abuse.

4.2 *Whistleblowing in Foreign Policy—Sergeant Joseph Darby and Specialist Ron Ridenhour*

The whistleblowing actions of Sergeant Joseph Darby were significant in uncovering questionable behavior at the Abu Ghraib prison complex in Iraq. It appears that the relatively low-ranking Darby took it upon himself to try to reveal behavior that he instinctively felt was not right. As previously noted, Darby surreptitiously passed on disturbing images of Iraqi prisoner abuse. The simple act of slipping a compact disc under a door of an investigatory body brought on a cascade of revelations that informed the American public about offensive behavior in Iraq. On January 13, 2004, Darby slipped the CD under a door and before long the American public widely viewed the incriminating photos. Due to Darby's revelations, in 2006 former Secretary of State Colin Powell wrote a letter to Senator John McCain where Powell stated that the world was beginning to doubt the moral basis for America's fight against terrorism. Powell asserted that actions in Iraq would put US troops at risk and that the United States should remind its soldiers of their moral obligations with respect to those in custody.

In 2005, Senator John McCain implored Congress to pass a clear statement regarding treatment of detainees. McCain proposed prohibition on cruel and degrading treatment of anyone in US custody. He also recommended that the military establish the Army Field Manual as the standard for interrogation of all detainees held in DOD custody. McCain stated that the enemy we fight has no respect for human life or human rights but it is not about who they are; it is about American values and who we are. The Senate agreed with McCain that torture was anathema to American values. On October 5, 2005, the Senate affirmed its commitment to establish uniform standards for interrogations. In a statement to the Senate, McCain stated, "We fight not just to preserve our lives and liberties but also our morals, and we will never allow terrorists to take those away. In this war that we must win—that we will win—we must never simply fight evil with evil" (Koven 2008, p. 167).

Ron Ridenhour represents another foreign policy whistleblower that enhanced accountability. In 1968, Army Specialist Ridenhour heard accounts of a US massacre at a village in South Vietnam. Ridenhour interviewed a number of the participants, and after he returned to the United States, he sent registered letters to 30 government officials asking for an investigation. Officials could not easily dismiss Ridenhour's claims as he honorably served in the military as a helicopter door gunner and a team leader of long-range reconnaissance patrols. In one of the letters, Ridenhour describes the account of a fellow GI about how US soldiers were "slaughtering villagers like so many sheep." According to the account, Ridenhour heard from Sergeant Larry La Croix that men under the command of a lieutenant (later identified as William Calley) were dragging men, women, and children of all ages out of bunkers and hooches and putting them together in a group. Calley then ordered an M-60 set up and the people were killed. La Croix said that he bore witness to this procedure at least three times. The three groups were of different sizes: one of about 20 people, one of about 30 people, and one of about 40 people.

In the letter that Ridenhour wrote, he notes that other GIs estimated that the population of the village (later identified as My Lai) had been 300 to 400 people and that very few, if any, escaped. Ridenhour makes a passionate appeal for an investigation. In one letter, he states: "I remain irrevocably persuaded that if you and I do truly believe in the principles, of justice and the equality of every man, however humble, before the law, that form the very backbone that this country is founded on, then we must press forward a widespread and public investigation" (Ridenhour 1969). President Richard M. Nixon, Defense Secretary Melvin R. Laird, and members of Congress, including his congressman, Representative Morris K. Udall, of Arizona, received Ridenhour's letter.

The Ridenhour accusations ultimately led to two separate investigations and an array of criminal charges. One of the investigations (Peers Commission) accumulated 20,000 pages of testimony and as an outcome of their report, army lawyers recommended that 14 officers including brigade commander Oran Henderson, assistant commander for the Americal Division George Young, and Americal Division leader Samuel Koster should be charged. Only Lieutenant Calley received any sentence. Calley received a sentence of life imprisonment on March 31, 1971. After the sentence, Calley spent about three and a half years under house arrest at Fort Benning until he was paroled on September 10, 1975 (Koven 2008, p. 146).

5 Conclusions

Just as community police departments have a responsibility to protect the security of citizens at the local level, and the FBI assumes responsibilities at the national level, organizations such as the CIA and NSA have obligations to protect citizens against international threats. Given the inherent secrecy of agencies such as the NSA, many activities take place beyond the awareness of ordinary citizens or even congressional representatives. As recounted by former NSA contract worker Edward Snowden, modern-day capabilities for information collection are immense. The issue is whether policing and security powers of public officials are used judiciously and legitimately. Citizens desire safety, yet they also desire to be free of an oppressive police state. Revelations at the local level indicate that law enforcement agents have been engaged in questionable behavior. At the national level, agents infiltrate organizations and collect wiretap recordings of individual suspects. Agencies such as the CIA and NSA command immense budget resources with few details provided about how they expend those resources.

According to the most famous quotation of English historian Lord Acton (John Dalberg-Acton 1834–1902), power tends to corrupt and absolute power corrupts absolutely. A less famous aphorism of Lord Acton is that bureaucracy is the weapon and sign of a despotic government, inasmuch as it gives whatever government it serves, despotic power. In accord with Lord Acton's warning, law enforcement bureaucracies must walk the tightrope of protecting citizens while at the same time ensuring basic liberties and freedoms. This is not an easy task given the human nature and the inclination of the "good guys" to become intoxicated with their power. History shows that societies can lose their freedom through the actions of those who claim to be its fiercest defenders. All societies have the capacity to move along a continuum from absolute freedom to a "police-state-light" stage, to a complete loss of freedom in an "absolute police-state" condition. Awareness of the necessity for accountability and institutions strong enough to enforce accountability is a first step toward protecting average citizens from abusive state power.

References

Aid, M. M. (2009). *The secret sentry: The untold history of the National Security Agency.* New York: Bloomsbury Press.

Anderson, D. L. (2002). *The Columbia guide to the Vietnam War.* New York: Columbia University Press.

Bamford, J. (2002). *Body of secrets.* New York: Anchor Books.

Burns, T. L. (1990). The origins of the National Security Agency: 1940–1952. *Center for Cryptologic History, National Security Agency, Series V, 1.* Retrieved September 4, 2018, from https://permanent.access.gpo.gov/gpo73503/origins_of_nsa.pdf

Daddis, G. (2012). The problem of metrics: Assessing progress and effectiveness in the Vietnam War. *War in History, 19*(1), 73–98.

Daugherty, W. J. (2004). *Executive secrets: Covert action and the presidency.* Lexington: University of Kentucky Press.

Devine, M. E. (2018, June 18). Intelligence community spending: Trends and issues. *Congressional Research Service.* Retrieved September 20, 2018, from https://fas.org/sgp/crs/intel/R44381.pdf

Esman, A. R. (2014, June 24). *European reports show NSA's successes.* Retrieved September 12, 2018, from https://www.investigativeproject.org/

Fitzgerald, B. (2006). Alum's book credits CIA analyst with uncovering Vietnam 'numbers gap.' *BU Today.* Retrieved September 17, 2018, from http://www.bu.edu/today

Friedman, U. (2012, January 3). The ten biggest American intelligence failures. *Foreign Policy.* Retrieved September 21, 2018, from https://foreignpolicy.com/2012/01/03/

Gellman, B., & Miller, G. (2013, August 29). 'Black budget' summary details U.S. spy networks successes, failures, and objectives. *Washington Post*. Retrieved September 20, 2018, from https://www.washingtonpost.com/world/national-security/

Greenwald, G. (2014). *No place to hide: Edward Snowden, the NSA, and the U.S. surveillance state*. New York: Metropolitan Books.

Koven, S. G. (2008). *Responsible governance: A case study approach*. Armonk: M.E. Sharpe.

Mathews, R. (2017). Iran-Contra affair. *Encyclopedia Britannica*. Retrieved January 11, 2017, from https://www.britannica.com/event/Iran-Contra-Affair

MacAskill, E. (2011, October 21). Iraq rejects US request to maintain bases after troop withdrawal. *The Guardian*. Retrieved September 29, 2018, from https://www.theguardian.com/

McCoy, A. W. (2006). *A question of torture: CIA interrogation, from the cold war to the war on terror*. New York: Henry Holt.

Mestrovic, S. G. (2007). *The trials of Abu Ghraib: An expert witness account of shame and honor*. Boulder: Paradigm.

Murry, G. (2018). *The on-going battle for the soul of the army*. Retrieved September 17, 2018, from http://smallwarsjournal.com/

National Security Agency Releases History of Cold War Intelligence Activities. (2008). *The National Security Archive*. Retrieved September 12, 2018, from https://nsaarchive2.gwu.edu

Nelson, S. (2018, February 27). Trump sends Congress record high 'black budget' spy funding request. *Washington Examiner*. Retrieved September 11, 2018, from https://www.washingtonexaminer.com/

Ransom, H. H. (1970). *The intelligence establishment*. Cambridge, MA: Harvard University Press.

Ridenhour, R. (1969). *A letter from Ron Ridenhour regarding the My Lai massacre (1969)*. Retrieved September 27, 2018, from https://alphahistory.com/

Weinstein, A. (2011, October 25). *5 presidents with the biggest approval ratings declines*. Retrieved September 29, 2018, from https://listosaur.com/

Zelizer, J. (2018, February 27). Why the Russia investigation could be more like Iran-Contra than Watergate. *The Atlantic*. Retrieved September 26, 2018, from https://www.theatlantic.com/

PART III

Conclusions

CHAPTER 7

Conclusions

1 Introduction

Bureaucracies are intended to be neutral tools. Bureaucrats are unelected officials who have great power due to their positions within formidable organizations. Power comes from the resources they command and their discretion in how they choose to use those resources. The core issue remains that of ensuring that government bureaucracies work in the interests of the people and do not become powers unto themselves. This is the focus of the chapter and the entire book. For democracies to work as envisioned by democratic theorists, the ability of government agencies to operate independent of popular oversight must be constrained, abuses must cease, and the people should have greater awareness of agency practices. Greater accountability can be obtained; however, one should not expect all government agencies to welcome it.

2 Accountability Problem of Bureaucrats as Policymakers

The law enforcement bureaucrat exercises broad discretion in their operations, often behind a curtain of secrecy. Today the wall of secrecy is eroding with new technology, yet for many organizations the wall remains. At the local level, policing actions that previously went unreported or misreported are now subject to greater scrutiny. The ease by which average citizens can video record police actions has increased accountability and raised questions

S. G. Koven, *The Case Against Bureaucratic Discretion*,
https://doi.org/10.1007/978-3-030-05779-4_7

about police behavior. Video recordings have shown police officers shooting and abusing citizens who do not appear to pose an imminent threat to the officers. The recordings raise the question of local police acting as prosecutor, judge, jury, and executor without due process of law.

The "blue wall" of silence hinders accountability. Fellow officers do not want to "rat out" their colleagues or report serious violations of protocol. If the organization does not dismiss the "bad apple" officers, misbehavior continues. The organizational hierarchy may even tolerate or reward illegal behavior in the name of aggressive law enforcement. They do not want to expose problems in their department or they are willing participants in fostering the behavior. Those who suffer the consequences of the loss of accountability are citizens who increasingly grow to hate and distrust the police. The consequence of this slippery slope is "out of control" police and federal government law enforcement agents who act with immunity confident that no one will hold them accountable for their actions. The ultimate outcome can be a loss of confidence in the fairness, legitimacy, and neutrality of the government.

In addition to the local police, national-level organizations such as the Federal Bureau of Investigation (FBI) also instill fear among many members of the population. Citizens are less likely to capture FBI shootings than local police abuses; however, the history of the FBI is replete with an absence of accountability and violations of civil liberties. The FBI chief J. Edgar Hoover built a massive organization that infiltrated organizations, listened to private conversations, and assembled huge numbers of files on the lives of individuals suspected of being threats to the state. The FBI assembled files on the sex lives and alcohol use of influential individuals in order to gain organizational power through intimidation. Hoover's abuses are legendary. Critics today castigated FBI Director James Comey for his actions in both the Hillary Clinton email investigation and the leaking of memos of a meeting with Donald Trump. In theory, the FBI does not engage in partisan politics, yet both Hoover and Comey violated that directive. Democrats were critical of Comey's decision to send a letter to Congress about the reopening of Clinton's email investigation. They questioned his public press conference where he called Clinton and her top aides extremely careless. He nevertheless seems to conclude unilaterally that no reasonable prosecutor would bring such a case. The press conference was the first time the FBI disclosed its prosecutorial recommendation publicly. Comey also received criticism for drafting an exoneration letter for Hillary Clinton before the investigation was complete.

FBI Director James Comey again came under suspicion when he arranged for a university lawyer to leak to the press a memo he wrote after a private meeting with President Trump. The memo asserted that Trump had asked him to end the FBI's investigation into former National Security Advisor Michael Flynn. In testimony before Congress, Comey stated that he asked a law professor friend to share the contents of his memo because he thought that might prompt the appointment of a special counsel. Two days after the *New York Times* published the story about Comey's memo, the assistant director of the Department of Justice (DOJ) appointed Robert Mueller as a special prosecutor to investigate Russian meddling in the 2016 election. It appears in both the Clinton and Trump matters, the FBI went beyond their mandate to influence electoral behavior. This intrusion represents a slippery slope where government agents act as protectors of the people in terms of what information the people need to know about possible criminal behavior of leading American politicians. It is naïve to think such disclosures do not influence perceptions and voting behavior.

At the international level, security agencies such as the National Security Agency (NSA) and Central Intelligence Agency (CIA) function at even higher levels of secrecy than local or national law enforcement organizations. The CIA has expanded its operations over the years to include a wide range of shrouded missions. Much of the activities of the CIA exist beyond the awareness of average citizens. Periodically, abuses are uncovered and the public demands greater accountability. Such accountability, however, may be an anomaly. As described previously, jarring images of prison abuse at Abu Ghraib prison complex revealed CIA procedures that seemed to defy American standards of decency.

As under-the-radar organizations dealing with foreign adversaries, both the CIA and the NSA exercise broad discretion. In theory, the behavior of these organizations can be controlled by representatives of the people. In reality, however, control may be difficult. Institutions (such as Congress and the media) are possible means to limit unwarranted behavior. Media exposure may empower politicians to call for a reversal of policy. The moral outrage expressed by Senator John McCain in appearances before Congress was effective in altering "rough interrogation" policies of prisoners in Iraq. Corrective action ensued.

Discretion can be abused at the local, national, and international levels as aforementioned examples indicate. The book also describes instances where discretion, in regard to the decision to engage in "whistleblowing," produced some disinfecting light or corrective action. Police officer Frank

Serpico's decision to go to the media about widespread corruption in the New York City Police Department (NYPD) led to an investigation. The Knapp Commission investigation informed the public about unlawful practices and put pressure on officials to institute reform. Dr. Sam Foote's decision to defy the chain of command and provide the press with information about manipulation of wait times for veterans seeking treatments led to some firings and greater oversight of the system. Specialist Joseph Darby's actions in informing the Army Criminal Investigation Division about prisoner abuse at Abu Ghraib led to a change in policy, demotion in rank, and prison sentences for some of the participants. Retired Army Specialist Ron Ridenhour's decision to send a letter to influential members of Congress sparked investigations into the My Lai massacre in Vietnam. This led to a criminal conviction of Lieutenant William Calley and a necessary review of army behavior. Edward Snowden's decision to reveal NSA practices led to a greater awareness of the extent to which the government collects information on Americans and others.

A common thread running through the examples of public servants taking it upon themselves to expose disturbing activities is a deep uneasiness with observed practices. This seems to arise from an innate sense that something is wrong and they have a profound responsibility to redress the harm. They perform what they view as an honorable, moral, and virtuous act in order to right perceived wrongs. Their actions do not directly lead to society heaping rewards upon them. Some like Japanese diplomat Chiune Sugihara are viewed as a hero (many years later) for saving innocent lives. For others, the moral act of defying authority to reveal abuse comes with costs. Fellow officers ostracized Serpico, Veterans Administration (VA) officials pressured Foote into early retirement, Ridenhour became bitter about the My Lai investigation he considered a whitewash, Darby's identity was revealed by former Secretary of Defense Rumsfeld against his wishes after assurances of anonymity, and Snowden remains a fugitive, subject to arrest.

Despite the costs associated with defying the organization, principled individuals follow some sort of inner voice that directs them to act. The fact that these individuals exist and that their exposures are acted upon by the legitimate institutions (be they the courts, organizational hierarchy, Congress, or others) provides a ray of hope that discretionary actions can produce self-correcting behavior.

The core issue of the bureaucracy-democracy debate has always revolved around the fear that the people will no longer control their destinies through the election of representatives who are at least somewhat responsive to their wishes. The dark side of the bureaucracy-democracy conundrum is the fear that the better educated, better informer, professional managers will function as a permanent ruling class handing down mandates and making policy for the unwashed masses. In theory, the professionally trained, neutrally competent managers will establish more efficient, more effective, and less corrupt government. Society as a whole as well as individuals in society will benefit from the superior performance of the permanent class of bureaucrats who have access to more information and exercise better judgment than the judgments of average citizens. In reality, we should not be so quick to accept this vision. James Madison instructs readers in 1788 that if men were angels, no government would be necessary. Government is necessary since men are mortal, not angels. Bureaucrats need to be accountable for their actions; structures need to hold them accountable. As stated in 1914 by former Supreme Court Justice Louis Brandeis, sunlight is the best of disinfectant. There is no guarantee that the so-called educated classes will provide better government for the masses than representative democracy where the people empower their representatives. When power is concentrated, there is always a danger that it will be used for personal gain rather than for the general good.

3 Proposals to Foster Democratic Accountability

How to hold governments accountable is an enduring question. A number of observations are in order to address this question. First, one must be aware of misbehavior; sunlight is beneficial. One cannot address problems if one is ignorant of their existence. This question of awareness falls within the realm of whistleblowing. In the absence of whistleblowing, negative situations may perpetuate. Whistleblowing, however, is not without costs to the individual whistleblower. People who step forward with information place themselves at great personal risk. Those who blow the whistle should be aware of the potential risks they face. These risks include possible loss of employment, demotion, ostracism, or job reassignment, among others. Whistleblower protections may help although much evidence exists that retaliation by employers occurs. Protections can embolden people to expose wrongdoing; however, whistleblowers act at their own peril.

Second, organizations can exercise internal oversight. It is possible that in some organizations, higher officials do not know about abuses. In these instances, a better communication flow is necessary. It is also possible superiors in organizations are aware of abuses and either tolerate or encourage them. In these more serious cases, wholesale "house cleaning" may be essential to alter the organizational culture. Organizational cultures are difficult to change but not impossible. Bringing in an outside "change agent" as the head of the agency represents one strategy to enact change from the top down. This can be problematic if large proportions of organizational members resist the changes. Top-down leaders must convince members that change is beneficial rather than simply impose orders and demand compliance. Alternatively, change may occur from within the body of the organizations through training of employees, punishing the "rotten apples," or rewarding the good actors.

Third, as has become evident in recent years, media exposure can produce a firestorm of attention, which can lead to short-term or longer-term corrective action. Media attention can lead to firing specific personnel, replacing agency heads, electoral change, policy change, or organizational change. Finally, legislative bodies such as Congress have oversight authority over governmental agencies. Oversight can result in increased or decreased budgets. Hearings may uncover abuse and provide the public with a sense of how well or poorly agencies are performing their duties. This chapter describes how each of these tools may hold bureaucrats accountable.

3.1 Stronger Whistleblower Protections

Lawmakers recognize the crucial service whistleblowers provide in holding organizations accountable for wrongdoing. Many state and federal laws encourage whistleblowers and protect them from workplace retaliation. Congress initially addressed whistleblower rights in the Civil Service Reform Act of 1978. In 1989, Congress passed the Whistleblower Protection Act to strengthen and improve protection of federal employees, to prevent reprisals, and to help eliminate wrongdoing. The Whistleblower Protection Act protects workers by clarifying the procedure by which employees could report wrongdoing and workplace retaliation. The 1989 law also established the Office of Special Counsel (OSC) to represent whistleblowers. This law and the subsequent Whistleblower Protection Enhancement Act of 2012 enabled whistleblowers to obtain back pay and benefits, recoup attorneys' fees, and retain a clean record. It mandates that those who retaliate and whistleblowers may be subject to disciplinary action such as demotion, removal, suspension, and fines.

Passage of whistleblower legislation did not eliminate dangers to those that reported violations. Svara (2015, p. 154) notes that for fiscal year

2011, four out of five whistleblowers were dissatisfied with their interactions with the OSC. As previously discussed, New York City police officer Frank Serpico did what he thought was right in exposing widespread corruption in the NYPD. He suffered for the experience. Serpico received a gunshot wound to the face in 1971 and became a pariah. At the time of the shooting, fellow officers refused to make a dispatch to police headquarters, indicating that an officer was shot. The two officers who had accompanied Serpico to the scene of a crime did not follow him into the scene. This raises the question of whether colleagues brought Serpico to a place to be murdered. There was no formal investigation. Upon retirement, Serpico complained that he did not receive the respect he thought he deserved because he violated the police code of silence. Serpico was the first police officer in the history of the NYPD to step forward to report and subsequently testify openly about systemic corruption.

Treatment of the VA whistleblowers was not as egregious as the treatment of Serpico; however, whistleblowers suffered consequences. In 2013, Dr. Sam Foote of the Phoenix VA hospital lodged a formal complaint against a VA executive. The hospital then assigned to him an increased patient caseload. Foote moved up the date for his retirement and began to collect information for an Office of Inspector General (OIG) complaint. The complaint would allege that up to 40 veterans died while awaiting care from the Phoenix VA system. The VA did not totally ignore Foote's action and dispatched an inspector general team to Phoenix. In addition, Foote went to the media with his story of questionable reporting of patient wait times. Others such as Dr. Katherine Mitchell, a physician at the VA, corroborated much of Foote's information. The VA ordered audits of the department's more than 900 medical facilities. Foote's revelations ultimately led to the resignation of VA Secretary Eric Shinseki in 2014. Foote was not pleased with generating the intensity of animosity at an institution where he spent 24 years of his life trying to help veterans. He noted that rather than acclaim, dedicated colleagues in Phoenix were threatened, spit at, and insulted (Wagner 2014).

The whistleblowing actions of Foote exposed serious fraud but did not seem to have long-term effects on the massive veterans' bureaucracy. During and after the worst scandal in VA history, not only did the VA continue the practice of giving bonuses to those that manipulated records, but also paid nearly half the bonuses in 2014 to the exact same employees as the previous year. Instead of triggering audits, forensic investigations, and prosecutions, the status quo seems to have prevailed. Of the seven most troubled facilities cited in 2014, only in Phoenix, the epicenter of the scandal, did the bonus dollars materially fall. In the troubled Veterans Affairs centers at Hines, Memphis, Central Alabama, and Biloxi, Mississippi, bonuses paid during 2014 increased. In Albuquerque and Miami, bonuses decreased, but still were higher than in 2012. The VA terminated only eight employees out of a total VA payroll of 341,000 employees due to the wait time scandal. At the peak of the VA scandal, in June 2014, the US House of Representatives voted unanimously to end the practice of bonuses; however, the Senate never took up the legislation (Andrzejewski 2015).

The legendary whistleblower of Watergate fame (Deep Throat) maintained relative anonymity from 1972 until 2005 when the number two person at the FBI's (Mark Felt) family revealed his identity in a *Vanity Fair* magazine article. The courts convicted Felt in November 1980 of conspiring to violate the constitutional rights of Americans. President Reagan pardoned Felt seven months after the conviction. He disappeared from public view for a quarter of a century and unequivocally denied that he had been Deep Throat. Felt's motivations for speaking to the media about Watergate are unclear. Some claim that Felt, a J. Edgar Hoover loyalist, was bitter when President Richard Nixon did not appoint him FBI director. Nixon appointed an FBI outsider, L. Patrick Gray, to lead the FBI after Hoover's death. Felt died in 2008 at the age of 95. He remained relatively anonymous while the reporters who Felt fed information to gained glory and fame.

Whistleblowers serve a vital function for democracies. They provide inside information about organizations where abuses occur. Often they are castigated by their fellow employees for not being a "team player," for "ratting out" others, or for being a "showboat." In many cases, whistleblowers suffer serious consequences. Government officials often provide lip service about the value of whistleblowers. The reality in many instances, however, contradicts the rhetoric. For example, Barack Obama initially pledged that his administration would encourage, rather than punish government whistleblowers. His presidential transition webpage in 2008 proclaimed the need to empower federal employees as "watchdogs of wrongdoings and partners in performance," and to "strengthen whistleblower laws to protect federal worker." Despite the rhetoric, Obama's Justice Department increased the number of prosecutions of whistleblowers for violating the Espionage Act of 1917. In the Obama administration, federal prosecutors charged eight leakers with espionage, more than all other administrations combined. Obama viewed the people who revealed secrets of his administration as criminal leakers, rather than heroic actors.

The two biggest cases of espionage whistleblowing in the Obama administration involved Chelsea Manning and Edward Snowden. Manning received a 35-year sentence for giving hundreds of thousands of secret documents to WikiLeaks. Obama commuted Manning's sentence three days before the end of his presidency. Obama believed the Manning case differed significantly from that of Snowden since Manning went through the military criminal justice process and acknowledged wrongdoing. In contrast, according to the White House, Snowden fled into the arms of an adversary and sought refuge in a country that made a concerted effort to undermine confidence in the US democracy (Olmsted 2018, p. 225).

The anecdotal evidence suggests that idealistic people are still willing to step forward to reveal abuses within their organizations. In some instances, such as the case of Mark Felt (Watergate), Ron Ridenhour (My Lai), and Joe Darby (Abu Ghraib), the whistleblowing action led to real changes. Regarding other whistleblowers such as Frank Serpico and the NYPD or Edward Snowden and the NSA, long-term changes are harder to discern. Nevertheless, whistleblowing remains an effective means to shed light on the darker corners of abusive organizations. Government officials can enhance accountability by reducing the negative personal consequences that individuals suffer when making difficult decisions to uncover abuses.

3.2 Better Organizational Oversight

Organizations can take on lives of their own. They develop internal norms and expectations; they make decisions regarding hiring, firing, promotion, and demotion. These internal sets of cues have a tremendous impact on what the overall nature of the organization will resemble. The internal norms determine the basic culture and "feel" of a given agency. Since the organization is more durable than the transitory chief executive, be they presidents, governors, or mayors, the organization provides a sense of stability and continuity for workers. Democratic accountability occurs when the aims and methods of organizations correspond with the general desires of the people. Problems of democratic accountability arise when organizations or individual bureaucrats seek personal goals regardless of the public will (Niskanen 1971) or when organizations/individual bureaucrats seek to impose their visions by fiat without regard to popular sentiment.

In a deviation from the ideals of democracy, the protections from day-to-day oversight that bureaucrats and organizations enjoy may lead to the creation of semi-autonomous fiefdoms. These fiefdoms in turn may adopt patterns of behavior that are contrary to popular wishes and contrary to constitutional protections of citizens. This is especially true regarding national security and law enforcement organizations. Local police may profile people for arrest or harassment, they may use excessive force, they may fine and harass certain groups more than others, and they have discretion that can have an immediate impact on neighborhoods. National-level organizations such as the FBI have disregarded constitutional protections through wiretaps and collecting files. The organizations then try to use files or dossiers to blackmail or destroy people's lives. Law enforcement organizations have infiltrated groups in order to create additional chaos and instigate illegal behavior. Internationally oriented security organizations such as the NSA may collect billions of pieces of information on residents in an area. Any sense of privacy is lost in the modern era when the government monitors all manners of communications daily. Organizations such as the CIA engage in actions that many individuals find reprehensible.

Oversight is necessary in order to limit organizational abuses. The oversight can be internal or external. It can be top down or bottom up. Internal oversight occurs when the organization itself determines that things are not working and begins to take steps to remedy the situation. External oversight occurs when those outside the organization demand change and insist on better accountability. Top-down oversight can occur if organizations place new and different leaders at the top of the administrative hierarchy. Bottom-up oversight is possible if personnel at lower levels of the hierarchy act to ensure responsible behavior.

Media coverage and congressional actions may exert enough external exposure of policies (such as "rough interrogations" or "speed traps" in minority neighborhoods) to alter those policies. Internal pressure may produce change when organizational personnel adopt different modes of behavior. The most direct strategy to change an organization's culture is to put a new head in place such as a new police chief, new FBI, CIA, or NSA director. This may have an immediate short-term effect as personnel adopt in order to comply with new priorities. The long-term effect subsides, however, unless significant numbers of personnel in the bowels of the organization willingly embrace the new directions. Change that is more permanent will occur in street-level organizations (such as local police forces) only if the street-level bureaucrats embrace the change.

Organizations have tools to enact adjustment. They can train and retrain workers in order to better align with sentiments of the majority. They possess an array of "carrots" and "sticks" to apply in efforts to shape behavior within the organization. Organizations can choose to reward some behavior and punish others. They can expeditiously identify and try to rid themselves of "bad actors." They can effect better communication within the organization so that higher-level officials are aware of internal norms. Organizations can more clearly proscribe and prescribe. They can exhort workers to be more responsive to external cues.

3.3 Responsible Media Attention

Democracies require an informed electorate. A free and open press is a basic prerequisite for citizens to form opinions and express those opinions at the polls. Media attention therefore can affect elections; elections in turn can empower new sets of legislators, legislators can make new policy and bureaucratic organizations are responsible to implement the new changes. The media therefore is an essential link in the chain from the people to the policy to the implementation. A break in the media link (as in a state-controlled press or a press that completely lacks credibility) ruptures the chain and undermines democratic accountability.

The media has been under attack at various times in history but informing the electorate with a diversity of opinion remains essential. The impact of a monopoly of information (as in a state-run media) erodes the ability of the people to receive truthful information and to correct abusive behavior. The outpouring of communication from blogs, websites, late-night comedians, Google searches, and other sources enhances the diversity of opinion. This may polarize society in "echo chamber," yet a free and open discourse is preferable to a news monopoly that characterizes state-run societies. Administrations often try to influence the media and conflict may emerge between leaders and reporters. In early 2017, Donald Trump proclaimed on Twitter that the nation's news media was "the enemy of the American people." He specifically cited the "failing" *New York Times*, NBC News, ABC News, CBS, and CNN.

The Trump administration blamed news organizations for stymieing his agenda and referred to the media as the "opposition party." He asserted that much of the media in Washington, DC, along with New York and Los Angeles speaks not for the people, but for the special interests. Critics of Trump claimed that he displayed similarities with Richard Nixon in trying to divide the country, and make the conduct of the press the issue, instead of the conduct of the president. They continued to assert that Trump's attack on the press echoed the language of autocrats who seek to minimize dissent (Grynbaum 2017).

Wall Street Journal reporter Bret Stephens (2017) expresses the view that journalists have a responsibility to separate truth from falsehood, which is never more important than when powerful people insist that falsehoods are truths, or that there is no such thing as truth. Stephens notes that we are living through a period in which the executive branch of government is engaged in a systematic effort to create negative opinions about news organizations. He claims that Trump routinely describes reporting he dislikes as fake news, calls for journalists to be fired, and lobbies to rewrite libel laws in order to more easily sue the press. Critics of the Trump administration maintain that one of the goals of the Trump presidency is to depose mainstream media in favor of media outlets such as *Breitbart News*.

The danger of media attacks is present in the threat that strong leaders will define truth as what one can get away with and that falsehood can be stronger than truth, if it is sold to the people on a large enough scale. This parallels with the dictum of Soviet leader Joseph Stalin that the death of one man is a tragedy but the death of a million is a statistic. If one always lies, it is almost impossible to remember any one particular lie; outrage is victim to its own ubiquity; one can only cry "wolf" so many times. Trump's attacks land on an already weakened opponent. Stephens reports that in 2017, just 17 percent of adults aged 18–24 read a newspaper daily, down from 42 percent at the turn of the century. In 2017, there were fewer than 33,000 full-time newsroom employees, a drop from 55,000 in 1997.

Despite the efforts to discredit news, there is evidence that media exposure of wrongdoing has had an impact on behavior of individuals and organizations. The Trayvon Martin shooting in Sanford, Florida, received major news coverage. The Pew Research Center that tracks weekly news coverage concluded that the Martin killing received the highest level of sustained coverage of any story with a major racial component. At one point, about one-third of Americans (35 percent) said they were following news about the case very closely, making it one of the top stories in 2012 in terms of the level of public attention (Anderson 2013).

A timeline of the Florida shooting suggests that media coverage can affect outcomes (Dahl 2013). The Florida timeline notes that on February 26, 2012, George Zimmerman (a neighborhood watch volunteer) shot Trayvon Martin while the 17-year-old was walking back from a convenience store in Sanford, Florida. Zimmerman tells police he killed the teen in self-defense after a scuffle. The police take Zimmerman into custody but release him; they do not file any charges. On March 13–15, 2012, *The Atlantic*, the *Huffington Post*, and the *New York Times* all run stories about the Trayvon Martin shooting. Cable news stations and morning news programs interview Martin's parents and their attorney. Shortly later the DOJ announces it will investigate the shooting. On April 3, 2012, the FBI announces it has opened an investigation. The Seminole County State's Attorney office then stated it would convene a grand jury and charges Zimmerman with second-degree murder. On June 20, 2012, the city fires the Sanford police chief and on June 10, 2013, a trial begins. Despite the exoneration of Zimmerman, in the absence of media attention, it is conceivable there would be no arrest and no trial. In addition, there might not be scrutiny of the police chief and his subsequent firing.

A second example of media attention to questionable behavior relates to Abu Ghraib. In 2003, the Associated Press published a lengthy report on inhumane treatment, beatings, and deaths at the Abu Ghraib prison complex and other American prisons in Iraq. Based on interviews with released detainees, the Associated Press report notes the use of dogs to attack inmates, inmates made to wear hoods, and inmates humiliated in other ways. However, the report gained little notice. Visual images changed the situation dramatically. In 2004, the US television news magazine *60 Minutes II* (a franchise of CBS) broadcast a story that included photographs depicting the abuse of prisoners. The investigatory reporter, Seymour M. Hersh, published an article in *The New Yorker* magazine that documents abuses in detail. Later media coverage includes previously unreleased photos and videos broadcast by SBS, an Australian television network.

The media coverage appears to have had some effect. The Abu Ghraib prison closed in 2014. The US military court-martialed and convicted nine enlisted army soldiers of crimes committed at the Abu Ghraib prison: seven military police, and two soldiers from Military Intelligence (MI). The army took other action against some officers for crimes at Abu Ghraib. Brig. Gen. Janis Karpinski, commander of a Military Police (MP) brigade, was relieved of command, demoted to colonel, and received a letter of reprimand. Colonel Thomas M. Pappas, commander of an MI brigade, was relieved of command, and received a letter of reprimand and a monetary fine. The US government meted out numerous prison sentences. Among the soldiers receiving high levels of media attention, Corporal Charles Graner received a ten-year prison sentence and a dishonorable discharge. The army reduced his rank to private. Private First Class Lynndie England received a sentence of three years in prison and a dishonorable discharge. Staff Sergeant Ivan Frederick II received a sentence of eight years in prison and the forfeiture of pay. He also received a dishonorable discharge and a reduction in rank to private (Follman and Clark-Flory 2006). Graner served six and a half years; Frederick served four years; England served one year and five months.

Media attention did not prevent all local police officers or volunteer watch officials (i.e. "wannabe" cops) from abusing their authority. Attention to obvious abuses, however, can lead street-level cops to think twice before taking disastrous action. A high level of media exposure may lead police organizations to make incremental changes to their internal controls. For example, authorities may sanction "bad apple" soldiers and reward good actors. They may implement new procedures and different training. Media exposure may also pressure national policymakers to alter or reverse policies of organizations such as the CIA and MP. In the absence of the highly toxic pictures of Abu Ghraib prison and the flood of negative media attention that ensued, there is much less chance that prisoner interrogation policies would have changed.

3.4 *Legislative Oversight*

In the early years of the progressive movement, Woodrow Wilson (1885) declared that oversight of administration was as important as legislation. Wilson, along with others, considered legislative oversight to be a necessary condition for democratic governance. However, there is no definitive formula for how much oversight is required for an effective system of checks and balances. Oversight is critically important to ensure accountability and transparency and to provide a link between public policy and the will of the people. Democratic theorists acclaim oversight. In addition, various statutes require it. With the Legislative Reorganization Act of 1946, Congress required its standing committees to exercise "continuous watchfulness" of administrative agencies. The goals of legislative oversight are to detect and remedy failures and to exercise effective controls (McGrath 2013, p. 371).

Congress has legitimate authority over administrative agencies. The Legislative Reorganization Act of 1946 specifies three types of congressional oversight over the bureaucracy: fiscal oversight (control over money), legislative oversight (do programs work?), and investigatory oversight (inquiries into economy, efficiency, and effectiveness). Each of these oversight responsibilities falls under a separate committee. Authorizing committees are responsible for legislative oversight. Committees and subcommittees may hold hearings and require agencies to submit reports. In addition to the committee oversight, Congress can use the four agencies Congressional Research Service (CRS), General Accountability Office (GAO), Office of Technology Assessment (OTA), and Congressional Budget Office (CBO) to monitor bureaucratic performance. The GAO is best equipped to perform the task of oversight; however, there are serious limitations on its ability to conduct oversight (Riley 1987, p. 79).

Bureaucratic agencies have strong incentive to have good relations with congressional representatives. Riley (1987, p. 98) states that "Congress has managed to reserve for itself the final say on which agencies live and which die, on what sort of departmental home they will have, and on which programs the will administer, what legal authority they will have to administer them with, and how much money they can spend as they do it." In reality, congressional oversight is less robust. Many view congressional oversight as sporadic and reactive. The conventional view of congressional oversight is that Congress lacks the wherewithal to monitor the administrative process because of the sheer size and diversity of today's bureaucracy. In addition, many in Congress lack the expertise to monitor complex areas of the bureaucracy, and the bureaucracy seeks to preserve its autonomy through control of information. Pressure from the president, interest groups, and other actors may also limit oversight.

Scholars present various explanations for inadequate congressional oversight. Scher (1963) notes that people in Congress must make rational choices about how to allocate their time and energy. They realize that how they prioritize competing demands is likely to be crucial to electoral success and job security. Highly visible issues can provide substantial opportunities for legislators to build name recognition and project themselves as guardians of the public trust. This attention, however, is the exception rather than the rule. The norm is that people in Congress find many reasons to avoid oversight responsibilities except in high-profile cases. A multitude of factors supports the decision to neglect oversight.

Scher (1963) identifies seven key reasons why congressional representatives might avoid their oversight responsibilities. First, without the incentive of high-profile exposure, people in Congress would rather be associated with popular, district-serving legislation and individual constituent services than with typically unnoticed hearings on agency performance. Second, committee members tend to view government agencies as impenetrable mazes and to believe that any serious effort at penetrating them poses hazards for the inexpert congressperson, which outweigh any conceivable gain. Third, congressional representatives who have established mutually rewarding relationships with agency personnel tend to be reluctant to initiate or become actively engaged in a close review of that agency's affairs. Fourth, people in Congress tend to view their personal contacts with the agencies as more efficient than committee investigations for serving constituent and group needs. Fifth, committee members will tend to avoid agency review if they expect it will provoke costly reprisals from powerful economic interests. Sixth, representatives who perceive they can gain personally by loyalty to the president avoid close examination of the performance of agency officials appointed by the chief executive. Seventh, unless there are compelling reasons to alter normal committee life by taking on an agency, committee members are likely to consider it easier and less costly not to.

A typical pattern of congressional review of many agencies therefore is one of no review for long periods, or no review at all. In specific circumstances, agencies are more likely to be subject to oversight. Reviews of regulatory agencies are more likely to occur when the leadership of the majority party believes it can cause embarrassment to opposition leaders by holding them responsible for the performance of agency appointees. A pattern of unfriendly agency decisions or the thwarting of friendly decisions can also spark a review of agency performance. Congressional members may become aware of unfriendly agency decisions because of communications from economic groups whose interests the congressperson shares. Oversight may also occur because friendly representatives determine a limited investigation may be less damaging than a broader agency examination (Scher 1963).

4 Finding a Balance Between Responsiveness and Arbitrary License

4.1 Peril to Democracy of an Unresponsive Bureaucracy

The danger to democracy of unresponsive bureaucracy is intuitively obvious. Examples from this book update the perennial issue of how bureaucrats "flying under the radar" may become a force unto themselves, operating with minimal responsiveness to the will of the public. Street-level bureaucrats maintain power and use their discretion in manners that can enhance or erode the basic legitimacy of the state. In a broad conception of the law enforcement bureaucrat, they are seen as those who patrol the streets, apprehend suspects, utilize force, compile files, listen to conversations, interrogate terrorists, and fight wars. Precisely how they operate, in carrying out broad mandates from legislatures or executives, is subject to wide latitude. Individuals may abuse their authority and act in manners that are antithetical to both constitutional maxims and public desires. In such cases, a loss of both accountability and legitimacy occurs. Democratic checks on bureaucratic power erode; the people lose power; the expert bureaucrats gain in their ability to rule by fiat. An apathetic public encourages movement down this slippery slope of rule by technocrats.

Citizens may be apathetic, yet they expect at least a modest level of systems maintenance that includes but is not limited to keeping the streets safe, educating children for gainful employment, respecting human rights, protecting the privacy of law-abiding individuals, and not plundering the public treasury. Generally speaking, many citizens wish to pursue their private lives with a minimum of interference from the government. They take a laissez-faire attitude toward government as long as the ship of state appears to be sailing in relatively calm waters. High-profile images of shocking behavior, however, rupture the sense of calm and force citizens to confront abuses. Disturbing images force people to question what is going on in their government. Public pressure, in turn, foreshadows some type of corrective action even if the corrective action is largely symbolic.

Images provide a valuable window into government behavior. Questions arise. Citizens demand to know whether behavior is anomalous or represents standard operating procedures. They want to know who approves of procedures. They are particularly awakened when behavior fundamentally contradicts prevailing norms of society. They question whether bureaucracies are profoundly "broken" and in need of major restructuring. Will minor tweaks be sufficient? People want to know how corrective action can occur. Policy therefore is reactive, yet a reactive policy in response to genuine concerns of the public is preferable to a perpetuation of "broken" administration.

Accountability is consistent with democracy. Under the principles of democratic theory, the "people" rule. In reality, however, the power of the people is constrained by a variety of forces. Apathy, disgust, or the rationalistic conclusion that participation does not matter limits voting by average citizens. After years of political neglect, people may simply conclude that it does not matter whether politician A or politician B wins office and that the outcome will be the same. Other problems with popular rule exist. Slick advertising campaigns that wealthy special interests fund may manipulate voters. Advertisers bombard people with misinformation and contrary information. In addition, legislative actions such as gerrymandering can limit the power of voters. Voters whose voice is consistently overwhelming by others in their voting district may feel disenfranchised. Employers and others may intimidate voters. Voters may simply be too disillusioned to waste their gas money to go to the polls.

The fundamental peril that bureaucracy poses to democracy is that of stealth rule by a cabal of experts. Under this scenario, nonelected careerists whose everyday actions go undetected accumulate power. They begin to act as self-contained units; they decide for themselves the type of action that is necessary. The public has the ability to replace mayors, governors, presidents, city council members, or congressional representatives; however, they are less able to influence police officers, CIA interrogators, Infantry lieutenants, or FBI officials. This loss of accountability has real consequences. It is not true that what the public does not know cannot hurt them. Secret behavior can hurt individual citizens as well as the organic state when unelected professionals misbehave, unofficially make policies, and disregard the interests of the people.

The new world of iPhones, blogs, cable television, and Internet chatter can expose bureaucrats to a greater degree of scrutiny. This can shatter their sheltered world and inform citizens of abusive behavior. Major disruptions in bureaucratic equilibrium can occur when stark images (such as naked prisoner pyramids) awaken the slumbering public. More accountability occurs when the media exposes wrongdoing, the public responds, and administrators listen. A basic premise of democratic theory is that the people are more knowledgeable about "where the shoe pinches" than are the technical experts. They know where the breakdowns occur since they suffer the consequences. A bureaucratic vision can be profoundly antithetical to the democratic vision; popular checks on bureaucracy are necessary.

4.2 *Control of Bureaucracy Through Public Awareness (Communication), Transparency (Truthfulness), and Responsiveness (Elections)*

The threat administrative officials pose to ideals of democracy is as old as time. American scholars of the public administration were well aware of the threat and the need to protect the prerogatives of elected officials. Leonard D. White (1945, p. 1) notes that since the English Revolution of 1688 it has been a part of the Anglo-American tradition that elected representative assemblies control the policies and acts of the executive branch of government. This doctrine is "firmly embedded" in the American state and "universally accepted" throughout the nation. Despite such acceptance, however, White contends there is suspicion that a "vast body of officials" have "escaped the possibility of control" since "within the administrative system there has developed a capacity for self-direction." Elected officials therefore must be on guard against abuse, be it arrogance, stupidity, or corruption. Representatives have weighty responsibility because "the elected representative is the principal protection of the humble citizen against abuse of the great powers which officials possess" (p. 11).

Three means of democratic control are that of (1) communication, (2) truthfulness, and (3) responsiveness. As discussed in this text, one cannot fix what one does not know is a problem. Whistleblowing therefore is essential to accountability. The disillusioned police officer, the indignant VA doctor, the distraught war veteran, the alarmed active duty soldier, and others all have played vital roles uncovering wrongdoing of government agents. Added to the mix today is the ease in which people capture disturbing behavior on video and deliver material to the mass media. The mass media is all too willing to deliver upsetting images to the public. Communication therefore can produce such a level of discomfort at the highest levels of government that some sort of corrective action is necessary. Pictures such as those at Abu Ghraib are therefore necessary to alter status quo norms.

Second, some degree of transparency and truthfulness is necessary in order to confront harmful abuses. Agencies must be able to admit wrongdoing before they will accept change. If police departments resist allegations that graft exists or that some deadly action is unwarranted, then corrective action will never occur or will be temporary at best. If the highest levels of government discredit through lies or deception internal or external reports of violations, then the reports have no impact. The reports will remain silent, sitting on dusty shelves in distant offices. The forces of the status quo in efforts to avoid embarrassment may simply overwhelm the forces of change that wish to right the apparent wrongs of agencies. If the status quo prevails, the organization benefits in the short term. Deception and misinformation receive a reward. Positive change fails to gain traction.

A final arrow in the quiver of those fighting for accountability is that of electoral responsiveness. One does not expect average citizens to be aware of all abuses in vast bureaucracies. One does not expect average citizens to have the time or interest to become comprehensively informed about behavior even if information is available. Furthermore, the flood of contradictory information in the mass media (i.e. "spin") may lead average citizens to conclude that information collection may not help them make good electoral choices. On the contrary, information accumulation may simply reinforce existing prejudices or produce fodder for gossip with little discussion of real policy alternatives or real insight on who best represents their interest.

Elections, however, may represent the last best hope for accountability. As long as the ballots are not completely corrupted and money does not comprehensively manipulate perceptions, there is a possibility for system reform. Electoral realignments periodically occur. These realignments can wash away the corrosion of the older regime and can begin to institute change in bureaucratic organizations. Government appointees can set forth new policies and alter the fundamental culture of agencies. Fundamental realignments, however, are not normal occurrences. In US national elections 1860, 1896, 1932, and 1980 represent periods of displacement of "in" coalitions with "outs." The fact that such change was possible suggests that the average voter still has the ability to enact change. Voters may be apathetic, slow to react, and not always well informed. Like the proverbial donkey, you might need to hit them over the head with a large piece of lumber to get their attention. Nevertheless, the electorate still appear to be the firmest bulwark against the apocalyptic visions of continuous gains in power of the nonelected, unaccountable, self-interested, nonresponsive technocrats who operate in accord with their own sets of imperatives.

5 Conclusions

Accountability is the bedrock of individual and organizational behavior. Organizations, particularly law enforcement organizations, possess a great deal of discretion and many of their operations are not subject to ordinary review. Some actions "fly under the radar" in that they are not widely known, not publicized, and not scrutinized. This can lead to abusive behavior by actors that are not very responsive to the general desires of the people. The danger of nonresponsive bureaucracies can be countered by strong institutions. Legislatures, executives, the media, and free elections all play a role. Strengthening these institutions can work to diminish the threats bureaucracies pose to democratic responsiveness.

References

Anderson, M. (2013). As the Trayvon Martin case goes to trial, remembering a major media event. *Pew Research Center*. Retrieved August 20, 2015, from http://www.pewresearch.org/

Andrzejewski, A. (2015, May 24). The VA scandal one year later. *Forbes*. Retrieved October 8, 2018, from https://www.forbes.com/

Dahl, J. (2013, July 12). Trayvon Martin shooting: A timeline of events. *CBS News*. Retrieved October 9, 2018, from https://www.cbsnews.com/

Follman, M., & Clark-Flory, T. (2006, March 14). Prosecutions and convictions. *Salon*. Retrieved October 9, 2018, from https://www.salon.com/

Grynbaum, M. M. (2017, February 17). Trump calls the news media the 'Enemy of the American People.' *New York Times*. Retrieved October 9, 2018, from https://www.nytimes.com

McGrath, R. J. (2013). Congressional oversight hearings and policy control. *Legislative Studies Quarterly, XXXVIII*(3), 349–376.

Niskanen, W. (1971 [1994]). *Bureaucracy and public economics*. Cheltenham: Edward Elgar.

Olmsted, K. (2018). Terror Tuesday: How Obama refined Bush's counterterrorism policies. In J. E. Zelizer (Ed.), *The presidency of Barack Obama* (pp. 212–226). Princeton: Princeton University Press.

Riley, D. R. (1987). *Controlling the federal bureaucracy*. Philadelphia: Temple University Press.

Scher, S. (1963). Conditions for legislative control. *Journal of Politics, 25*(3), 526–551.

Stephens, B. (2017, February 26). Don't dismiss president Trump's attacks on the media as mere stupidity. *Time*. Retrieved October 9, 2018, from https://time.com/

Svara, J. (2015). *The ethics primer for public administrator in government and non-profit organizations*. Burlington: Jones & Bartlett Learning.

Wagner, D. (2014, May 31). The doctor who launched the VA scandal. *AZCentral*. Retrieved October 8, 2018, from https://www.azcentral.com/

White, L. D. (1945). Congressional control of the public service. *American Political Science Review, XXXIX*(1), 1–11.

Wilson, W. (1885). *Congressional government*. Boston: Houghton-Mifflin.

References

Aid, M. M. (2009). *The secret sentry: The untold history of the National Security Agency*. New York: Bloomsbury Press.

Anderson, D. L. (2002). *The Columbia guide to the Vietnam War*. New York: Columbia University Press.

Anderson, M. (2013). As the Trayvon Martin case goes to trial, remembering a major media event. *Pew Research Center*. Retrieved August 20, 2015, from http://www.pewresearch.org/

Andrzejewski, A. (2015, May 24). The VA scandal one year later. *Forbes*. Retrieved October 8, 2018, from https://www.forbes.com/

Apperley, A. (1999). Hobbes on democracy. *Politics, 19*(3), 165–171.

Appleby, P. (1949). *Policy and administration*. Tuscaloosa: University of Alabama Press.

Associated Press. (2018, July 17). Judge: Trial in Laquan McDonald shooting to start Sept. 5. *Miami Herald*. Retrieved July 17, 2018, from https://www.miamiherald.com/news/

Baker, A., Goodman, J. D., & Mueller, B. (2015, June 13). Beyond the choke-hold: The path to Eric Garner's death. *New York Times*. Retrieved July 16, 2018, from https://www.nytimes.com/2015/06/14/

Bamford, J. (2002). *Body of secrets*. New York: Anchor Books.

Bardach, E. (1977). *The implementation game: What happens after a bill becomes a law*. Cambridge, MA: MIT Press.

Bart, C. K. (1997, November–December). Sex, lies, and mission statements. *Business Horizons*, pp. 9–18.

Bart, C. K. (1998). Mission matters. *The CPA Journal, 68*(8), 57–58.

Beetham, D. (1996). *Bureaucracy* (2nd ed.). Minneapolis: University of Minnesota Press.

S. G. Koven, *The Case Against Bureaucratic Discretion*,
https://doi.org/10.1007/978-3-030-05779-4

Bertram, C. (2017, Summer). Jean Jacques Rousseau. In E. N. Zalta (Ed.), *The Stanford encyclopedia of philosophy*. Retrieved March 28, 2017, from https://plato.stanford.edu/archives/sum2017/entries/rousseau/

Birzer, M. L. (2017). Racial profiling: The intersection of race and policing. In M. J. Palmiotto (Ed.), *Police use of force* (pp. 81–111). Boca Raton: CRC Press.

Bok, H. (2014, Summer). Baron de Montesquieu, Charles-Louis de Secondat. In E. N. Zalta (Ed.), *The Stanford encyclopedia of philosophy*. Retrieved March 28, 2018, from https://plato.stanford.edu/archives/sum2014/entries/montesquieu/

Brennan, G., & Buchanan, J. (1980). *The power to tax: Analytical foundations of a fiscal constitution*. Cambridge: Cambridge University Press.

Bronstein, S., Griffin, D., & Black, N. (2014, June 24). VA deaths covered up to make statistics look better, whistle-blower says. *CNN*. Retrieved August 23, 2018, from https://www.cnn.com/

Burke, J. (1986). *Bureaucratic responsibility*. Baltimore: Johns Hopkins University Press.

Burns, T. L. (1990). The origins of the National Security Agency: 1940–1952. *Center for Cryptologic History, National Security Agency, Series V, 1*. Retrieved September 4, 2018, from https://permanent.access.gpo.gov/gpo73503/origins_of_nsa.pdf

Carter, D. L., & Barker, T. (1991). Administrative guidance and control of police officer behavior: Policies, procedures, and rules. In T. Barker & D. L. Carter (Eds.), *Police deviance* (2nd ed.). Cincinnati: Anderson Publishing Co.

Champion, D. J. (2001). *Police misconduct in America*. Santa Barbara: ABC-CLIO, Inc.

Christiano, T. (2015, Spring). Democracy. In E. Salta (Ed.), *The Stanford encyclopedia of philosophy*. Retrieved March 6, 2018, from https://plato.stanford.edu/archives/spr2015/entries/democracy/

Clayton, E. (n.d.). Aristotle: Politics. *Internet Encyclopedia of Philosophy*. Retrieved March 16, 2018, from https://www.iep.utm.edu/aris-pol/

Cohen, J. (2000). *Politics and economic policy in the United States* (2nd ed.). Boston: Houghton-Mifflin Company.

Cooper, T. L. (1990). *The responsible administrator* (3rd ed.). San Francisco: Jossey-Bass.

Cooper, T. L. (1998). *The responsible administrator* (4th ed.). San Francisco: Jossey-Bass.

Daddis, G. (2012). The problem of metrics: Assessing progress and effectiveness in the Vietnam War. *War in History, 19*(1), 73–98.

Dahl, R. (1956). *A preface to democratic theory*. Chicago: University of Chicago Press.

Dahl, R. (1961). *Who governs? Democracy and power in an American city*. New Haven: Yale University Press.

Dahl, R. (1967). *Pluralist democracy in the United States: Conflict and consent.* Chicago: Rand McNally.

Dahl, R. (1982). *Dilemmas of pluralist democracy.* New Haven: Yale University Press.

Dahl, R. (2001). *How democratic is the American constitution.* New Haven: Yale University Press.

Dahl, J. (2013, July 12). Trayvon Martin shooting: A timeline of events. *CBS News.* Retrieved October 9, 2018, from https://www.cbsnews.com/

Daugherty, W. J. (2004). *Executive secrets: Covert action and the presidency.* Lexington: University of Kentucky Press.

Davey, M., & Smith, M. (2015, November 24). Chicago protests mostly peaceful after video of police shooting is released. *New York Times.* Retrieved July 16, 2018, from https://www.nytimes.com/2015/11/25/

Davis, K. C. (1969). *Discretionary justice: A preliminary inquiry.* Baton Rouge: LSU Press.

Denhardt, K. G. (1988). *The ethics of public service: Resolving moral dilemmas in public organizations.* Westport: Greenwood Press.

Devine, M. E. (2018, June 18). Intelligence community spending: Trends and issues. *Congressional Research Service.* Retrieved September 20, 2018, from https://fas.org/sgp/crs/intel/R44381.pdf

DiIulio, J. (2014). *Bring back the bureaucrats. West.* Conshohocken: Templeton Press.

Dobel, J. P. (1999). *Public integrity.* Baltimore: Johns Hopkins University Press.

Domhoff, W. (1967). *Who rules America?* Englewood Cliffs: Prentice Hall.

Domhoff, W. (2018). *Who rules America?* Retrieved April 26, 2018, from https://whorulesamerica.ucsc.edu/power/

Edy, J. (2018). Watts riots of 1966. *Encyclopedia Britannica.* Retrieved July 2, 2918, from https://www.britannica.com/event/Watts-Riots-of-1965

Emeka, T. Q. (2018). Detroit riot of 1967. *Encyclopedia Britannica.* Retrieved July 11, 2018, from https://www.britannica.com/event/Detroit-Riot-of-1967

Esman, A. R. (2014, June 24). *European reports show NSA's successes.* Retrieved September 12, 2018, from https://www.investigativeproject.org/

Etzioni-Halevy, E. (1983). *Bureaucracy and democracy: A political dilemma.* London: Routledge & Kegan Paul.

Fayol, H. (1916 [1987]). General principles of management. In J. M. Shafritz & J. S. Ott (Eds.), *Classics of organization theory* (2nd ed., pp. 51–66). Chicago: The Dorsey Press.

Finer, H. (1936). Better government personnel. *Political Science Quarterly, 51*(4), 569–599.

Finer, H. (1941). Administrative responsibility in democratic government. *Public Administration Review, 1*(4), 335–350.

Fitzgerald, B. (2006). Alum's book credits CIA analyst with uncovering Vietnam 'numbers gap.' *BU Today.* Retrieved September 17, 2018, from http://www.bu.edu/today

Foer, F. (2018, September). How ICE went rogue. *The Atlantic*, pp. 56–70.

Follman, M., & Clark-Flory, T. (2006, March 14). Prosecutions and convictions. *Salon*. Retrieved October 9, 2018, from https://www.salon.com/

Friedman, U. (2012, January 3). The ten biggest American intelligence failures. *Foreign Policy*. Retrieved September 21, 2018, from https://foreignpolicy.com/2012/01/03/

Friedrich, C. J. (1935). *Problems of the American public service*. New York: McGraw-Hill.

Friedrich, C. J. (1940 [1972]). Public policy and the nature of administrative responsibility. In F. Rourke (Ed.), *Bureaucratic power in national politics* (2nd ed.). Boston: Little, Brown.

Friend, C. (n.d.). Social contract theory. *Internet Encyclopedia of Philosophy*. Retrieved March 26, 2018, from https://www.iep.utm.edu/soc-cont/#SH2b

Frug, G. E. (1984). The ideology of bureaucracy in American law. *Harvard Law Review, 97*(6), 1276–1388.

Fry, B., & Raadschelders, J. (2008). *Mastering public administration: From Max Weber to Dwight Waldo* (2nd ed.). Washington, DC: CQ Press.

Galster, G. (2012). *Driving Detroit: The quest for respect in the motor city*. Philadelphia: University of Pennsylvania Press.

Garrett, T. A., & Rhine, R. M. (2006, January/February). On the size and growth of government. *Federal Reserve Bank of St. Louis Review, 88*(1), 13–30. Retrieved January 31, 2017, from https://files.stlouisfed.org/files/htdocs/publications/review/06/01/GarrettRhine.pdf

Garrett, R. S., Thurber, A., Fritschler, A., & Rosenbloom, D. (2006). Assessing the impact of bureaucracy bashing by electoral campaigns. *Public Administration Review, 66*(2), 228–240.

Gaus, J. M. (1936). The responsibility of public administrators. In J. M. Gaus, I. D. White, & M. Dimock (Eds.), *The frontiers of public administration* (pp. 26–44). Chicago: University of Chicago Press.

Gellman, B., & Miller, G. (2013, August 29). 'Black budget' summary details U.S. spy networks successes, failures, and objectives. *Washington Post*. Retrieved September 20, 2018, from https://www.washingtonpost.com/world/national-security/

Gerth, H. H., & Mills, C. W. (1958). *From Max Weber: Essays in sociology*. New York: Oxford University Press.

Godfrey, R. (2018, July 11). What 'Abolish ICE' actually means. *The Atlantic*. Retrieved August 15, 2018, from https://www.theatlantic.com/politics/archive

Goldstein, J., & Santora, M. (2014, August 1). Staten Island man died from chokehold during arrest, autopsy finds. *New York Times*. Retrieved July 16, 2018, from https://www.nytimes.com/2014/08/02

Goodsell, C. T. (2011). *Mission mystique: Belief systems in public agencies*. Washington, DC: CQ Press.

Greenwald, G. (2014). *No place to hide: Edward Snowden, the NSA, and the U.S. surveillance state*. New York: Metropolitan Books.

Gruber, J. E. (1987). *Controlling bureaucracies*. Berkeley: University of California Press.

Grynbaum, M. M. (2017, February 17). Trump calls the news media the 'Enemy of the American People.' *New York Times*. Retrieved October 9, 2018, from https://www.nytimes.com

Gulick, L. (1925). Principles of administration. *National Municipal Review, 14*(7), 400–403.

Gulick, L. (1937 [1969]). Notes on the theory of organization. In L. Gulick & L. Urwick (Eds.), *Papers on the science of administration* (pp. 3–45). New York: Augustus M. Kelly Publishers.

Gutmann, A., & Thompson, D. (1996). *Democracy and disagreement*. Cambridge, MA: Harvard University Press.

Gutmann, A., & Thompson, D. (1998). *Democracy and disagreement*. Princeton: Princeton University Press.

Gutmann, A., & Thompson, D. (2004). *Why deliberative democracy?* Princeton: Princeton University Press.

Halperin, M., Clapp, P., & Kanter, A. (2006). *Bureaucratic politics and foreign policy* (2nd ed.). Washington, DC: Brookings Institute.

Hinkle, H., & Levinson-Waldman, R. (2018, July 30). The abolish ICE movement explained. *Brennan Center for Justice*. Retrieved August 15, 2018, from https://www.brennancenter.org/

Holland, M. (2017, September 10). The myth of deep throat. *Politico Magazine*. Retrieved August 6, 2018, from https://www.politico.com/magazine/story/

Interview with Paula Pedene: Triumph of a PR Hero and Whistleblower. (2016). Retrieved August 23, 2018, from http://www.irispr.com/blog/

Israel, F. L. (1986). *The FBI*. New York: Chelsea House Publishers.

Jackson, M. (2009). Responsibility versus accountability in the Friedrich-Finer debate. *Journal of Management History, 15*(1), 66–77.

Jarrett, G. (2018). *The Russia hoax*. New York: HarperCollins Publishers.

Jeffreys-Jones, R. (2007). *The FBI: A history*. New York/New Haven: Yale University Press.

Johnson, M. (2003). *Street justice: A history of police violence in New York City*. Boston: Beacon Press.

Johnson, C. (2018, June 14). *Report condemns FBI violations in 2016 Clinton probe but finds no political bias*. Retrieved August 4, 2018, from http://www.npr.org

Kaufman, H. (2006). *The forest ranger: A study in administrative behavior* (Special reprint ed.). Washington, DC: Resources for the Future.

Klein, C. (2015, March 6). *Remembering Selma's 'Bloody Sunday'*. Retrieved July 2, 2018, from https://www.history.com/news/selmas-bloody-sunday-50-years-ago

Korab-Karpowicz, W. J. (n.d.). Plato: Political philosophy. *Internet Encyclopedia of Philosophy*. Retrieved March 14, 2018, from https://www.iep.utmdu/platopol/

Koven, S. G. (2008). *Responsible governance: A case study approach*. Armonk: M.E. Sharpe.

Koven, S. G. (2015). *Public sector ethics: Theory and applications*. Boca Raton: CRC Press.

Koven, S. G. (2017). Causes and consequences of crisis. In A. Farazmand (Ed.), *Global encyclopedia on public administration, public policy and governance*. Cham: Springer International Publishing.

Koven, S. G., & Göetzke, F. (2010). *American immigration policy: Confronting the nation's challenges*. New York: Springer.

Koven, S. G., & Koven, A. C. (2018). *Growth, decline, and regeneration in large cities: A case study approach*. New York: Routledge.

Kristov, L., Lindert, P., & McClelland, R. (1992). Pressure groups and redistribution. *Journal of Public Economics, 48*(2), 135–163.

Landler, M. (2017, September 7). Hillary Clinton, in book, regrets not striking back at James Comey. *New York Times*. Retrieved August 2, 2018, from https://www.nytimes.com

Lind, D. (2018, March 7). *Jeff Sessions's lawsuit against California's "sanctuary" laws, explained*. Retrieved August 20, 2018, from https://www.vox.com/

Lindsay, A. D. (1947). *The modern democratic state*. New York: Oxford University Press.

Lindsay, A. D. (1980). *The essentials of democracy*. Westport: Greenwood Press Publishers.

Lippmann, W. (1922). *Public opinion*. New York: Harcourt, Brace and Company.

Lippmann, W. (1925). *The phantom public*. New York: Harcourt, Brace and Company.

Lipsky, M. (2010). *Street-level bureaucracy: Dilemmas of the individual in public services*. New York: Russell Sage Foundation.

Long, N. (1949). Power and administration. *Public Administration Review, 9*(3), 257–264.

Lowi, T. (1969). *The end of liberalism*. New York: W.W. Norton.

Lutrin, C., & Settle, A. (1985). *American public administration: Concepts and cases* (3rd ed.). Englewood Cliffs: Prentice-Hall Inc.

Maggetti, M. (2010). *Legitimacy and accountability of independent regulatory agencies: A critical review*. Center for Comparative and International Studies, ETH Zurich and University of Zurich. Retrieved February 27, 2018, from https://www.ethz.ch/content/dam/ethz/special-interest/gess/cis/cis-dam/

Marini, F. (1969). John Locke and the revision of classical democratic theory. *Western Political Quarterly, 22*(1), 5–18.

Mark, M. (2015, November 6). Amid Kim Davis backlash, Kentucky Gov.-Elect Matt Bevin to remove clerks' names from state marriage licenses. *International Business Times*. Retrieved May 21, 2018, from http://www.ibtimes.com/

Markon, J. (2015, July 6). California killing inflames debate on illegal immigrants, 'sanctuary cities.' *Washington Post*. Retrieved August 19, 2018, from https://www.washingtonpost.com/

Mathews, R. (2017). Iran-Contra affair. *Encyclopedia Britannica*. Retrieved January 11, 2017, from https://www.britannica.com/event/Iran-Contra-Affair

Mayhew, D. (2015). Robert A. Dahl, question, concepts, proving it. *Journal of Political Power, 8*(2), 175–187.

MacAskill, E. (2011, October 21). Iraq rejects US request to maintain bases after troop withdrawal. *The Guardian*. Retrieved September 29, 2018, from https://www.theguardian.com/

McCoy, A. W. (2006). *A question of torture: CIA interrogation, from the cold war to the war on terror*. New York: Henry Holt.

McGrath, R. J. (2013). Congressional oversight hearings and policy control. *Legislative Studies Quarterly, XXXVIII*(3), 349–376.

Meier, K. (1993). *Politics and the bureaucracy* (3rd ed.). Belmont: Wadsworth Publishing Company.

Meier, K. (2010). Governance, structure, and democracy: Luther Gulick and the future of public administration. *Public Administration Review, 70*, S284–S291.

Meier, K., & O'Toole, L. (2006). *Bureaucracy in a democratic state*. Baltimore: The Johns Hopkins University Press.

Mestrovic, S. G. (2007). *The trials of Abu Ghraib: An expert witness account of shame and honor*. Boulder: Paradigm.

Mill, J. S. (1861 [1991]). *Considerations on representative government*. Buffalo: Prometheus Books.

Miller, F. (2017, Winter). Aristotle's political theory. In E. Zalta (Ed.), *The Stanford encyclopedia of philosophy*. Retrieved March 16, 2018, from https://plato.stanford.edu/archives/win2017/entries/aristotle-politics/

Mitchell, K. (2015, December 14). *Written testimony of Dr. Katherine L. Mitchell*. Retrieved August 23, 2018, from https://www.veterans.senate.gov/imo/media/doc/

Montesquieu, C. (1748). *The spirit of laws*. Retrieved April 1, 2018, from http://oll.libertyfund.org/titles/montesquieu-complete-works-vol-1-the-spirit-of-laws

Murry, G. (2018). *The on-going battle for the soul of the army*. Retrieved September 17, 2018, from http://smallwarsjournal.com/

National Security Agency Releases History of Cold War Intelligence Activities. (2008). *The National Security Archive*. Retrieved September 12, 2018, from https://nsaarchive2.gwu.edu

Nelson, S. (2018, February 27). Trump sends Congress record high 'black budget' spy funding request. *Washington Examiner*. Retrieved September 11, 2018, from https://www.washingtonexaminer.com/

Nice, C., & Fisher, P. (2016). *Public budgeting* (2nd ed.). San Diego: Birkdale Publishers.

Niskanen, W. (1971 [1994]). *Bureaucracy and public economics.* Cheltenham: Edward Elgar.

O'Leary, R. (2006). *The ethics of dissent: Managing guerrilla government.* Washington, DC: CQ Press.

Olmsted, K. (2018). Terror Tuesday: How Obama refined Bush's counterterrorism policies. In J. E. Zelizer (Ed.), *The presidency of Barack Obama* (pp. 212–226). Princeton: Princeton University Press.

Ostrom, V. (1973). *The intellectual crisis in American public administration.* Tuscaloosa: University of Alabama Press.

Palmiotto, M. J. (2017a). Police use of force. In M. J. Palmiotto (Ed.), *Police use of force* (pp. 13–34). Boca Raton: CRC Press.

Palmiotto, M. J. (2017b). Use of force throughout history. In M. J. Palmiotto (Ed.), *Police use of force* (pp. 1–11). Boca Raton: CRC Press.

Pateman, C. (1970). *Participation and democratic theory.* Cambridge: Cambridge University Press.

Pateman, C. (1996). Democracy and democratization. Presidential address: XVIth world congress, IPSA. *International Political Science Review, 17*(1), 5–12.

Pennock, J. R. (1960). The problems of responsibility. In C. J. Friedrich (Ed.), *Responsibility* (pp. 3–27). New York: Liberal Arts Press.

Perrow, C. (1979). *Complex organizations: A critical essay* (2nd ed.). Glenview: Scott Foresman.

Pfiffner, J. P. (2001). Presidential appointments: Recruiting executive branch leaders. In G. C. Mackenzie (Ed.), *Innocent until nominated: The breakdown of the presidential appointments process* (pp. 50–80). Washington, DC: Brookings Institute.

Pfiffner, J. P. (2013). The paradox of President Reagan's leadership. *Presidential Studies Quarterly, 43*(1), 81–100.

Plant, J. F. (2018). Responsibility in public administration ethics. *The Public Interest, 20*(Supplement 1), S33–S45.

Policing Immigrant Communities. (2015). *Harvard Law Review, 128*(6), 1771–1793. Retrieved December 22, 2018, from https://harvardlawreview.org/2015/04policing-immigrant-communities/

Postell, J. (2017). *Bureaucracy in America: The administrative state's challenge to constitutional government.* Columbia: University of Missouri Press.

Powers, R. G. (2004). *Broken: The troubled past and uncertain future of the FBI.* New York: Free Press.

Putnam, R. D. (1976). *The comparative study of political elites.* Englewood Cliffs: Prentice Hall.

Putnam, R. D. (1977). Elite transformation in advance industrial societies: An empirical assessment of the theory of technocracy. *Comparative Political Studies, 10*(3), 383–411.

Rainey, H. (2003). *Understanding and managing public organizations* (3rd ed.). San Francisco: Wiley.

Ransom, H. H. (1970). *The intelligence establishment*. Cambridge, MA: Harvard University Press.

Ridenhour, R. (1969). *A letter from Ron Ridenhour regarding the My Lai massacre (1969)*. Retrieved September 27, 2018, from https://alphahistory.com/

Riley, D. R. (1987). *Controlling the federal bureaucracy*. Philadelphia: Temple University Press.

Robertiello, G. (Ed.). (2017). *The use and abuse of police power in America*. Santa Barbara: ABC-CLIO.

Roberts, A. (1994). Demonstrating neutrality: The Rockefeller philanthropies and the evolution of public administration, 1927–1936. *Public Administration Review, 54*(3), 221–227.

Rohr, J. (1989). *Ethics for bureaucrats: An essay on law and values* (2nd ed.). New York: Marcel Dekker.

Rosen, J. (1996, December 29). In search of common ground. *New York Times*. Retrieved April 7, 2018, from https://search-proquest-com.echo.louisville.edu/docview/

Rosenstein, R. (2017). *Memo for the Attorney General*. Retrieved August 4, 2018, from https://www.bbc.com

Rourke, F. E. (1984). *Bureaucracy, politics, and public policy* (3rd ed.). Boston: Little Brown & Company.

Schein, E. (2004). *Organizational culture and leadership* (3rd ed.). San Francisco: Jossey-Bass.

Scher, S. (1963). Conditions for legislative control. *Journal of Politics, 25*(3), 526–551.

Schubert, G. (1960). *The public interest*. Glencoe: Free Press.

Schugurensky, D., & Myers, J. P. (2001). *Walter Lippmann and John Dewey debate the role of citizens in democracy*. Retrieved April 24, 2018, from http://schugurensky.faculty.asu.edu/moments/1922lippdew.html

Schumpeter, J. (1943 [1976]). *Capitalism, socialism and democracy*. New York: Harper and Row.

Shafritz, J., & Ott, S. (1987). *Classics of organization theory* (2nd ed.). Chicago: Dorsey Press.

Shear, M. D. (2018, April 16). Nursing election grievances, Hillary Clinton supporters curse Comey. *New York Times*. Retrieved August 1, 2018, from www.nytimes.com

Smith, M. (2018, July 15). Chicago police fatally shoot man, and then a crowd confronts officers. *New York Times*. Retrieved July 15, 2018, from https://www.nytimes.com/2018/07/15/

Spicer, M. (1998). The science of administration, the founders, and theories of political association. *International Journal of Public Administration, 21*(2), 299–321.

Stephens, B. (2017, February 26). Don't dismiss president Trump's attacks on the media as mere stupidity. *Time*. Retrieved October 9, 2018, from https://time.com/

Stillman, R. (1987). *The American bureaucracy.* Chicago: Nelson-Hall.
Svara, J. (2015). *The ethics primer for public administrator in government and non-profit organizations.* Burlington: Jones & Bartlett Learning.
Tassava, C. (2008, February 10). The American economy during World War II. *EH.Net Encyclopedia.* Retrieved February 27, 2018, from http://eh.net/encyclopedia/the-american-economy-during-world-war-ii/
Theoharis, A. G. (2004). *The FBI & American democracy: A brief critical history.* Lawrence: University Press of Kansas.
Thompson, D. (1970). *The democratic citizen: Social science and democratic theory in the 20th century.* New York: Cambridge University Press.
Thompson, V. (1975). *Without sympathy or enthusiasm: The problem of administrative compassion.* Tuscaloosa: University of Alabama Press.
Turner, H. A. (1956). Woodrow Wilson as administrator. *Public Administration Review, 16*(4), 249–257.
United States Department of Homeland Security. (2017). Retrieved January 11, 2017, from https://en.wikipedia.org/wiki/United_States_Department_of_Homeland_Security
United States Department of State. (n.d.). *The oversight powers of Congress.* Retrieved May 28, 2018, from http://countrystudies.us/united-states/government-14.htm
Vick, J. (2015). Participatory versus radical democracy in the 21st century: Carole Pateman, Jacques Rancie're, and Sheldon Wolin. *New Political Science, 37*(2), 204–223.
Wagner, D. (2014, May 31). The doctor who launched the VA scandal. *AZCentral.* Retrieved October 8, 2018, from https://www.azcentral.com/
Waldo, D. (1948). *The administrative state: A study of the political theory of American public administration.* New York: Ronald Press.
Walker, S. (2015). *The new world of police accountability.* Thousand Oaks: Sage.
Wallenfeld, J. (2018). Selma march. *Encyclopedia Britannica.* Retrieved June 19, 2018, from https://www.britannica.com/event/Selma-March
Weinstein, A. (2011, October 25). *5 presidents with the biggest approval ratings declines.* Retrieved September 29, 2018, from https://listosaur.com/
Weisman, S. (1983, October 10). Watt quits post; President accepts with 'reluctance.' *New York Times*, p. A1.
White, L. D. (1945). Congressional control of the public service. *American Political Science Review, XXXIX*(1), 1–11.
Will, G. (2017, February 25). 'Big government' is ever growing, on the sly. *National Review.* Retrieved January 9, 2017, from http://www.nationalreview.com/article/445230/
Wilson, W. (1885). *Congressional government.* Boston: Houghton-Mifflin.
Wilson, W. (1887). The study of administration. *Political Science Quarterly, 2*(2), 197–222.

Wilson, J. Q. (1975). The rise of the bureaucratic state. *The Public Interest, 41*, 77–103.

Wilson, J. Q. (1989). *Bureaucracy*. New York: Basic Books.

Woll, P. (1963). *American bureaucracy*. New York: W.W. Norton & Company.

Zelizer, J. (2018, February 27). Why the Russia investigation could be more like Iran-Contra than Watergate. *The Atlantic*. Retrieved September 26, 2018, from https://www.theatlantic.com/

Index

S. G. Koven, *The Case Against Bureaucratic Discretion*,
https://doi.org/10.1007/978-3-030-05779-4

FSC
www.fsc.org
MIX
Papier | Fördert
gute Waldnutzung
FSC® C083411

Kolibri 360 GmbH
Ferdinand-Jühlke-Straße 7
99095 Erfurt, Deutschland
produktsicherheit@kolibri360.de